STATUS

STATUS

WHY IS IT EVERYWHERE?
WHY DOES IT MATTER?

Cecilia L. Ridgeway

Russell Sage Foundation   NEW YORK

THE RUSSELL SAGE FOUNDATION

The Russell Sage Foundation, one of the oldest of America's general purpose foundations, was established in 1907 by Mrs. Margaret Olivia Sage for "the improvement of social and living conditions in the United States." The foundation seeks to fulfill this mandate by fostering the development and dissemination of knowledge about the country's political, social, and economic problems. While the foundation endeavors to assure the accuracy and objectivity of each book it publishes, the conclusions and interpretations in Russell Sage Foundation publications are those of the authors and not of the foundation, its trustees, or its staff. Publication by Russell Sage, therefore, does not imply foundation endorsement.

LIBRARY OF CONGRESS
CATALOGING-IN-PUBLICATION DATA
Names: Ridgeway, Cecilia L., author.
Title: Status : why is it everywhere? why does it matter? / Cecilia L. Ridgeway.
Description: New York, New York : The Russell Sage Foundation, [2019] |
    Includes bibliographical references and index.
Identifiers: LCCN 2019022886 (print) | LCCN 2019022887 (ebook) | ISBN 9780871547842 (paperback) |
    ISBN 9781610448895 (ebook)
Subjects: LCSH: Social stratification. | Social status. | Equality. | Power (Social sciences)
Classification: LCC HM821 .R47 2019 (print) | LCC HM821 (ebook) | DDC 305—DC23
LC record available at https://lccn.loc.gov/2019022886
LC ebook record available at https://lccn.loc.gov/2019022887

The paper used in this publication meets the minimum requirements of American National Standard for Information Sciences—Permanence of Paper for Printed Library Materials. ANSI Z39.48-1992.

Text design by Linda Secondari.

RUSSELL SAGE FOUNDATION
112 East 64th Street,
New York, New York 10065

10 9 8 7 6 5 4 3 2 1

CONTENTS

ABOUT THE AUTHOR

CECILIA L. RIDGEWAY is Lucie Stern Professor in the Social Sciences, Emerita, in the Sociology Department at Stanford University.

ACKNOWLEDGMENTS

I WANT TO thank the Center for the Advanced Study of the Behavioral Sciences at Stanford University for a stimulating fellowship year in 2012–2013, when I formed the initial idea of writing a book in order to come to terms with the subtle but pervasive power of status processes—something I had studied for most of my academic career but which remained, in a deep way, slightly mysterious, not just to me but to other scholars. After my year at CASBS, I had the idea of pursuing this project and some notes. But it was an invaluable sabbatical year as a visiting scholar at the Russell Sage Foundation in New York in 2016–2017 that actually gave me the time and intellectual support needed to do the real, focused work of working through the ideas and writing core chapters. RSF put me in the company of some wonderful scholars, gave me a beautiful office, and said, "Do it." This book simply never would have happened without that support, and I am very grateful to the foundation for that. RSF gave me a generous fellowship, but I must also thank the deans of the School of Humanities and Sciences at Stanford for the additional financial support that made it possible for me and my partner, Robert N. Parker, to relocate to New York City for ten months. And speaking of Rob Parker, it was always his voice saying, "You can do it," when I was in the wilderness on this project that actually got me through. Finally, I want to thank three very thoughtful reviewers, who took the time to give me expert comments, and Suzanne Nichols, RSF's publications director, who helped me work with this feedback to greatly improve the manuscript. We never do things alone, but only with and through all these others.

CHAPTER 1

WHAT IS STATUS AS A FORM OF INEQUALITY?

WE SEE STATUS virtually everywhere in social life, if we think to look for it. It suffuses everyday possessions, the cars we drive, the clothes we wear, the food brands we prefer, and the music we listen to. More significant aspects of our lives are equally marked by status, like the neighborhood we live in, our occupation, or our educational background. Even the organizations we work for carry more or less status value, as we can be acutely aware when we describe them to others. Think about what is at stake, for instance, in how you will be viewed at a social gathering when someone asks, "What do you do anyway?" Whether we like it or not, status is also attached to our social identities, like our sex, race or ethnicity, age, and social class background. And of course, in every interpersonal group we enter, implicit (or explicit) status differences quickly emerge and we find ourselves ranked up or down in the process.

Why is status everywhere? Why does it matter if it is? Defined simply, status is a comparative social ranking of people, groups, or objects in terms of the social esteem, honor, and respect accorded to them. But what is status really? That is, why does status develop and how does it work? What is its significance for our lives?

Notice that I said, "We see status everywhere . . . *if* we think to look for it." Oddly enough, we usually do not think about it, at least not explicitly, even though it permeates our lives. And if we do knowingly think about status, we don't often credit it with much consequence. We think of it as a relatively trivial aspect of social life, a social vanity. And yet, people give every appearance of being deeply motivated by status concerns. Teenagers look for "respect" on the streets, as do CEOs in the boardroom. A father boasts about "my daughter the lawyer." Billionaires care about their public status as one of the world's richest people, above and beyond the exchange value of their massive fortunes. Why is this? What is the nature and power of status as a social process—that is, as something people "do"? And what is the nature and power of status as a form of social inequality—a structure of advantage and disadvantage that shapes people's life outcomes? What is the significance of status for broader patterns of inequality in an advanced industrial society such as the contemporary United States? These are the core questions that this book addresses.

In taking on these questions, my goal is to make a case for what I refer to as the "deep story" behind status as a form of social inequality.[1] Rather than providing a descriptive review of empirical research on status hierarchies or offering a how-to guide for attaining status, I want to inquire into the fundamental nature of status as a form of inequality distinct from more familiar forms of inequality based on power or wealth. What is it and why do we do it? Or better, *how*—according to what processes—do we do it? To answer these questions, I develop a conceptual account of what I claim underlies status hierarchies and status evaluations. Although my goals are analytical, I develop this account out of a close consideration of current empirical research on status processes. I further attempt to show how my account of what status is, at root, helps explain some of its distinctive characteristics: that it is everywhere in social life, affecting individuals and groups alike, and that it is an ancient form of inequality that nevertheless interpenetrates modern meritocratic institutions. I also argue that it plays a unique and powerful role in the creation and maintenance of durable patterns of inequality based on social differences such as gender, race, and social class.

To preview my account, I argue that status evaluations and status hierarchies are everywhere because they emerge from a fundamental tension in the human condition. From infancy on, people are cooperatively interdependent with others to achieve what they need and want in life, from the means of basic survival to what it takes to make them happy. Survival itself requires entering into social relationships and coordinating efforts with others to produce what is required and desired in life. We are, after all, born helplessly dependent on years of support from others, and even as we grow into independence our ability to find sustenance, shelter, and a meaningful life is deeply dependent on working with others.

In a fundamental sense, then, we are a group species in which individuals need to organize with others to make it. But this deep cooperative interdependence coexists with and, indeed, creates an equally fundamental competitive interdependence among individuals. When people coordinate their efforts to achieve something, questions necessarily arise about the terms on which their relationship will be conducted and how the spoils of their joint efforts will be divided. Who will be the center of attention? According to whose will and judgments will joint actions be determined? How much effort will each contribute, what costs must each endure, and what share of the benefits produced by the group will each get? Everybody has an unavoidable interest in forming cooperative endeavors with others, but everybody also has an interest in maximizing what they get from those endeavors.

Status hierarchies, I claim, are a human invention to manage social situations that are characterized by cooperative interdependence to achieve valued goals and competitive interdependence to maximize individual outcomes. I argue that status hierarchy, as a structural form, is a sociocultural *schema* or blueprint, a set of learned and shared rules, for organizing social relations in order to manage this basic tension between overarching cooperative interdependence and the competitive interests among individuals nested within it. For clarity, I will call this argument I put forth the *cultural schema theory* of status.

William Sewell, following Anthony Giddens, has argued that social structures have a dual nature, consisting of a cultural schema, or set of implicit rules for enacting the structure, and the material distribution of resources and behaviors that result from that enactment.[2] The cultural schema of status, I argue, is a structural schema in this sense. It is a cultural blueprint people use to organize their behavior with others in cooperative, goal-oriented situations that, when enacted, produce a behavioral status hierarchy.

As we will see in the next chapter, the cultural schema of status, by my theoretical account, is actually twofold. It consists of a deeply learned, taken-for-granted norm for status allocation and a more explicit, changing, and historically contingent set of shared status beliefs about social differences that are believed to indicate greater or lesser status worthiness and value for the shared goal effort. This twofold schema is explained in much more detail later. For now, it is useful to think of it as a norm of status allocation that acts as the social grammar—the rule for organizing status relations—and a set of status beliefs that act as the changing vocabulary through which the grammar is enacted to produce status hierarchies in different contexts. As this description suggests, when I refer to the status schema as *normative* in nature, here and throughout, I use the term in the sociological sense that denotes a cultural rule that is enforced by social sanctions rather than in the more philosophical sense of prescribing an ideal.

My claim that status is, at root, *cultural* in nature and based in a normative schema, is, of course, controversial. After all, status hierarchy is a social form with deep roots in human history. It is also one that appears to be both universal in human societies and ubiquitous throughout social life.[3] Cognizant of this, several scholars argue that status hierarchies have evolutionary roots in our primate heritage.[4] Yet, as we will see, status nevertheless clearly functions as a sociocultural process based on shared cultural beliefs, evaluations, and expectations.

I take up the evolutionary question in the next chapter since it is basic to an account of status hierarchies. As we will see, doing so provides a framework for understanding how and why a cultural schema of status might develop and take the form that it does. In the end, I argue that status is a form of inequality that may be laid on evolutionary residues but is not reducible to them. In a sense, then, status is something like language in that it is a social form that is deeply cultural and socially learned, but also something to which we may be predisposed to learn and respond.

So why is status everywhere? And why does it matter? First, because tensions between cooperative interdependence and competitive interests are fundamental to the human condition, situations that are characterized by them are everywhere. When people find themselves in such situations, they draw on the taken-for-granted cultural schema of status to anticipate how others are likely to behave in the situation and figure out how to behave accordingly themselves in order to both achieve the shared goal and maximize their own outcomes. Thus, people implicitly pull status into goal-oriented, collectively interdependent situations. In this way, status becomes a basic building block of group organization across a wide variety of social contexts. It is so chronically available as a social relational schema that people use it to make sense of and organize intergroup relations as well as interpersonal relations if the groups are linked in mutual interdependence, like business firms in a market or ethnic groups in a society. And because of the twofold nature of the status schema, as we discuss later, status among individuals in local contexts and status among groups in the larger community are inherently linked. In these ways among others, status becomes interwoven with the larger structure of socioeconomic inequality in society. In particular, status processes drive inequality based on group differences such as race, gender, and social class. And as it does, status, with its connotations of greater or lesser worthiness and esteem, legitimates such inequality in terms of perceived "merit."

A second reason why status matters and is everywhere is that people care deeply about it.[5] As a social ranking of esteem and respect, status is a public representation of the social value that a community or society attaches to one person (or the groups to which they belong or the objects they own) compared to another. We who are so deeply dependent on our relations with others in the group or community care for good reason about how much that group seems to value us.

People care about their social worth, their status, quite as much as they care about money and power. In the classic film *On the Waterfront,* the character played by Marlon Brando famously laments, "I could have been a contender, I could have *been* somebody." The familiar yearning to "be someone" in life is not so much about money and power as about being publicly seen and acknowledged as worthy and valuable by the community. So status is not merely an instrumental cultural device for managing common situations; it is a deeply felt and highly consequential personal ranking. Anything that so arouses our instrumental and emotional interests will be highly salient to us in our environment, making status something we will see as well as read into almost any context.

Not surprisingly, then, status spreads through association, as we notice things in our environment that carry high or low status value and we link other things associated with them with that status value.[6] This is a third reason why status is everywhere around us. As we will see, the spread of status is the process by which objects acquire status value from their owners or producers and confer it in turn on their consumers. An admired athlete, for instance, adopts a particular style of sneakers and the kid on the street buys the same sneakers to impress his friends. In "rubbing off" (that is, spreading) among individuals and groups through association, status, both high and low, creates a politics of association among them that is consequential for inequality.

In brief outline, this is the perspective on status that this book develops. The goals are to understand how status works both at the micro level of interpersonal relations and at the level of status rankings among groups and to understand their significance as systems of inequality. Before going much further, however, we need more information on what status hierarchies actually look like as social phenomena and how they can be distinguished from other inequality processes. For instance, what do we see and experience when we observe or take part in the development of a status hierarchy in an interpersonal context? Once we have a descriptive sense of what interpersonal status hierarchies are like, we can use that to unpack the defining characteristics of a status hierarchy. That, in turn, will give us at least an initial sense of how the characteristics of status hierarchies might relate to the organizational problems that people face in situations of cooperative interdependence to achieve valued goals. The next task will be to clarify the differences between status hierarchies as a form of inequality and inequalities based on power or wealth (that is, the possession of valued material resources). I conclude this chapter with a brief outline of how the chapters that follow take up the major questions to which this book is addressed.

The Phenomenon of Status Hierarchies

The most powerful experiences that most people have with status are interpersonal. We are all familiar with joining a group of others who are focused on some shared activity or project at work or perhaps in the classroom at school. There is an initial period of orientation and uncertainty as you try to gain a quick sense of who the others are and what that means in comparison to you. The others in the group are speaking up and talking about what the group is working on together, and maybe you jump in too with your own thoughts. But whether you speak or not, it rapidly becomes apparent that some individuals are doing more of the talking than others. And others are reacting by paying more attention to and offering more approval for the comments of some than others. Soon others are following the more prominent individuals' lines of thought in their own comments. In as little as a few minutes, an implicit status hierarchy seems to emerge. Some individuals are treated as more valued, esteemed, or respected than others, holding the group's attention when they speak or act. Others find themselves cast in a supportive role: they react to the comments of the esteemed members but gain less attention from others when they offer their own thoughts.

To most people, this experience of the emergence of an interpersonal status hierarchy is entirely familiar, but also a little mysterious in that it is hard to say after the fact exactly how it happens. The hierarchy emerges implicitly, through multiple small behaviors that they as individuals participate in but rarely notice in the ongoing give-and-take of interaction. As a result, it often feels like the hierarchy just emerges organically, through a process by which some individuals are revealed to be "better," more important, and more influential than others. Although the emergence of the hierarchy may be experienced as a little mysterious, people are usually acutely sensitive to their "place" once it does. High-status members bask in the group's approval. Low-status members may be appreciative of the high-status members and feel glad to be included with them in the group, but they may also sometimes wonder how they ended up on the bottom.

This simple, familiar experience of the emergence of interpersonal status hierarchies provides a useful starting point for gaining a broader understanding of the social phenomenon of status rankings. As part of my cultural schema theory of status, I argue that interpersonal status hierarchies lie at the heart of status rankings more broadly because they are the most direct source and product of what I have referred to as the basic cultural schema of status as an organizational form of social relations. Therefore, it is helpful to use interpersonal status hierarchies as an initial model for understanding the fundamental features of status hierarchies as an organizational form. We can leave for later chapters a detailed discussion of the connection of this form to the development of status hierarchies among groups and social objects. In general, my concern in this book is with status between individuals in interpersonal hierarchies and status between groups of individuals in society, such as races, genders, or occupations. These are the relations, I argue, that are most informative about the deep story about status as a form of inequality. I deal only glancingly with status relations among corporate actors, like firms in a market, and then mostly to comment on their link to status as a cultural schema.

Behavioral Indicators of Interpersonal Status

The modern study of simple interpersonal status hierarchies began with Robert Freed Bales's classic studies in the 1950s.[7] His findings provide a more systematic behavioral portrait of status relations that is useful for fleshing out our description of interpersonal status hierarchies. Bales created small, socially homogeneous, and initially leaderless groups from the sophomore men in his Harvard classes. He gave the groups a decision-making task to work on together and observed what happened—recording how the students acted toward one another and organized their behavior. The groups met multiple times, always working on a shared task.

One of the first things Bales observed was that inequalities in interaction developed quickly within each group and then stabilized, often within ten minutes or so, but almost always before the end of the fifty-minute session.[8] Once they developed, these patterns of unequal interaction persisted and guided interaction in subsequent group sessions. Typically, one group member emerged who talked substantially more than the rest, frequently addressing the group as a whole and not just other individual members. This group member was also more likely to be asked his opinions by others in the group. The remaining members also varied in how much talking they did, with some saying relatively little while others spoke more. More prominent members who did more of the talking in the group tended to receive more positive reactions to their suggestions from others and generally experienced fewer disagreements. In the end, the members who talked more in the group and received more positive reactions to their comments were also the ones more likely to be ranked by their fellow members as having the best ideas and doing more to guide the group.[9]

Note the correlated pattern of inequalities that developed in these groups. Differences in members' participation and prominence (who was the center of attention? who directed the conversation?) were also associated with other members' evaluative reactions to them (who gained their approval? with whom did they disagree?) and assessments of them (who was thought to have better ideas compared to another?). These inequalities in participation and evaluation were associated in turn with differences in influence over the group activities. Such correlated inequalities in prominence and participation, evaluation, and influence are the behavioral indicators of an interpersonal hierarchy of esteem and influence—a status hierarchy.[10] If behavioral inequalities like this developed so rapidly and reliably even in these unstructured groups of social equals, Bales reasoned that status hierarchies are likely to emerge in any goal-oriented, cooperative group.[11] And, indeed, studies of mock juries composed of men and women with different social and occupational backgrounds soon showed that similar behavioral hierarchies developed just as rapidly in socially diverse groups as well.[12]

The correlated behavioral inequalities established by these early studies became the foundation for *status characteristics and expectation states theory*, which is currently the conceptually most developed and empirically best-documented theory of interpersonal status hierarchies.[13] We will examine this sociological theory and the evidence behind it in much greater detail in later chapters. For now, it is worth highlighting how it points toward the pressures created by cooperative goal-interdependence as the instigation for the emergence of the behavioral hierarchy.

The theory argues that when people come together to work on a cooperative task or goal, they are faced with a problem of figuring out how to behave, assuming that they want to accomplish the goal. Should they put themselves forward or wait for others to begin? To manage this dilemma, they use the social cues they read from one another to form implicit anticipations of how useful they believe another's contributions to the group effort are likely to be compared to their own and those of other group members. These implicit, often unconscious *performance expectations* shape their behavior toward others in self-fulfilling ways. The higher the performance expectation they form for another compared to their self-expectation, the more likely they are to hesitate and wait for the other to speak first, ask for her opinions, evaluate positively what she says, and, when disagreements occur, change their opinion to agree with her so that she becomes influential in the group. In this way, group members' efforts to anticipate whose suggestions will best help them achieve their shared goal leads them, by acting on those expectations, to behave toward one another in such a way that creates a behavioral hierarchy of participation and prominence, evaluation, and influence.

As I make a case for the theory that status is based in a normative cultural schema, my effort is not aimed at challenging or contradicting the established account of status characteristics and expectation states theory. Rather, my intention is to go beyond that theory in an effort to tell a deeper, more encompassing story about status. I do this by describing normative cultural processes that undergird the social judgments and behavioral processes that status characteristics and expectations theory describes.[14]

Before going on, we also need to acknowledge the cultural context of Bales's classic status studies; that context conditionalizes his specific findings about talking more as a sign of status. The more general behavioral indicator of interpersonal status, rather than talking, is prominence, being the center of attention, the person listened to when (or if) he or she speaks and whose opinion is sought by others. In the context of American culture, which values individualism and instrumental assertiveness, this is often also the person who speaks up and talks more than others, but it is commanding the group attention (along with receiving positive evaluations and wielding influence) that is the real behavioral indicator of status.[15] In general, throughout this book, the focus will be on status in the contemporary American context even though some aspects of my argument, such as those in regard to evolutionary accounts or the basic claim about the roots of status in a cultural schema, have more general applicability.

Distinguishing Characteristics of Status

With a more concrete sense of what an interpersonal status hierarchy looks and feels like when we see it in everyday social contexts, we can now take a more analytic approach. What are the distinguishing characteristics of status hierarchies? Once again, I start by addressing this question in terms of interpersonal hierarchies and then connect it to status rankings between social groups in society. Since the status rankings of objects, such as a BMW automobile compared to a Kia, derive from the status ranking of the individuals or groups with which they are associated, I do not deal with them separately here.

The definition of status that I gave earlier—status is a comparative social ranking in terms of esteem, honor, and respect—is usefully simple, but deceptively so. It requires some unpacking to gain a full, descriptive appreciation of what status is as a social phenomenon. First, notice that status is an evaluative *relation* between two or more actors, one of whom is ranked higher in comparison to the others. So no actor can have high or low status except in relation to some implied other, and status is always a rank order or hierarchy of evaluation among actors. This does not mean that the lowest-ranked actor has no esteem or respect in the group or community, but that the low-ranked actor is relatively less esteemed than higher-ranked actors.[16] Status is inherently relational and evaluative in this way whether the actors ranked are individuals in an interpersonal hierarchy or groups in a larger community or society.

Second, notice that status is a *social* ranking. This is the trickiest part of the definition because it implies several different but important points about status that are essential to understanding its nature. If we say that one person is higher status than another, the question immediately arises, on what basis? As a rank order of social esteem, status implies a *shared, collective standard of what is worthy of respect.* Both actors are compared and ranked against this standard of value.

This referent standard exists external to the two actors as the shared perspective of a *group* on what is of value—what "counts"—and how these actors rank in relation to it—that is, which of them is better at what counts.[17] Thus, the status relation between two actors, self and other, inherently involves an implicit third party, the group, with its standard of value and comparative judgments of self and other.[18] Since groups can have different standards of value, what counts and makes someone high status in one group, say of athletes, will not necessarily count in another group, such as a group of computer hackers. Thus, status is an inherently *multilevel* relation that implies actors at one level who are nested within an encompassing group that shares a particular, socially defined standard of value. Once again, this is true for both individuals in an interpersonal group and status rankings among groups in society.

If status is a social ranking of self compared to another, according to a group standard, then an actor's status is fundamentally dependent on the evaluations and reactions of *others.*[19] Understanding this is central to understanding status dynamics. As the classic sociologist Erving Goffman pointed out long ago, status cannot be seized or possessed like material goods.[20] Instead, status is more like a reputation. A person can take actions to claim it, but it must be granted by others in the group or context through their reactions to that claim. In Bales's groups, for instance, an individual could take the initiative to speak up and make a claim on the group's attention, but others had to react positively to his claim by listening with approval to what he said and accepting his arguments. That status is *given,* not taken, is one of its fundamental features.

Therefore, when two actors judge their status in relation to one another, they do so by drawing on a shared group standard. This standard is, in effect, a *cultural* belief shared by the group or surrounding society, so that status rankings are inherently based on sociocultural processes of shared beliefs and evaluations. Furthermore, since the actors have a shared recognition of the group standard by which they are compared, both the higher-status actor and the lower-status actor also share their recognition of the social fact of their relative rank. They understand how they are viewed by the group or community. In the status hierarchy of high school, for instance, both the prom queen and Suzie Glutz know where each other stands.

In this sense, status hierarchies are *consensual*—the same information about relative ranks is known and shared by both high- and low-ranking actors.

It is not surprising that high-status actors recognize and accept their rank. It is a distinctive aspect of status hierarchies, however, that low-status actors like Suzie Glutz also recognize, as a matter of social reality, that, whether they like it or not, they rank lower according to the group standard.[21] This does not mean that lower-status members of the group necessarily view their lower status as what they really deserve, although they may do so, but they do recognize that this is how they are seen in the eyes of the group. Understanding how the distinctive consensual aspect of status hierarchies comes about and its implications for the importance of status as a form of inequality in society will be an important focus of future chapters.

Finally, because status is a social ranking from the shared perspective of the group, the group acts as a kind of social observer for actors that gives their status rankings a *public* character. That is, people experience status rankings as evaluative judgments that exist not only in their own eyes but also, for better or worse, in the eyes of a relevant group audience of others. Much of the emotional significance of status for individuals derives from this sense of the publicness of the approval or disapproval that status rank confers. Status rankings go to the heart of the relationship between the individual and the group even as they also reflect relationships between one actor compared to another.

Managing the Cooperative-Competitive Tension

I have made the claim that status hierarchies are a human invention to manage social situations that are characterized by cooperative interdependence to achieve a valued goal and competitive interdependence to maximize individual benefits in the situation. Now that we have a descriptive sense of what interpersonal status hierarchies look and feel like and what their defining characteristics are, a basic question arises. If status hierarchies supposedly address the problems and tensions created by cooperative interdependence to achieve shared goals, how do they do this? Do they offer a kind of organizational solution to these problems?

Situations of cooperative goal interdependence pose several problems for the people involved in them. The first and most basic problem is to find a means for organizing the collective efforts of the participants to accomplish the valued goal together as a team or group. Organizing a collective effort involves motivating individuals to work on the shared goal effort instead of just waiting for others to do so or focusing on personal concerns. It also involves coordinating the diverse, occasionally conflicting contributions of the various group members into a unified line of group action to achieve the goal. The second problem posed by the situation is closely related to the first. This is to manage each member's competitive interest in running the group effort on her own terms in order to maximize her personal share of the collective rewards that the group produces through its efforts.

As an organizational form, status hierarchies solve these problems rather neatly by offering esteem and influence to members in proportion to what the rest of the group perceives as the usefulness of their contributions to the shared goal effort. There is overwhelming evidence that status hierarchies do operate this way. That is, esteem and influence are granted by group members in exchange for a recipient's perceived value for the group effort.[22] Recall that the members of Bales's groups who became more prominent were those perceived as having the "best ideas" for solving the group task.

In such a system for granting status, status acts as a reward that incentivizes contributions to the collective effort, thereby addressing the motivation problem. And because status brings influence as well as esteem, greater influence over group decisions and actions is also allocated to those perceived as making the best contributions to the group effort. In this way the status hierarchy provides a system for resolving disagreements among members and coordinating them into a joint action. Finally, the status hierarchy manages the competitive interest problem as well by incentivizing members to compete to make (or at least appear to make) the best, most useful contributions to the group goal effort. In this way, the status hierarchy harnesses individual competitive interests to the shared collective interest to maximize the group's goal attainment efforts. This may not always fully solve the competitive interest problem, but it does at least redirect and mitigate it.

As several scholars have pointed out, the solutions that status hierarchies provide for people when they are faced with achieving a shared, valued goal make status hierarchies a *functional* system for organizing collective goal attainment.[23] Status hierarchies have at least the potential to enhance a group's performance and productivity in pursuing collective goals compared to groups without a status hierarchy.[24] At the very least, status hierarchies make group efforts more efficient by managing disagreements, redirecting competitive interests, and coordinating actions into a joint effort. And to the extent that group members, in granting status, accurately discern who among them can make the most valuable contributions (as we will see in future chapters, this is a big "if"), the status hierarchy improves the quality of the group effort. Because status is granted for *perceived* value to the group effort and perceptions can be biased or manipulated, some scholars have argued that status hierarchies are best understood as a "boundedly functional" organizational solution to the problems of cooperative goal attainment.[25]

In my own analyses, I endorse the main points of this boundedly functional account. But that said, a critical reader would be forgiven for asking if this picture of status hierarchies is not just a bit too neat and tidy. Aren't there other ways to organize social hierarchies? And if there are, why should status systems predominate? What about people's simple desire for dominance, to be in charge, whether or not the group thinks they have something valuable to offer to the shared goal effort? And even if status hierarchies are more functional, that does not explain how they might develop or persist as a social form. We cannot simply rest on the presumption that status hierarchies are functional as an explanation for why status is everywhere. We need to take seriously evolutionary arguments about hierarchy formation among people to understand how status hierarchies might develop and take the form that has been documented in the empirical evidence. Such an analysis, which is the project of the next chapter, sets the foundation for my claim that status hierarchies are based on a normative cultural schema.

Status, Power, and Resources

I mentioned at the outset that I wished to understand the nature of status as a form of inequality that is distinct from more familiar forms of inequality based on power or wealth. So how is status different from power and wealth? That is the next question we need to consider.

As the classic sociologist Max Weber pointed out, power, as a distinctive basis of inequality, is based on the ability to get the other to comply despite his or her resistance.[26] Power, in other words, is not dependent on persuasion or consent, even if that may occur. Rather, it is based on the ability to control the other by forcing compliance even without consent. This is different, as Weber also observed, from the kind of soft power that status brings, which is the power of influence. Status, as esteem and attention, gives the actor an enhanced ability to persuade others to go along, particularly in relation to the goal effort. It does not, by itself, provide the capacity to force them to comply.

Power in a relationship derives from one actor's control over valued resources on which another actor depends, as the sociological theory of *power-dependence* has shown.[27] Resources are anything, material or cultural, that the other values and needs. The more another depends on a resource we control, the more power we have to force that other to do what we want by threatening to withhold the valued resource or rewarding compliance. Thus, power is rooted in the control of valued resources.

An implication of this analysis is that power and wealth are closely related forms of inequality. Wealth is commonly understood as the possession of valued material resources like money or land. Wealth is by no means the only valued resource whose control confers power. Control over positions in organizations or valued symbolic resources like titles or prizes can also confer power. But inequalities in wealth clearly convert to inequalities in power under a broad range of social circumstances.

How are these intertwined processes of power and wealth different from inequality based on status? First, while status exists in the evaluations of an actor by others and thus is given, not owned, wealth and power are taken and possessed. As we will see, people's dependence on others for the evaluations that give them high or low status is central to the dynamics by which status hierarchies work and legitimate larger structures of inequality. Second, power and wealth are more directly rooted in material inequalities—resources and their control. Status, by contrast, is fully cultural in nature. That is, it is created by beliefs shared by a group or community about "what counts" and "who counts more" according to that standard. The basis of status inequality in cultural beliefs begins to hint at why I might argue that status is, at root, a cultural schema for organizing social relations in certain circumstances. Such hints, of course, are not fully sufficient to make that argument, but they do point to cultural features of status for which a deep story of status must account.

As a form of inequality based on cultural beliefs, then, status is indeed rather different from the more directly material inequalities of power and wealth.[28] And yet, once status develops in an interpersonal hierarchy or between social groups in a community, it often, even typically, co-occurs with differences in power and resources.[29] Actually, as we will see over subsequent chapters, the relationship between status, on the one hand, and power and wealth, on the other hand, is largely reciprocal. Emerging as high status (that is, more esteemed and valued) in a group working together on a shared goal positions the actor to receive a higher share of whatever resources flow from the group's goal efforts. And greater control over those resources often converts to a classic power advantage.

Status hierarchies, with their shared assessments of who is "better" and more valuable than whom, often mediate between individuals and their access to valued resources and positions of power. This is especially the case for interpersonal status hierarchies that develop within organizations like schools, workplaces, and government or health institutions. These are the institutions that distribute the valued life outcomes by which we typically measure social inequality more broadly, such as income, education, a good job, or health care.[30] And as we will also see in future chapters, inequalities in wealth and power can lead over time to the emergence of cultural status beliefs that portray the rich and powerful as also "better" at what is culturally valued, giving them added advantages in maintaining their privileged position.

Thus, status, though quite distinct as a form of inequality, nevertheless shapes and is shaped by power and wealth. It is precisely through this interweaving of inequality processes that status inequality, rooted though it is in interpersonal hierarchies and shared cultural beliefs, nevertheless manages to play a significant role in creating and maintaining durable patterns of material inequality even in an advanced industrial society with ostensibly meritocratic institutions. These are among the processes that we will explore in future chapters.

What Is Ahead?

Over the next six chapters I develop my argument that status is based on a deeply learned cultural schema and show that this cultural schema theory accounts for both why status is everywhere in social life and how status plays a powerful role in the creation and maintenance of durable patterns of inequality based on social differences between groups in society. The first task, taken up in chapter 2, is to make the case for status as a cultural schema in contrast to evolutionary accounts of interpersonal hierarchies as based on dominance and on prestige. As we will see, the key issue for us is not so much whether these evolutionary theories are valid as it is that they are theories of dyadic rank formation. Other research shows that there is a significant degree of contingent uncertainty in the way dyadic contests are assembled into a single hierarchy in groups of three or more.

This uncertainty, I argue, creates an opportunity for the formation of social norms in the group to collectively govern status allocation. The motivation for the formation of such norms is group members' shared interest in exercising some control over a would-be dominator who would use prominence in the group to pursue personal benefits rather than contribute to the shared goal effort from which all members will benefit. I make a case for why this leads to a twofold schema of a basic norm of status allocation (status for perceived value) and a set of shared cultural status beliefs about social differences that allow coordination about judgments of perceived value to the group. I describe the implications of this normative schema for the nature of the consensus by which status hierarchies operate. I also note the remaining tensions between group members' cooperative and competitive interests, which simmer behind this normative consensus and affect the dynamics of status hierarchies.

Chapter 3 takes the analysis of status as hierarchy governed by a normative cultural schema and asks what this tells us about why people value and pursue status as ardently as they pursue money and power. The first task, of course, is to show evidence that people do care about status in this way. As we will see, there is good evidence that people vigilantly monitor their own and others' status in social situations, react strongly to perceived status threats, and actively pursue status across many situations. When we examine the ways in which people care about status, we see that the tensions among group members that emerge in the struggle for status are revealing: they show us how the normative dynamics of status hierarchies work. One of the questions the chapter takes on is how status hierarchies maintain sufficient stability to function in the face of people's competitive concerns about status.

The basic norm of status allocation that I propose in my cultural schema theory, status for perceived value, is consistent with evidence we have already reviewed and likely to be uncontroversial among scholars of status. The second part of the proposed schema, shared cultural status beliefs that link social differences among individuals to presumptions about what is likely to be their greater or lesser value to the group, will be less familiar. Chapter 4 unpacks status beliefs and describes the important role they play in making status a form of inequality that matters not only among individuals in interpersonal contexts, but for broader patterns of social inequality in society. As common knowledge cultural beliefs, status beliefs are the means by which actors coordinate their judgments of who is more valuable and worthy of esteem to create a consensual status hierarchy. But as they do so, they link the status of the social difference groups to which people belong, such as races or genders or occupations, to the prominence and influence they attain in interpersonal contexts. In this way, rather than random noise, interpersonal status processes become consequential for larger patterns of inequality based on group differences. In addition to discussing how status beliefs develop, this chapter looks at the role of status beliefs about groups in the spread of status beyond groups of individuals to corporate groups like law firms or restaurants. Considering this final issue allows us to consider the necessary conditions for the evocation of status as a social form and the limits of those conditions.

The previous chapters disaggregate various aspects of status structures to see how status works as a form of inequality. Chapter 5 pulls these threads together to examine how status processes play out for people as they make their way through their everyday experiences. We start with the basic observation that if interpersonal status is accorded for perceived value to the group, what the group values, and therefore who will be higher status, depends on the nature of the group's context and goals. From here we turn to a more systematic and empirically documented account of the emergence of interpersonal status hierarchies and the factors that affect who ends up where in the hierarchy. This is where we take a close look at status characteristics and expectation states theory's account of performance expectations that are shaped by status characteristics, assertive versus deferential behavior, and social rewards in the situation. We also look at legitimacy, authority, and backlash against challenges to the status hierarchy as well as techniques by which individuals overcome the effects of status characteristics that disadvantage them. Given our interest in the links between interpersonal status processes and larger patterns of inequality, the chapter concludes by noting three types of systematic bias produced by the framing effects on interpersonal hierarchies of status-valued group identities like gender or race. These are the evaluative biases summarized as status bias, legitimacy bias, and associational preference bias.

Biases created by status-valued group identities set the stage for chapter 6, which argues that status is everywhere and matters not only because it addresses a common human condition, but also because it shapes the nature and stability of larger patterns of socioeconomic inequality between social groups in society. Drawing on arguments by the social theorist Charles Tilly, I examine how status processes consolidate material inequality with categorical group differences, thus promoting, in turn, the durability of these patterns of material inequality.[31] When a group difference is status-valued according to widely shared status beliefs, it gives individuals, holding constant their current levels of resources and power, an added advantage (or disadvantage), based on their group identity alone, in gaining access to future resources and power. Thus, status, as a form of inequality, gives patterns of inequality based on social differences like gender or race an autonomous capacity to reproduce themselves. This occurs not only directly through interpersonal status processes but also indirectly through organizational practices and procedures that are created through interpersonal processes. Finally, status beliefs stabilize structures of inequality by legitimating them on the basis of merit, an effect that, ironically, can lead to the everyday denial of status bias and advantage in an achievement-oriented society like the contemporary United States.

Having come full circle from microlevel interpersonal status processes to macrolevel structures of inequality, the book concludes in chapter 7 with a brief summary that pulls together the diverse threads of the cultural schema account of status to provide a final claim for the significance of status as an ancient form of inequality that continues to powerfully shape our society and daily lives.

CHAPTER 2

FOUNDATIONS FOR A CULTURAL SCHEMA OF STATUS

IT IS NO accident that status hierarchies arise most sharply in social situations that are characterized by cooperative interdependence to achieve a valued goal and competitive interdependence to maximize individual benefits in the situation. Concerns about status, influence, and whose views will carry the day, for instance, come to the fore at committee meetings or project deliberations at work. We see this as well in classroom discussions. We even see it in families when collective decisions are at stake, like whether to move to accommodate one family member's new job offer or where to take the family vacation. Status hierarchies, I have argued, are a human cultural invention to manage just such situations. Indeed, as we saw in the last chapter, a number of scholars have pointed out that status hierarchies, as they are commonly observed, offer a boundedly functional organizational solution to the problems that these situations of cooperative interdependence create for people.[1] Yet functionality for cooperative goals is not by itself sufficient to explain how or why interpersonal status hierarchies develop as a social form and come to have the behavioral nature that they do. We need a deeper answer.

My own search for such an answer has led me to argue that status hierarchies result from a deeply learned cultural schema of norms—a set of shared social rules—for allocating standing and coordinating behavior in such situations. According to the cultural schema theory I propose, the status schema is twofold, consisting of a basic norm of status allocation and a set of shared status beliefs about social differences believed to indicate greater or lesser worthiness and value for the shared goal effort. But how might the problems of managing situations of cooperative goal interdependence give rise to such a twofold normative schema?

In answering this question, we also need to take into account long-standing arguments about the evolutionary roots of hierarchy formation among humans and other primates.[2] Some might find it controversial to claim that status hierarchies are governed by a cultural schema, given such arguments. I argue, however, that the cultural schema of status may be built on a platform of evolved responses but is not reducible to them. Status hierarchies are like language in this way—fully cultural in nature, but something we may be predisposed to develop.

To begin this inquiry, we need to look more deeply into the dynamics of hierarchy formation and the tensions and conflicts of interests it involves among individuals who are cooperatively interdependent to achieve something they want or need. Among these tensions and conflicts are those addressed by evolutionary arguments about human hierarchies.[3] This inquiry will be useful in its own right, as it reveals the dilemmas that hierarchies entail for people in such situations. But most important for us here, this inquiry is necessary for specifying the foundations of what I have called the cultural schema of status—that is, the shared social rules for enacting status hierarchies. It will also provide a foundation for my argument that the schema of status is twofold, entailing both a basic norm of status allocation and a shared set of status beliefs. Finally, our inquiry into the dynamics of hierarchy formation will show us the limits of the rules for status, where they break down, and what other factors are involved.

Most research on status follows the functional approach to understanding status hierarchies and focuses on the situational problems that people face when cooperating to achieve a valued goal.[4] This includes research associated with status characteristics and expectation states theory, which, as I mentioned in chapter 1, is currently the best-developed theory of status hierarchies in goal-oriented, cooperative groups.[5] Such research typically makes no explicit assumptions one way or the other about possible evolutionary roots for the behavioral dynamics it documents empirically.

There is, however, a long-standing approach that does turn to evolutionary theories of hierarchy formation to explain status dynamics, and it has gained renewed attention in recent years.[6] For many years, some scholars have argued that, beneath it all, human hierarchies, like those of many other animals, are formed through *dominance* relations based on intimidation, and that this has evolutionary roots.[7] A second, more recent evolutionary theory of hierarchy formation posits that people have evolved an additional tendency to form hierarchies based on *prestige*.[8] I will begin by considering the nature of dominance hierarchies and their implications for managing situations of cooperative goal interdependence, in comparison to status hierarchies. I take an especially deep dive into the issue of dominance behavior in interpersonal hierarchies, not only because of long-standing debates but also because of the light it shines on the emergence of norms for status allocation. Next I consider evolutionary arguments about prestige as the basis for hierarchy.

As we will see, evolutionary theories of hierarchy formation are arguments about the establishment of ranks between any two individuals based on differences that affect their individual fitness.[9] Yet there is a second-level problem of concern to us here, one that these evolutionary theories of hierarchy do not address in sufficient detail. How are these dyadic ranks assembled into a shared hierarchy in a group of three or more, as most goal-oriented human groups are?[10] Considering this problem leads us to the more complex question of the contingent dynamics of hierarchy formation in groups larger than simple self-other dyads. What is the role of third parties in such groups? As we will see, third-party dynamics lie behind the formation of a normative cultural schema of status. We will examine how these dynamics specifically create the conditions for the development of a twofold cultural status schema. Finally I consider what this examination suggests about the nature of the group consensus that governs the status hierarchy, the limits of that consensus, and the enduring tensions between leaders and followers in the status hierarchy.

What about Dominance?

Everybody agrees that in status hierarchies, some members defer to the choices and influence of others. But what, really, is the basis of their deference? Although we like to think that we defer to others whom we respect for their good ideas and efforts, could it be that we are mostly just intimidated by them? This is the basis of the dominance perspective on interpersonal hierarchies.[11] Dominance relations are based on implied *threat*, so a dominance hierarchy is a rank order based on fear and intimidation.[12] Joey Cheng and her colleagues argue that we can no longer ignore the evolutionary roots of human hierarchies and the continuing role this gives dominance relations in everyday status hierarchies.[13]

One long-standing approach that has argued for the importance of dominance relations in everyday status hierarchies is that of Allan Mazur.[14] It provides a good illustration of the arguments and evidence in favor of the dominance perspective. Human hierarchies, by this approach, share basic commonalities with other animal hierarchies, despite also having many distinctive differences. Like other animals, humans can engage in dominance acts, which are displays designed to implicitly threaten and stress the other, creating in the other unpleasant physical arousal. A teenager on the street, for instance, "grills" another with an aggressive eye-to-eye stare. Directing such behaviors toward another creates a dominance contest in which one person tries to outstress the other. The one who feels the most uncomfortable breaks the tension by backing down and deferring. Some dominance acts from our evolutionary heritage include physical behaviors like an erect, assertive posture, aggressively direct eye gaze, and firm, assertive facial gestures.[15] Mazur suggests that dominance acts can also include more socially constructed signs of power (and the implicit ability to threaten), like social authority.[16]

Mazur acknowledges the extensive evidence that, in everyday status hierarchies, most deference relations are established in an apparently voluntary, cooperative way.[17] That is to say, one person simply defers to another without engaging in an obvious dominance contest, such as a stare-down or other such intimidation. In a book club, for instance, after one member says, "I think the author means this," a second members says, "I disagree. The author is not saying that, but this." The first member falls silent or perhaps mumbles, "Maybe you are right."

Mazur argues that, despite appearances, the actual basis of the deference in this situation is still dominance. In such voluntary, uncontested deference, by his argument, one person is simply reading the dominance signs of the other and implicitly realizing that he or she would lose an overt contest or argument. It makes sense to defer without a fight if a fight would be costly and unlikely to succeed. Indeed, the principal value in forming dominance hierarchies is that doing so provides a system for distributing a pool of available resources with a minimum of costly fighting. In that sense, dominance hierarchies are classic "pecking orders" in which the most dominant gets first access to the valued goods, followed by the next and the next in the rank order. Dominance hierarchies, then, are potentially quite as efficient as status hierarchies in distributing resources, as understood by the functional account.

The context that produces status hierarchies, however, is one in which people are interdependent not just to distribute existing goods but to produce new valued goods through the pursuit of a valued goal. How would a dominance hierarchy organize people for collective goal attainment? It seems clear that the more dominant members could force the less dominant members to work on the collective goal effort. This would be a classic system of exploitation because the most dominant members could then take the largest share of the collective goods produced by the less dominant members. This suggests that a dominance hierarchy could also be used to organize a group of people to produce valued new goods.

Note, however, that in comparison to a status hierarchy, a dominance hierarchy is an inefficient organization for collective production.[18] A dominance hierarchy does not incentivize the most dominant members to work directly on the productive efforts. Instead, the most dominant members spend their efforts controlling the less dominant members and forcing them to engage in productive labor. As a result, a dominance hierarchy, by not employing the most dominant members in the goal effort, does not fully mobilize the available energies and talents of the group in the productive effort. Furthermore, since dominance hierarchies are based on fear and threat of attack, the less dominant members have an incentive to get away from the hierarchy if they can or to organize to overthrow the dominator. Thus, dominance hierarchies are potentially less stable than status hierarchies. By this logic, then, groups organized according to a classic dominance hierarchy are likely to be less productive and less effective in pursuing collective goals than those organized by a status hierarchy.

This, of course, is another way of saying that dominance hierarchies are not as functional for people trying to attain a cooperative goal as a status hierarchy would be. But that brings us back to the point that functionality is not a sufficient explanation for why people would form one or another kind of hierarchy. What, then, do we make of the dominance explanation for interpersonal deference hierarchies?

There is evidence that people do experience some aggressive physical gestures and stances as commanding and even intimidating and may sometimes react with deference.[19] Indeed, many readers may recognize from their own experience occasional exchanges in which another person tried to stare them down or spoke to them in an implicitly threatening manner, even in a work- or goal-oriented context. In a much-noted incident during the 2016 U.S. presidential debates, for instance, Donald Trump walked up behind Hillary Clinton and loomed aggressively over her as she was speaking. Evolutionary theorists argue that it is only reasonable to expect that humans would continue to have in their evolved repertory of behavioral responses some form of deference dynamics based on dominance.[20] Thus, we cannot dismiss agonistic dominance as a possible source of deference in interpersonal hierarchies. But the occasional exhibition of dominance behavior does not mean that dominance relations are the typical foundation of interpersonal hierarchies of influence and deference—what we have called status hierarchies.

Prestige: A Second Evolutionary Approach

As we noted in the last chapter, there is overwhelming evidence that, in conditions of cooperative interdependence, people grant influence and deference to others in proportion to their perceived ability to make valuable contributions to the shared goal effort.[21] In an effort to come to grips with this evidence, scholars interested in positing evolutionary roots for human hierarchy formation have argued that people are likely to have evolved a second type of deference response based on *prestige*.[22] Deference based on prestige is more similar to status as we have used the term in that it is based on respect and admiration freely granted to another because of that other's perceived ability to offer useful cultural information.[23]

Drawing on cultural evolutionary arguments about people's evolved social learning capacities, Joseph Henrich and Francisco Gil-White propose that people may have further evolved a response to esteem and honor those who appear to offer superior "information goods."[24] The idea is that by giving status and deference to those with superior information, the deferrer gains an opportunity to come closer to the superior person and learn his or her skills and information, which provides an evolutionary advantage. Henrich and Gil-White suggest that adding the prestige argument allows evolutionary accounts to address questions such as "Why did people defer to Steven Hawking in his wheel chair?"[25] Following this general line of reasoning, Cheng and her colleagues argue that both dominance and prestige-for-expertise exchanges remain parallel, evolved sources for influence and deference in interpersonal hierarchies.[26] Their studies provide some evidence consistent with this argument.[27]

What implications can we draw from this review of evolutionary approaches that might assist us in finding a deeper answer to the question of why status hierarchies have the behavioral nature that they do—a nature described by but not fully explained by the functional account? First, it is clear that dominance dynamics do occur in social relations. People display occasional motives to aggressively take charge regardless of others' desires. Such motives are likely to play a role in the background of status hierarchies even if such hierarchies are generally organized according to shared cultural rules for granting status in exchange for the perceived usefulness of one's contributions to the group effort. Second, although dominance dynamics occur, even arguments from evolution no longer favor dominance as the sole or primary basis for hierarchy formation among people.[28] These same evolutionary arguments, however, do not fully explain how dominance and prestige systems might work together in the formation of hierarchies. Thus, major questions remain unanswered.

Status, Prestige, and Dominance

If everyday status hierarchies are not typically simple dominance hierarchies, are they then just developed prestige hierarchies, as evolutionary theorists have described them? The answer, I propose, is, not quite. We need not deny that people may have evolved responses to defer to those with superior informational skills to observe a further, important point. Such a simple self-other exchange of prestige for information does not adequately capture the nature of interpersonal status hierarchies as they have been empirically documented. For this and reasons to be addressed shortly, I argue that the prestige account, like the dominance account, cannot fully explain these hierarchies.

In the prestige argument, respect and esteem are freely given, in ways similar to what we know about status hierarchies, in exchange for the perceived value of what a person offers.[29] But value in the prestige account is informational value to the individual deferrer and may or may not involve value to the group's goal effort, so it is not quite the same as what we see in status hierarchies. Furthermore, from the empirical evidence on status hierarchies, "value to the group," as groups seem to judge it, is more than just expertise—understood as "superior information goods"—as important as that is. It is perceived as capacity to contribute to the group's goal attainment, which I call *performance capacity*.[30] Performance capacity involves not only task-relevant skills and abilities ("information goods") but also the *agentic* effort and *group-oriented motivation* to apply those skills and abilities to the collective goal effort.[31] In the book club, for instance, the person who becomes high status and influential will not just be the one who has literary training, but the one who takes the initiative to speak up and use her literary skills to help the group members come to a satisfying, mutual understanding of the book under discussion.

Research has shown that it is possible to analytically distinguish, at least in laboratory studies, the contributions of task skills and abilities, agentic effort, and group-oriented motivation to the status and influence an individual attains in a cooperative group.[32] As we will see in later chapters, the relative importance of these elements for status varies with the specific circumstances of the group. In general, however, task skills and abilities and agentic effort work together to jointly feed an impression of a member's *goal-related competence,* which makes up the core component of perceived performance capacity in cooperatively interdependent, goal-oriented groups.[33] Given our focus in this chapter on such contexts, in what follows I discuss performance capacity in terms of perceived competence at the group goal. Some status researchers use competence more narrowly to refer only to skills and abilities (information goods).[34] I use the term more broadly, however, to refer to the *combination of abilities and effort* directed to the group goal.[35] I return to the question of how *group-orientation* comes into the picture toward the end of the chapter. As we shall see, group-orientation, which is a sense that a person is willing to work in the group interest, not just for self, can set framing bounds on the value to the group of that person's perceived competence.[36]

For now, the important point is that status hierarchies as we empirically observe them are much more like prestige hierarchies than dominance hierarchies, but that they involve an assertive element and a collective, group-orientation that is missing from the pure prestige account. The importance of agency in status dynamics hints at how cultural rules for granting status may manage people's dominance tendencies by incentivizing actors to redirect their energies from self-focused, domineering behaviors into agentic, proactive efforts in service to the collective task. These agentic task efforts have the effect of making the actor seem more competent and valuable to the group and thus earn status and influence.[37]

In the final analysis, we are left with the empirical evidence that status hierarchies are predominantly based on exchanges of status for perceived value to the group, but we still do not have an explanation for why this should be the case. To address this basic question, we need to dig deeper into the dynamics of hierarchy formation. And to do that, we need to consider that hierarchies in groups of more than two people involve more than the simple question of whether one person defers to another. As we shall see, whatever the validity of evolutionary approaches based on dominance and prestige, they are limited by being theories of self-other, dyadic deference relations. In groups of three or more, the formation of hierarchies critically involves the reactions of third-party members who are bystanders to the deference relation between any two members.[38] As we shall see, understanding the role of third-party members is central to understanding the emergence of cultural norms that govern status hierarchies.

The Contingent Dynamics of Hierarchy Formation

An implicit assumption behind many arguments about interpersonal hierarchies is that the hierarchy that emerges is determined by *individual differences* in the traits (strength, expertise) or states (flush with confidence, feeling down) that participants bring to the setting. Note that the evolutionary arguments about dominance and prestige necessarily follow this individual differences logic because they focus on individual fitness and dyadic deference relations. But the settings in which status hierarchies develop—ones in which people are cooperatively interdependent—typically involve groups or teams of more than two people.

Is the individual differences assumption about hierarchy formation reasonable in groups larger than a dyad? The sociologist Ivan Chase has long investigated this question. Early on, he showed that, as a logical matter, associations between prior individual differences and rank position would have to be very high for individual differences to fully determine linear hierarchies in groups larger than a dyad.[39] There is no question that prior differences of various sorts are in fact factors that significantly predict where individuals will end up in the hierarchy. But do they fully determine that position? Using experiments and other evidence, Chase and his colleagues have clearly demonstrated that, even with simple animals like fish and chickens, individual differences, while predictive, cannot entirely account for the hierarchies that emerge in groups of three or more.[40]

If individual differences do not fully determine hierarchical ranks, what does? Chase and Kristine Seitz describe evidence clearly suggesting that the answer lies in contingent behavioral processes involving three or more individuals.[41] The specific, detailed nature of these contingent behavioral processes that finally structure the hierarchy is not fully resolved in Chase's research. But the point remains that on the basis of both logical and empirical evidence, this research shows that hierarchy formation is not just an aggregation of individual pairwise deference relations. Instead, the formation of hierarchies in groups of three or more has a substantial element of *contingent uncertainty* that depends on social dynamics among the individuals in the larger group.

I argue that the sensitivity of hierarchy formation to larger social dynamics, which is apparent even among simple animals, creates a critical *organizational space* for people in which cultural norms for hierarchy formation can emerge regardless of whether they have evolved reflexes for deference to dominance or prestige. In simple dyads, one person may reflexively admire and defer to another with little thought or, alternatively, reflexively be intimidated into quick deference. But in a larger group she may react differently. And even if she does not react differently, the ultimate consequences of her deference for the hierarchy may depend on the contingent reactions of other members. The key to understanding why and how status hierarchies are based primarily on deference for perceived value to the group (that is, performance capacity) lies in understanding the reactions of third-party members who are bystanders to the deference relations between any two members. This analysis provides the foundation for understanding how a normative schema could emerge that governs status relations in the hierarchy through a process at the cultural level. This cultural status schema may be laid upon a platform of evolved deference responses but is not reducible to them.

Third Parties and Collective Hierarchy Formation

To understand the possible effects of third-party members on the development of interpersonal deference hierarchies, it is helpful to start by recalling the basic interests that the hierarchy creates for individuals in deciding to defer or not to another group member. Under conditions of collective goal interdependence, each individual has a clear, rational interest in deferring to other members on the basis of their apparent competence at the goal effort, understood broadly as performance capacity. Doing so will maximize the group's goal success and thus increase the pool of valued rewards in which the individual, as a group member, will share. On the other hand, the individual also has a competitive interest in being in charge, regardless of personal competence, in order to maximize control of whatever rewards are generated.[42] In the face of such conflicting interests, what would make an individual member reliably defer to others based on apparent performance capacity?

To answer this question, consider how goal interdependence not only shapes members' interests for their own deference behavior but also gives them an interest in *other* members' deference behavior.[43] Members have a distinct interest in all others granting deference to others on the basis of apparent competence at the goal effort, since this will increase the pool of collective rewards available for them to share. This means that it is in each member's interest that *others'* status be given on the basis of apparent performance capacity, whatever they want for themselves.

Thus, although group members may have conflicting interests for their own status, they have a clear and uncontested interest in seeing that others receive status in exchange for performance capacity. As a result, if they perceive one member to be more competent at the goal effort than a second member, they are likely to pressure the second member to defer to the first member. For instance, if I really want us to succeed at our goal and I think that person over there has much better ideas about how to do that than you do, then I want you to be quiet and let the person with the good ideas talk, and I am likely to pressure you to do that. But of course, you and all the other group members have the same sort of interest in my own deference behavior and may pressure me in the same way. Research by the sociologist Christine Horne has shown that interdependent exchange interests like this lead group members to form *norms* that they enforce.[44]

This suggests that, regardless of his or her personal desire to defer, each group member is likely to face pressure from every other member to defer on the basis of perceived competence at the goal effort. The result is to create a system of collective pressure on each member to defer on the basis of perceived performance capacity. Here we see a genuine social force that could tip hierarchy dynamics toward the formation of a normative system in which deference is exchanged for performance capacity when people are goal-interdependent.

Collective Constraints on Dominance

What are the implications of this social force for the use of dominance behavior to create deference relations based on intimidation? A dominance attack on another member is by definition threatening. Even if the dominator is trying to claim deference that is not justified by his or her apparent goal-related competence, the attacked member might reflexively submit. Other third-party members, however, who may witness this attack but are not the direct victim of it, are likely to be less reflexively threatened. And they have no interest in seeing this threatening but not competent member gain control in the group.

Following this reasoning, I argued a number of years ago that third-party members would intervene in a dominance attack against another member that was not justified by the member's apparent competence at the goal effort.[45] They would effectively form a coalition with the victim in resisting and attacking the dominator. The effect, then, of the interest all members have in *others* being granted status based on performance capacity would be to create an implicitly normative social control process that constrains the use of dominance behavior that is not justified by the group's collective goals.

This collective social control process should be effective in constraining unjustified dominance under most circumstances. Even a large or aggressive dominator is still only one person who would be outnumbered and typically overpowered by an opposing coalition of other members. Also, the group members' knowledge of their potential collective power over a dominator would reduce the credibility of the dominator's threat, further constraining the dominator's ability to gain reflexive deference even from the direct victim of his or her attack. As a result, the dominator would not typically succeed in gaining influence in the group under circumstances in which third-party members had the opportunity to intervene.

This is an argument from logic, but does it really work? David Diekema and I conducted an experiment to find out.[46] We created four-person, same-sex decision-making groups, seated them around a table, and gave them an incentive for making the best group decision that they could. Unbeknownst to the other participants, two members of each group were confederates. In half of the groups (the dominance condition), one of the two confederates (the main confederate) presented his or her arguments in an aggressive, commanding way and specifically interrupted and challenged the other confederate. In the other half of the groups (the control condition), the main confederate simply participated in a normal but active manner in the group discussion. The ideas and arguments that the main confederates put forth were the same in both conditions, so that they did not differ in objective task competence. We were interested in how the two other participants, who were third parties to the dominance attack, would react. We also were interested in how much influence the dominant confederates would end up with in their group, compared to the confederates in the control condition.

The results were quite interesting and supported our logical argument. The third-party participants did in fact intervene against the dominators. In both male and female groups, the other participants spontaneously attacked the attacker, challenging and speaking aggressively toward the dominant confederate. In the end, the dominator not only failed to gain any more influence over group opinion than the neutral confederate did but was actually perceived as less influential than the neutral confederate.

The evidence of this study suggests several points. Under conditions of goal interdependence, a kind of social control system does seem to develop that constrains the effectiveness of dominance used to claim rank beyond that justified by perceived competence. Christopher Boehm and his colleagues have described widespread anthropological evidence for such constraints on domineering behavior over a large variety of human societies.[47] This social control system is seen most clearly in the behavior of third parties whose reactions shape the eventual results of a given dyadic dominance attack. Earlier I argued that the sensitivity of hierarchies to larger dynamics involving third parties creates a social space for cultural norms for hierarchy formation to develop. Norms are revealed by their enforcement. Indeed, Richard Emerson argued that a group norm is properly viewed as the voice of the coalition that would stand against you if you violated the norm.[48] From that perspective, the implicit coalitions that participants formed against the dominator in these studies reveal an emergent group norm enforcing perceived performance capacity, not dominance, as the appropriate basis of rank allocation when group members are goal-interdependent.[49] And an important effect of this norm is to control a would-be dominator who would take over the group without concern for the collective interest.

The Enforcement of Status-for–Perceived Performance Capacity

The Ridgeway and Diekema study showed resistance to dominance not justified by goal-related competence, but its design did not allow it to also show that perceived performance capacity was the actual basis of influence and status in those groups.[50] A large research literature, including that associated with status characteristics and expectation states theory, has clearly demonstrated that perceived goal-related competence is the typical primary basis of status in goal-oriented groups.[51] Few of these studies, however, have examined dominance in the same study or demonstrated actual enforcement of a system in which status is expected to be granted in proportion to a member's perceived competence at the goal effort. A more recent study does so.

Cameron Anderson and Gavin Kilduff examined how individuals who are high in the personality trait of dominance, which is associated with acting in an assertive, firm, and self-assured manner, attain influence and status in face-to-face goal interdependent groups.[52] Through a series of studies of MBA students working in groups, the researchers found that dominant personalities did end up rated by their teammates as having high status and influence in their groups. But these dominant personalities did so by using their self-confidence and assertiveness to convince their teammates that they had superior competence at the group task. In other words, their teammates' perceptions of their task competence mediated their attainment of influence and status. They were not able to use "take charge" dominance behavior to directly claim status independent of convincing others that they were competent.

This study shows, as did Diekema and I, that under conditions of goal interdependence, group members were not willing to grant influence on the basis of dominant behavior alone.[53] But this study also shows that the actual basis for granting influence and status, even for dominant personalities, was perceived task competence. It shows something else as well. In the face of group pressure to show competence in order to attain status, dominant personalities turned their aggressive assertiveness toward the group goal effort in an active attempt to appear competent. Agonistic dominance behavior—that is, threatening, intimidating behavior—is not generally perceived as indicating competence.[54] In the Ridgeway and Diekema study, dominant confederates were actually perceived by their teammates as less competent than neutral confederates, despite the similarity of their substantive arguments. But as a variety of research has shown, proactive, task-directed behavior carried out in an assertive, confident, but not threatening verbal and nonverbal style does give the impression of competence, independent of actual competence.[55] Such behavior also generally leads to status.[56] And status, of course, is based on the groups' *perceptions* of each member's goal-related competence. This begins to suggest how people's personal desire for dominance can be incorporated into a normative status-for–perceived performance capacity system.

We began this chapter by asking why social deference hierarchies are primarily based on status-for–performance capacity relations. Although hierarchies like this are functional when people are interdependent to achieve a shared goal, we sought a more compelling explanation for why or how people should so reliably develop such a system. The answers we have found so far center on how goal interdependence causes group members to have interests not only as actors themselves but also as third parties to the actions of other members in the group. In particular, goal interdependence gives each group member an interest in ensuring that deference is granted to *other* members on the basis of perceived performance capacity rather than something else, such as dominance alone. This interest that each member has in the basis of deference granted to others creates an implicit motivation for group members to pressure each other into deferring to performance capacity and resisting other types of claims to status rank. And as we saw, this kind of situation, in which members not only share a collective goal but have interdependent exchange interests, has been demonstrated to give rise to group norms—that is, practices that the members will enforce with one another.[57]

For these reasons, I argue that this shared basis for pressuring each other to defer to perceived performance capacity is best conceptualized as the emergence of a social norm that defines status-for–performance capacity as the appropriate basis for rank allocation. In both the Ridgeway and Diekema study and the Anderson and Kilduff study, participants did seem to be acting as though they shared a normative understanding of what the appropriate basis for deference and status should be in their goal-oriented groups.[58] Shared norms that enforce deference for perceived competence in goal-interdependent contexts could explain why status-for-competence hierarchies so reliably develop in such contexts. Shared norms that govern status relations are *cultural* by definition. This cultural-normative system may be laid on the residue of evolutionary processes, particularly if these include social learning and the capacity to create shared culture. Yet this cultural-normative system is not fully reducible to these evolved responses.

The actual development of such norms, however, remains a little mysterious in the discussion so far. Yes, the interests created by goal interdependence provide a motivation for such norms. And yes, the contingent uncertainty of hierarchy formation beyond the dyad creates the opportunity for norms to emerge. But are such norms created de novo in each group, or are they drawn from a broader cultural understanding? How exactly do we get from the interests in a situation to a shared understanding that we might call a cultural schema of norms for enacting status hierarchies? This is the next question to address.

A Norm-Based Schema for Status Allocation

When a group of people are interdependent to achieve a valued goal, they have an interest in other group members receiving deference only in exchange for perceived ability to contribute to the goal effort. At the time David Diekema and I conducted our early study, I assumed that simply having this interest would be sufficient to induce group members to act on it by pressuring others to only claim status on the basis of perceived competence. I now think that this assumption underestimates the risk that group members would take in acting to pressure a fellow member without any assurance that other group members would support this action. In the example of that earlier study, third-party members intervened to attack the dominator who tried to seize rank without justification by competence and supported each other in implicit coalitions when they did so. But there is risk in attacking a threatening dominator. What made the participants implicitly assume that they would not stand alone if they stood against the dominator?

It seems likely that they felt safe acting as they did because they took for granted an implicit cultural norm that status should be earned through perceived competence, a norm that they assumed was shared by their fellow group members. If they assumed that this norm was "common knowledge" (that is, widely shared cultural knowledge that "everyone knows"), then it was reasonable to assume that their fellow group members would also use this norm as the basis of their behavior. By using the norm to anticipate their fellow group members' responses, they could act against the dominator with reasonable assurance that the other group members would support their actions.

This is an example of what game theorists describe as using "common knowledge"—which, of course, is cultural knowledge—to solve a coordination problem.[59] Common knowledge is something that you not only know but can assume others also know. If two people draw on the same set of assumptions about how to behave under given circumstances, they can anticipate each other's actions and coordinate their behavior smoothly.

Actors in status hierarchies certainly behave as though they were coordinating their behavior by means of a common-knowledge normative schema for allocating status. Indeed, it is difficult to account for the coordination that occurs in status hierarchies without presuming the existence of shared cultural rules for granting status—in other words, a normative schema for status relations. Even arguments that people have an evolved response to give prestige for superior information cannot fully account for this coordination in groups greater than dyads because of the contingent complexities of hierarchy formation that we discussed earlier. It is for these reasons that I treat status as a cultural schema or normative blueprint for organizing social relations under conditions of goal interdependence.

But how could a normative schema for status allocation develop in the first place, especially given the tensions between people's cooperative and competitive interests under conditions of goal interdependence? Goal interdependence gives group members an interest in pressuring others to grant status for perceived competence. But before acting on this interest, members need a way to anticipate how others in the group will react to their actions, since the ultimate costs or benefits of their actions are contingent on the others' reactions to them. Without a preexisting shared norm, how might they anticipate the others' reactions?

The members' knowledge that they are all oriented toward the same valued goal and are interdependent to achieve it creates a kind of co-orientation among the members.[60] Under these circumstances of co-orientation, it seems likely that members, if they recognize their own interest in having others defer to competence, will assume that the others oriented to the same situation will see things as they do. Thus, they will assume that the others also recognize this interest and will either support them or at least not resist them if they act on this interest. This presumption of shared interest is not as reassuring as a preexisting shared norm would be, but it does lessen to some extent the risk of acting on the interest. Assume, then, that a group member publicly acts on this interest by pressuring another to defer to competence or by supporting another's deference to competence. If others seem to accept this action in that they do not challenge it, then the action seems socially valid in the group.[61] That is, it gives the appearance of being consensually accepted in the group and, in that sense, implicitly normative and legitimate.

Through some process like this, which is similar to processes that have been empirically demonstrated in the development of other types of status beliefs, it is possible that the circumstances of goal interdependence could cause people to spontaneously invent implicit norms that deference and status should be granted to those who are perceived to be more competent at the goal effort.[62] Once such a norm exists, people can learn it by being treated according to it by others, and it could spread widely, as evidence has shown that other types of status beliefs do.[63] The fact that the norm does help the group more effectively coordinate its goal efforts might reinforce people's use of the norm in subsequent situations, thereby speeding its spread.

A Twofold Cultural Schema of Status

The foregoing is merely a logical analysis, of course. However, it is a plausible account that suggests that basic status norms might emerge and spread to become a shared schema fairly easily without any requirement that people somehow recognize the functionality of status norms as they develop them. Rather, they would merely try to coordinate with others to act on interests they share owing to the conditions of goal interdependence. A basic status norm forms as an unintentional by-product of this process. According to the cultural schema theory of status I propose, this *basic status norm,* as I call it, is the first component of the twofold schema that governs status hierarchies.

The nature of the basic status norm is simple: deference and status should be granted in proportion to an individual's perceived competence at the collective goal effort. This norm creates a constraining web of mutual expectations for deference to greater perceived competence. It means that each individual group member has a right to expect that others' status will be based on perceived competence, but it also means that other group members expect that individual member as well to defer to greater perceived competence.[64]

The normative expectation of other group members that the individual member will defer on the basis of perceived competence immediately confronts the individual with a second question. How can he or she figure out what the others will take to be a sign of greater or lesser competence at the group goal effort? Note that given the web of others' expectations that the individual member confronts, it is actually more important for the individual group member to find a way to understand what *others* understand as competence than to make an independent personal judgment of competence.[65] In other words, the individual group member is faced with a second coordination problem. I argue that people solve this second problem by developing shared cultural *status beliefs* about the attributes and behaviors that indicate higher or lower levels of status worthiness and specific or general competence.[66] In contrast to the normative character of the basic status rule, status beliefs are more descriptive in nature, capturing shared beliefs about differences among people that are culturally linked to status and competence.

Members of a goal-oriented group could forge such beliefs among themselves through discussion and negotiation, but populations of people who must regularly come together in cooperative interpersonal groups to attain valued goals are likely to develop sets of widely shared status beliefs. Evidence suggests that people form shared status beliefs quite easily and that such status beliefs are widespread in U.S. culture.[67] Status beliefs are associated with a wide variety of social distinctions in the United States, including gender, race, social class, education, age, and occupation.[68] In North America, there are also cultural beliefs linking assertive, agentic behavioral styles with greater status and competence.[69] As we will see in later chapters, status beliefs are fundamental both to the way people organize interpersonal status hierarchies and to the way status shapes relations among organizations and larger structures of inequality.

For the moment, however, the central point is that the sociocultural schema that people use to enact status hierarchies is twofold. This is the argument of the cultural schema theory of status for which I am making a case. We have an implicit, taken-for-granted, but fundamental basic status norm that we learn from experience and pass on to others through our behavior. This basic status norm is deeply embedded in our cultural understanding of how to organize everyday social relations in goal-interdependent circumstances. It acts as a kind of social grammar—a set of rules—for status relations. We combine this deeper, implicit normative schema with a more explicit, variable, and historically changing set of shared cultural status beliefs that we use to anticipate what others will judge as "better," more competent, and valuable. This is the second component of the status schema. Status beliefs are the changing social vocabulary through which people enact the grammar of the basic status norm to create diverse status hierarchies in varying contexts.

It is through this combination of a shared basic status norm and shared status beliefs that people are able to quickly form status hierarchies in the real time of interaction, even though these hierarchies are based on potentially complex assessments of competence. The trade-off, of course, is that the extent to which these hierarchies actually do put the most competent members in positions of greatest influence is dependent on the validity of status beliefs and the consequent accuracy of group assessments of the members' relative competence. As we saw with dominant personalities, appearances of competence can be manipulated.

The Nature of the Governing Status Consensus

This analysis of the sociocultural schemas that people use to enact status hierarchies sheds additional light on the nature of the consensus that governs status hierarchies. To function effectively, rank positions in a hierarchy must be at least roughly agreed upon. Both classic research and current studies do find substantial, if not perfect, agreement among group members on perceived status ranks.[70] Such a consensus could come about in two ways. Each member's "first-order" expectations for their own competence and status relative to others in the group could correspond with each other member's personal first-order expectations.[71] An example of a first-order consensus would be "I think you are better than me at this," and the member so addressed thinks that too.

Alternatively, members could agree at the level of second-order expectations about each member's relative competence and status in the group. The concept of second-order expectations is borrowed from status characteristics and expectation states theory.[72] It refers to people's perceptions of *others'* expectations about their relative competence and status in the group. For instance, "I think *they* think you are better than me at this" is a second-order expectation. A consensus based on second-order expectations would be an agreement about what others are likely to expect is the perceived competence and status rank of each member, including self. In such a consensus, we could all agree, for example, that others in the group think you are better than me at this, but that they also think I am better at it than that other person.

I have argued that the pressures that cause hierarchies to take the form of status hierarchies emerge through third-party dynamics and the need to anticipate the reactions of others in goal-interdependent settings. People solve these coordination problems through the development of status beliefs that allow them to agree on what others can be expected to expect in terms of relative competence, deference, and status. This shared agreement about what others will expect creates a web of mutual expectations among the group members that pressures each of them to defer to what the consensus holds is greater competence. Clearly, then, by this account, the consensus that creates and governs the status hierarchy is really a consensus at the level of second-order expectations about competence and status rank. Individual group members may or may not personally agree that they are less competent at the group goal than a given other member, but they do agree that others will assume, based on shared cultural beliefs, that they are less competent and expect them to defer.

What is the evidence to support this argument? Is the governing consensus of a status hierarchy really primarily a second-order consensus? Several studies suggest that it is. In a study of face-to-face, goal-oriented groups, Anderson and his colleagues had group members rate the status of each member as well as their own status in the group.[73] Members' ratings of others' status showed substantial agreement, suggesting that a second-order consensus about status rankings did exist in the group. Furthermore, group members were closely attuned to this second-order consensus. They accurately estimated others' views of their own standing in the group, showing that they were sensitive to others' expectations. They had good reason to be sensitive. When group members perceived their own status in the group to be higher than the other members perceived it to be, they were less liked and accepted in the group. In other words, for individual members of this group, "knowing your place" in terms of recognizing the status that other group members consider appropriate for them would be enforced by an implicit system of group pressure based on the second-order consensus.

An earlier study based in status characteristics and expectation states theory also examined what happens when a group member's own first-order expectations for competence and status compared to another disagrees with what that member thinks the other thinks (second-order expectations). Lisa Troyer and Wesley Younts gave study participants information suggesting that their teammates expected either higher or lower task competence from them than the participants expected for themselves.[74] When the participants then worked with their teammates on the group task, their behavior and influence were most strongly predicted by the others' expectations for them.

Another study explicitly demonstrates the importance of others' expectations in inducing group members to defer to superior competence. Deference to apparent superior competence, of course, is the foundation of status hierarchies. Cameron Anderson, Robb Willer, and their colleagues told study participants that they would be working together in four-person teams on a cooperative decision task.[75] Before beginning, however, they gave group members a test that purportedly measured their ability at the upcoming group task. Participants received feedback on their own score, which was manipulated to be relatively high or low in the group, as well as the scores of the other members. Half the participants, however, were told that while everyone would receive a list of all four team members' scores, these scores would be anonymous in that nobody would know which member achieved which score. The other half were told that all team members would know which member had which score. The researchers then asked participants whether or not they would prefer to be highly influential and high status in the upcoming group interactions. When participants thought that they had low ability compared to their teammates (first-order expectations), but also thought that their teammates did not know that (no second-order expectations), they expressed a preference for high influence and status in the group despite their low task competence. But when participants thought that the others did know they had scored low on task ability (clear second-order expectations), they said that they would prefer to have relatively low influence and status compared to their teammates. In other words, these participants' willingness to defer to superior competence resulted from the pressure of *others'* expectations rather than from personal doubts about their ability.

This evidence suggests that the consensus that governs the status hierarchy and enforces the norm of deference to perceived task competence is a second-order consensus. *It is a consensus among group members about what others can be expected to expect.* This "working consensus" can coordinate behavior in the group without members necessarily fully buying into it as what each "really deserves."[76] In fact, some evidence suggests that rank order disagreements (for example, I rank myself above you, but you don't) are not uncommon at the ego (first-order expectation) level.[77] It is likely that working consensus and the coordination that follows from it in everyday status hierarchies are possible only because consensus at the egoistic level of "what I want for me" is not necessary for working consensus to emerge and function. Instead, this more easily agreed upon second-order consensus creates a web of mutual expectations that is sufficient to create and enforce the status hierarchy.

Dominance Revisited

The power of the normative schema of status to constrain individual members' behavior and enforce a status-for-competence system in goal-oriented groups appears to be considerable. It is not unlimited, however. The possibility that people will want influence and status regardless of their task competence does not go away. Neither does people's tendency periodically to fall back on dominance behavior to get their way through intimidation. How does this work within a normative status-for-competence system, and when does such behavior break down the status system itself?

Status hierarchies require that some degree of agentic behavior on the part of members be employed in the group's collective goal effort. And high-status members, as those with the greatest influence over the group activities, are expected to proactively lead the group in its goal attainment efforts.[78] Thus, status systems create an opportunity for members to express their personal desires for dominance through assertive (but nonthreatening) task efforts that aim to persuade other members of their task competence.[79] In this way, individual desires for dominance can be subverted and incorporated within a normative status-for-competence system. The normative status system, in other words, manages dominance desires through carrots as well as sticks.

The specific nature of the group's goal or task matters here as well. Especially when the group's goals involve aggressive competition with other groups, as in an athletic team or a military unit, competence at the goal effort inherently involves the demonstration of aggressive, dominant behavior. Groups in these situations necessarily incorporate and esteem members who are skilled at dominance behaviors but who use these behaviors to help the group achieve its goals.[80] Yet there is an inherent tension in such groups between empowering aggressive members to express their dominance in the collective goal pursuit and the risk that those members will turn that dominance back on the group in a purely self-interested pursuit of power and rank.[81] It is easy to see that the web of expectations that constrain the use of raw dominance within the group could be broken down in a group that values aggressive dominance directed toward out-groups. In fact, violent gangs and criminal groups may be contexts in which the norms of the status hierarchy are often overcome and the hierarchy tips toward a classic dominance structure based on fear and intimidation.

Another context in which the use of dominance attacks may sometimes overwhelm the normative status-for-competence system has more to do with the strategic behavior of the dominator than with the nature of the group goal effort. A normative status system constrains the use of simple dominance to gain rank by giving other members an incentive to form implicit coalitions against the dominator while also giving members normative backing for such interventions against the dominator.[82] A determined and strategic dominator, however, could defeat the formation of opposing coalitions by isolating the other members and intimidating them one by one so that they fail to act to support anyone who resists the dominator. It seems likely that this occasionally happens in a wide variety of everyday groups, in the workplace and elsewhere. A strategic dominator at work, for instance, might come to your office when you are alone and threateningly demand that you not oppose him when he puts forth his plan at the meeting and that you not talk to others about this encounter. He could take others aside one by one and similarly threaten them. At the meeting, when he asserts his plan for control, no one speaks up to disagree, or if someone does, others are afraid to support him or her. The result is a type of dominance hierarchy, or at least a dominance relation between the group leader and group members.

There are limits, however, to the effectiveness of such dominance behavior. As noted earlier, dominance hierarchies give low-ranking members an interest in either leaving the group or subverting the leader as soon as they get the chance. As a result, dominance hierarchies tend to be unstable.[83] Mark Van Vugt and his colleagues, for instance, found that members of autocratically run groups were four times more likely to leave the group and go elsewhere than members of democratically led groups.[84]

The implicit adoption of a normative cultural schema for perceived competence as the appropriate basis for deference relations creates and enforces status hierarchies in the vast majority of goal-interdependent groups. But the desire for personal dominance and the use of intimidating behavior does not disappear. To some extent, dominance can be subverted and incorporated within the status system; the more overt dominance attacks that still break out on occasion can usually be quickly contained by the reactions of other group members. But under less common circumstances, genuine dominance hierarchies may supplant the typical status system altogether.

Tensions between Leaders and Followers

The fact that group members' self-interests and potential for dominance behavior never really go away within interpersonal status hierarchies creates a basic tension between leaders and followers in goal-interdependent groups.[85] There are many benefits of gaining high status and becoming an influential leader in the group.[86] Naturally, then, however, other group members may be a little suspicious of a claim for high status, wondering whether it is just a self-interested grab for influence and esteem. Oliver Hahl and Ezra Zuckerman show that this inherent motivational ambiguity behind a claim to high status explains why higher-status members are typically seen as more inconsiderate and inauthentic than lower-status members unless they give credible evidence of their prosocial intent.[87]

With grounds for suspicion, group members want some assurance that if they grant high status and influence to a claimant, he or she will use that influence to benefit the group. Members, in that sense, want to get a good deal for their deference.[88] Members need, of course, to be convinced that the claimant is sufficiently competent at the goal effort to be able to help the group and more competent than others who might otherwise lead the group. And as part of assessing competence, members typically value the claimant's agentic forcefulness toward achieving the goal effort. But they also need to know that the claimant's assertiveness is *group-motivated,* rather than primarily self-interested.[89] In other words, they need to trust the status claimant to be cooperatively oriented toward helping the group, not just benefiting self.

These tensions between followers and leaders cause group members to value *both* forceful, instrumental agency directed toward the task and signs of trustworthiness in a candidate for high status in the group. As we will see in later chapters, group motivation becomes a part of what it means to be perceived as *effectively* competent and deserving of deference in a status hierarchy. In that sense, the status-for-competence exchange embodied in the basic status norm is really an exchange for *bounded competence* in which the value to the group of a member's competence is framed by the member's cooperative or self-interested intent. This basic tension between putting yourself forward to be seen as competent and needing also to be seen as helpful and group-oriented gives the dynamics of status attainment a distinctive character. At least in Western culture, which values individual agency, status dynamics become a process of what Anderson and his colleagues have termed "micropolitics."[90] That is, individual members, like politicians, compete to convince the other members that they are more competent and trustworthy than another member and thus deserving of the other's "vote" for their high status.

Conclusion

As we have seen, it is the interests and tensions that people confront in cooperatively interdependent situations that give rise to a normative cultural schema for status relations. Among these tensions are people's occasional tendencies to resort to dominance and intimidation, which may have evolutionary roots. Another may be people's evolved interest in granting prestige to those with superior information goods. But while these dyadic tendencies simmer in the background of status relations, they do not illuminate the more complex problem of the *shared* interests that people have when they must cooperate to achieve something they want or need. In such situations, people share an interest in seeing *others* granted standing and influence in the group on the basis of their perceived value for the collective goal, whatever they want for themselves, since that will increase everyone's rewards from the goal effort. These shared, interdependent exchange interests provide a foundation for the emergence of a *normative process* of status allocation according to which group members pressure one another to defer on the basis of perceived value for the goal effort. This is the basic status norm.

The shared interests created by cooperative goal interdependence provide the incentive for people to develop a normative schema to manage status allocation. But it is the contingent uncertainty of hierarchy formation in groups of three or more that provides the opportunity for a normative cultural process to develop that manages deference and status in the face of individual interests and, possibly, evolved responses. Among the effects of the basic status norm is a set of both negative and positive sanctions for controlling would-be dominators who would take over the group without concern for the collective interest.

Enacting and enforcing the basic status norm, however, creates a second problem for people: they must now coordinate their judgments of others' perceived value to the group and, similarly, understand how others judge their own value in the group. I argue that people solve this problem by creating and drawing on shared common knowledge—cultural status beliefs. These are beliefs about social differences among individuals that are widely believed to indicate greater or lesser worthiness and competence that contributes to collective goals. As the social vocabulary through which people enact the basic status norm, status beliefs are essential to status as a form of inequality. For these reasons, I argue that status processes, at root, reflect the operation of a twofold cultural schema, consisting of the basic status norm and a historically changing set of status beliefs. This is the basis of the cultural schema theory of status. As we shall see in future chapters, much of the significance of interpersonal status hierarchies for larger patterns of inequality in society results from the effects of status beliefs acting through interpersonal hierarchies to shape social outcomes.

CHAPTER 3

WHY DO WE CARE ABOUT STATUS?

WE NEED TO take status inequality seriously if for no other reason than that we care so much about it. Things we care a lot about have the power to shape how we live and how satisfied we are with our lives. But why, really, do we care about status—about how esteemed we are in the eyes of the group compared to others? That is the question at the heart of this chapter. It implies a prior question, which is, of course, what is the evidence—beyond anecdotal stories—that people do care so very much about status? I have argued, for instance, that in the struggle for precedence that is behind inequality, people care as much about status as they do about money or power. What is the evidence for that argument? This is the first set of questions this chapter will address.

In figuring out why people care about status, we will see how the tensions among group members that emerge in the struggle for status reveal more about how the normative dynamics of interpersonal status hierarchies work. If people care so much about status, doesn't this mean that they will eagerly compete for it? I have argued that status hierarchies are normative systems for managing cooperative interdependence to achieve shared goals. Doesn't the competitive desire for status threaten the bounds of cooperation in the group? How do status hierarchies achieve any functional stability in the face of people's competitive concerns for status? And how do status hierarchies talk some members into accepting low status, as some must if the hierarchy is to function? What do the answers to these questions reveal about how status hierarchies work? Addressing this set of questions is a second goal of this chapter.

In our investigation of why people care about status, I focus on why they care about how they are ranked in esteem in interpersonal groups and social encounters. This focus flows from a basic contention of the cultural schema theory of status that I have been developing in this book. That theory claims that interpersonal status hierarchies lie at the heart of status rankings more broadly because they are the most direct source of the normative cultural schema, or "rules," that we use for enacting status as an organizational form of social relations. In the last chapter, we looked more closely at why this is the case and at the nature of those rules. Here we will keep the focus on interpersonal hierarchies because these are also the contexts in which individuals directly experience being treated by others as though they are valued by the group—or being treated as though they are not as valued or esteemed as others in the group.

Recall that status, unlike power or resources, is not taken and possessed, but rather given by others. It is in interpersonal contexts—or more broadly, *social relational contexts*—that people as individuals receive status. A social relational context is any situation in which people consider themselves in relation to another whom they have to take into account in order to figure out how to respond in the situation.[1] Such contexts can be direct interactions with another in person or through social media as well as indirect and even imaginative social relations, such as when a person listens to a politician speak about "people like us." This is where people see reflected in others' perceived treatment of them their comparative value to the group. Naturally, then, these are the contexts that most powerfully evoke people's concerns about status. Yes, people care about status in other contexts too. They care about the status of the brands of their cars or clothes, the status of their occupations and the places where they work, the status of the neighborhoods they live in. But these other status concerns most powerfully shape their personal experience by affecting the status with which they are treated by others in social relational contexts—dressed as they are, driving the car they do, living and working where they do, and embodying certain status-valued social identities like gender or race or social class.

Framing Considerations

To understand why people care about status, we need to start with a basic observation. People are fundamentally dependent on their social relations with others to survive and get the things they want and need in life. If you need social relationships to survive, then little can be more important to you than your standing with others. How you stand with others shapes their relative willingness to include you in their groups and the terms on which they will accept you there. Status is how others perceive your relative value to the group in terms of what you have to offer to the group's collective activities. As such, it is one of two central dimensions of your standing with others.[2] The second dimension of your standing with others is more familiar: how much do the others in the group like you, accept you, and treat you as someone who belongs to their group? But as we shall see, status is not reducible to liking and acceptance. It has its own independent effects.[3]

As this framing of the issue implies, our focus in this chapter will be on why people care so much about their own status. But since status is an inherently comparative relation—you are higher or lower in status than someone else in the eyes of the group or community—caring about your own status implies paying attention to the status of others as well.[4] The social psychologist Susan Fiske argues that there are two fundamental dimensions to our perceptions of others rooted in our basic survival dependence on relationships with others. We need to know "friend or foe" by reading signs of warmth and "how capable are they of carrying out their intentions," which we read through status.[5] These basic dimensions of our perceptions of others are simply the mirror of the dimensions of belonging and status that concern us about our own standing with others.

In thinking about why people care about status, we also need to keep in mind that high status brings direct benefits to those who receive it—esteem, attention, and influence among others. Recall that the functional account of status hierarchies discussed in previous chapters views status as an incentive system designed to motivate individuals to contribute as best they can to the group's effort to achieve its collective goals. But of course, for some to be high status in a group, others must be available to defer to them and accept lower status in the group. So considering the question of why people care about status also raises the issue of low-status members. What is in it for them to accept low status and continue in that role to contribute to the group goal effort? Do the normative rules of status provide any compensation for accepting low status in the group? These are among the considerations that will frame our inquiry into why people care about status. We need to start at the beginning, however, by first examining the evidence that people do care more than superficially about social status.

Do Individuals Really Care about Status?

Most people would readily concede that people are not indifferent to the esteem and respect with which they are treated by others. But is status really a powerful, motivating concern that evokes strong feelings and shapes a wide range of behaviors? The organizational behavior scholars Cameron Anderson, John Hildreth, and Laura Howland reviewed a broad range of social scientific research in an effort to resolve the question of whether the desire for status is a fundamental human motive in life.[6] To be considered "fundamental," they argue, status as a motive needs to meet four demanding criteria. First, the attainment of status (or lack thereof) needs to affect more than just temporary psychological functioning, like feeling up or down in the moment. It also has to have long-term, accumulating effects on a person's well-being—their self-esteem, happiness, and even health. Second, the desire for status needs to motivate a wide range of behavior directed toward its pursuit or the avoidance of its loss. Third, status also needs to be an end goal in itself that is not fully reducible to some other motive or goal, such as belonging (the desire for human attachments), which is already widely acknowledged to be a basic human motive.[7] Finally, the desire for status should be apparent across all human cultures.

Based on the wide-ranging evidence they review, Anderson and his colleagues conclude that the desire for status does indeed meet these criteria and should be recognized as a fundamental human motive. Among the many effects of status documented in the studies reviewed by Anderson and his colleagues are several that clearly demonstrate how concerned people are with their relative status in the eyes of others. Two that are especially illustrative for our concerns here are the attention people pay to the smallest signs of status, their own and others', and the emotional power of people's reactions when their status is threatened.

People Closely Monitor Their Own and Others' Status

People vigilantly monitor signs in social situations that give clues to their own and others' relative status.[8] They immediately notice and can become preoccupied with, say, the fact that one coworker has a corner office and others do not.[9] They quickly and almost automatically pick up another's displays of emotions, like pride or shame, that reveal his or her relative status in the situation.[10] And they are sensitive to nonverbal cues, like voice tone or eye contact, that reflect relative status position.[11]

Status differences in interpersonal contexts are often not explicitly acknowledged, even while they are enacted through multiple small signs and behaviors. Yet in an indicator of how carefully people attend to status, research shows that people are accurate perceivers of others' status as well as their own.[12] For instance, as one study showed, an individual's perception of each fellow group member's status was very similar to how the status of those group members was actually ranked, on average, by the group members as a whole.[13] I would argue that this happens in part because people follow shared cultural status beliefs about what the signs of higher or lower status are, so that they end up making similar judgments about who is higher or lower in status. According to the cultural schema theory, these status beliefs are one part of the twofold schema by which people enact status relations. We will discuss this more later, but for now the point is that people pay close enough attention to accurately estimate the status that another will be granted by others as well as by themselves.

For the same reasons, but perhaps more surprisingly, people also accurately perceive their own status in a group, despite the potential ego-costs of doing so. Anderson and his colleagues found that individuals' self-perceptions of their status were closely correlated with the average of their fellow group members' actual ratings of their status.[14] Indeed, in that study, individuals' own estimates of their status were as accurate an indicator of their actual standing in the group as was any other single member's estimate of their status. If we depend on others to survive and status is a central dimension of our standing with them, perhaps it is not surprising that we learn to accurately read our status in the eyes of others, whether we are happy with it or not.

People React Strongly to Perceived Threats to Their Status

People not only vigilantly monitor their own and others' status in the situation, but also react strongly to perceived threats to that status—as when, for instance, they feel that they have been treated with disrespect. These strong reactions are another sign that people care deeply about status. Research suggests that feeling disrespected typically provokes anger and is indeed one of the more common sources of anger in social relations.[15] It is not uncommon, for instance, to see people flash with anger even in a routine commercial encounter if they think the clerk involved has treated them disrespectfully.

Not only are people who feel disrespected often angry, but they may even respond with some sort of direct or indirect aggression against the perceived source of the disrespect. In a telling study, Vladus Griskevicius and his colleagues experimentally primed some participants to be concerned about status and then asked how they would react if someone accidentally spilled something on them at a party and didn't apologize.[16] Compared to participants who had not received this priming to think about status, those so primed said that they would aggress in some way on the spiller more strongly. In other words, the more focused people in the study were on status, the more likely they were to act aggressively in response to an act that could be taken as disrespectful.

There is evidence that this same emotional and behavioral response to perceived status threats is behind the "backlash" reaction that people from lower-status groups in society, such as women and people of color, sometimes encounter when they act assertively toward higher-status others, like men and whites. Research by the social psychologist Laurie Rudman and her colleagues, for instance, shows that the hostile, angry reaction frequently experienced by highly assertive women is not primarily due to any violation on their part of the stereotype that women should be warm and "nice."[17] Rather, this reaction comes from the perception that they are "too dominant" in a way that violates and disrespects the gender status hierarchy. Research has documented a similarly hostile resistance reaction to African American men who act highly assertively in a workplace context with white people.[18]

Sometimes threats or challenges to one's status-valued social identities, like race, gender, or class, come not from a specific interpersonal encounter but from broader patterns of social change that seem to imply that people from groups that had traditionally been reasonably high status are no longer as respected and valued in society as they feel they should be. Even these symbolic, more distanced status threats to people's identities can sometimes lead to angry and even aggressive backlash reactions when they become salient for them through media representations or public political commentary. Drawing on early work by Herbert Blumer and a wide body of social research, the sociologist Lawrence Bobo argues, for instance, that a great deal of hostile racial prejudice can be understood as reactions by those in higher-status racial groups to perceived threats to the racial status order.[19]

For some, reactions to perceived threats to the status of their valued social identities can even motivate support for political movements or candidates seeking to restrain or restrict resources for the challenging groups and reassert the status of their own group. In a clear demonstration of this, the psychologists Maureen Craig and Jennifer Richeson and the sociologists Rachel Wetts and Robb Willer conducted experiments in which they made salient for white participants the changing racial demography of the United States that will eventually make whites a minority.[20] Highlighting this shift evoked racial status threat in the white participants in both studies and led them to more strongly endorse conservative political ideologies in one study and oppose welfare programs in the other.

The social identities whose status is threatened need not be primarily racial identities, although that can be part of the equation as well. The sociologist Arlie Hochschild interviewed white working-class Louisianans who supported the conservative Tea Party movement and found them to be people who grew up seeing themselves at the respected center of America with the status of hardworking, traditional "middle Americans."[21] They now felt not only besieged by economic and social changes but also treated with contempt by coastal Americans and urban elites who looked down on them as ignorant, prejudiced hicks and who gave special privileges to other social groups who, they felt, hadn't worked as hard as they had.[22] They felt the status insult and were angry enough to seek political action against those "cultural elites."

The political scientist Katherine Cramer makes a very similar case in her 2016 book *The Politics of Resentment*.[23] She argues that a sense of being deeply disrespected (for instance, being viewed as "redneck racists") by urban elites is among the significant causes of support for iconoclastic political candidates like Wisconsin governor Scott Walker and President Donald Trump among Midwestern, rural, white voters. Based on her extensive interviews with rural Wisconsin voters, Cramer argues that this sense of not getting respect despite their hardworking contributions to society is just as important a driver of their political behavior as their sense of declining economic outcomes and reduced political control. Supporting this conclusion, her fellow political scientist Diana Mutz similarly argues in her analysis of voting in the 2016 U.S. presidential election that perceived status threat was among the factors that drove support for Donald Trump.[24]

What Makes People Care about Status?

In a basic way, we have already answered the question about what makes people care about status—through evidence that it is a fundamental motive for behavior and is related to people's dependence for survival on relationships with others and groups. In the last chapter, we noted plausible arguments that concern about social rank, including prestige, may have evolutionary roots.[25] In her examination, Fiske similarly argues that we are predisposed to perceive and emotionally respond to status.[26] In this book, I have argued that status hierarchies, as a form of social inequality, are not simply a fully determined product of evolutionary concerns about rank, although they are likely influenced by such concerns. Instead, I have argued, status hierarchies are best understood as a normative schema developed at the cultural level as a tool for managing a fundamental human circumstance—cooperative interdependence to achieve collective goals in the face of competitive individual interests. If experiences with status at the interpersonal and social relational levels are structured by a normative cultural schema, then this suggests that what makes people care about status involves more than just evolved reflexes. Our analysis of how people care about status—that is, the social psychological processes through which they care—would benefit from some further unpacking.

The normative schema of status, according to the cultural schema theory I have put forth, consists of a *basic status norm,* according to which deference and status should be granted in proportion to each group member's perceived value to the group goal effort (understood as goal-related competence and group motivation), and a set of shared *status beliefs* about the personal attributes and signs that indicate more or less status-worthiness and types of competences. We can think of status at the relational level as a set of social processes governed by these implicit cultural rules that are enacted repeatedly across the many contexts in which people are interdependent to achieve shared goals. From this perspective, we can ask, what are the incentives that these cultural rules of status create for the individuals who find themselves acting within them? Status creates its own *direct incentives* to pursue it through the normative rewards it distributes. But status processes also create a wide range of *indirect incentives* to pursue status through their impact on a person's sense of self and well-being.

Direct Incentives for Pursuing Status

The norms of status work by providing a range of incentives for individuals to contribute (or appear to contribute) to the group's goal effort and to do so to the best of their ability. Status—the esteem and honor that group members grant in exchange for valued contributions—is itself a potent reward, as attested by the evidence of how much people care about it. In addition to esteem, status hierarchies reward their higher-ranked members with greater attention. They are given the floor to speak their views, and when they do, others listen.[27] Higher-status members also receive more positive responses, like agreements and smiles, and fewer disagreements and other negative reactions from others than do lower-status members.[28] And because they are presumed to be more competent at the group effort, they have greater influence in the group. Finally, they receive a greater share of any external rewards or benefits that flow from success at the group effort.[29] This pattern—attention, positive responses, influence, and external awards coming to those with higher status—has been repeatedly documented in research associated with status characteristics and expectation states theory.[30]

Clearly, then, the basic status norm of exchanging deference and esteem for perceived contributions to the group has the effect of dangling a wide range of rewards in front of group members. These rewards work by going disproportionately to those who end up with high status. But this means, of course, that low-status members participate in granting these rewards to others but receive many fewer of them themselves. The very value of these rewards makes their lack a cost to be avoided if possible by pursuing higher status or avoiding the loss of status that has been attained. While the basic rule of the status exchange makes it clearly better to be high than low status in a group, it is worth noting that it does result in some payoff for low-status members as well. If by giving more competent members greater influence the group is more successful at its goals, then the low-status members will also receive a share, though a smaller share, of the benefits that flow from that success.[31] Also, low-status members, while seen as less competent than high-status members, are partially compensated by being regarded as "nicer"—warmer and more considerate—than high-status members.[32] We will return later in this chapter to the question of how the cultural norms of status incentivize acceptance of low status.

One of the more powerful effects of the rewards created by the basic status norm is to encourage group members to try to convince their fellow members that they have valuable contributions to make to the group. There is a wide range of evidence that people pursue status by trying hard to project an image of their instrumental value to the group.[33] By drawing on widely shared status beliefs about the behaviors, attributes, and other signs that are culturally assumed to indicate greater rather than lesser competence and status-worthiness, people can strategically represent themselves as offering as much value to the group—and therefore being status-worthy—as they can. And they can do so in a language of status signs that others are likely to understand.[34] For instance, people can take the initiative to speak up and offer distinct opinions about the group's efforts, make references to their own experience or expertise, and present themselves in as confident (rather than hesitant) a way as they can manage. The micro-political process this creates as people jockey for status, however, is significantly constrained by the fact that people bring to the group context status-valued attributes that they do not control, like gender, race, or class background, but that nevertheless powerfully shape others' impressions of their competence and status-worthiness.[35]

Indirect Incentives to Pursue Status

Acting in one situation after another in which valued rewards are distributed according to the norms of status exposes individuals not only to direct incentives to pursue status but also to indirect incentives through the impact of these experiences on their sense of self and well-being. A long tradition of research, particularly that associated with the sociological approach called *symbolic interaction,* has shown that people acquire their self-concept—that is, their sense of their attributes and social identities and the emotions attached to those—primarily from their interactions with others in their immediate, *local* environment.[36] As a result, everyday social interactions are a potent arena for the self. And if a great many of these everyday interactions are organized and pervaded by status rankings, then the outcomes of local status interactions will be a powerful source of feedback on the self. In particular, status interactions give meaning-laden feedback on the social value of aspects of the self.[37] How much do those in your local environment seem to value what you have to offer compared to others around you? Such feedback, especially as it accumulates over multiple interactions tends to affect your own sense of self-worth—your self-esteem and sense of well-being or happiness.

One of the powerful ways in which experiences in everyday status hierarchies are related to people's sense of well-being is in their effect on the emotions that are evoked in them as they find themselves acting as a high- or low-status participant in the group interaction. A wide variety of research shows that interpersonal status hierarchies systematically shape the emotional experiences of their participants.[38] When you are high status in a situation, others esteem you, offer you more smiles and positive feedback on your contributions, and give you credit when things go well in the group.[39] Not surprisingly, then, being high status evokes generally positive emotions and self-crediting emotions like pride.[40] In contrast, when low status, you get less attention from others and are more likely to be disagreed with or criticized. Low-status members are more likely to feel negative emotions like sadness and, when things go wrong for the group, self-blaming emotions like guilt or shame.[41] Even when things go right for the group, low-status members reap fewer emotional benefits, at least at a personal level, because the credit goes to the higher-status members for whose efforts low-status members feel appreciation.[42]

The links between status positions and emotions are so common and familiar that they are part of our implicit cultural knowledge. Earlier, we noted that people very quickly pick up on people's status-related emotions and use that to infer their actual status in the situation.[43] In fact, Larrisa Tiedens and her colleagues showed that people have shared cultural stereotypes of the emotions associated with status. When presented with vignettes in which people working together on a task are described as feeling pride, on the one hand, or sadness, guilt, or appreciation, on the other, participants assumed that the prideful member must be high status and the guilty or sad member low status.[44]

The effect of high status making people generally feel good about themselves and lower status making them feel less good and even sometimes sad would be another indirect incentive for people to care about status and prefer situations in which they can be higher rather than lower status. Anderson and his colleagues, in their review of research on the motivating power of status, describe a substantial body of research showing that, other things equal, people are more attracted to relationships, groups, and communities in which they would have reasonably high status rather than those in which they would be low status.[45] But of course, things are not always equal, and there can be trade-offs that make it worth joining groups where they would be low status.[46] Many people, for instance, would be eager to join a highly prestigious group even if they would be low status in it. Even more importantly, people often do not have the power to choose whether to belong to certain groups or communities (for example, the neighborhood they grow up in), and their choices to belong to some other groups may be greatly constrained by systems of power and authority in society (as in the workplace or at school).

Whatever the mix of social constraints and choices that determines the range of group contexts in which a person participates, status experiences in those contexts accumulate to affect his or her happiness and general subjective sense of well-being as well as self-esteem. Cameron Anderson, Michael Kraus, and their colleagues examined status differences among individuals across a diverse range of local group contexts, including friends, workplaces, and neighborhoods, and found that individuals' status in their groups consistently and strongly predicted their positive feelings and life satisfaction.[47] Status predicted well-being even controlling for how much people felt liked or accepted in their groups, showing again that status has its own effects independent of belonging. In a study that tracked MBA students during school and as they left and joined the workforce, the authors also found evidence that students' changes in status brought about corresponding changes in their subjective well-being.

Importantly, and consistent with what we have argued so far, in these studies by Anderson, Kraus, and their colleagues, it was status in *local* social relational contexts that mattered most for subjective well-being.[48] Thus, a plumber who is respected among her fellow plumbers might feel more subjective well-being than a physician who is low status among her colleagues. Similarly, it is status in local groups, especially face-to-face groups, that have the largest impact on self-esteem.[49] In a review of nine studies of respect in groups such as sororities, families, and living groups, for instance, Heather Smith, Tom Tyler, and Yuen Huo found strong correlations between how respected individuals were in their groups and their self-esteem.[50]

The Strength of Status as a Persistent Motivator

Clearly, people do care a great deal about status, and they have many good reasons for doing so. But in the struggle for precedence out of which inequality emerges, how do concerns about status stack up against other famous motivators, like power or money? If we are interested in status not just as an individual motive but as a widespread form of social inequality, this is an important question. Examining it opens further windows onto the nature of status as social normative process rooted in social relations.

Examples from history clearly show that the pursuit of status is undeniably in the mix for people along with the pursuit of money and power. In his foundational analysis of status as a social phenomenon in European society, Max Weber, showed that the acquisition of superior wealth or power is rarely sufficient for groups of people.[51] Typically, they quickly go on to seek distinction in their culture and manners in order to also acquire status superiority. And as we saw in Hochschild's, Cramer's, and Mutz's contemporary analyses of the drivers of political views among some sectors of American society, status concerns similarly are as or more important than economic or power concerns.[52]

Adding to this historical backdrop, two organizational behavior scholars, Nicholas Hays and Lindred Greer, have conducted a series of experiments and other types of studies to pit people's well-known motivation for power against the strength of their motivation for status.[53] One test of the strength of a motivator is whether, after getting some of it, rather than being satisfied, you want to seek even more of it. Power is often assumed to be addictive in this way, but as Hays and Greer note, what little research exists suggests that this is not really true. After acquiring a moderate amount of power, most people become less interested in gaining even more. But not so status.

In their studies, Hays and Greer found that the higher the status associated with a position, the stronger participants' preference for having that position. There was no point at which preference for higher status leveled off. But participants' preference for positions that increased in power did taper off, so that high-power positions were no more preferable than moderately powerful positions. In two experiments, Hays and Greer found that participants placed at the bottom of a social hierarchy worked harder to increase their power than their status; as participants rose in the hierarchy, however, they became less interested in more power and their desire for more status seemed to accelerate. In an archival study of the behavior of PGA golfers, they found a similar pattern of a preference for more power among golfers ranked at the bottom but a preference for more status among those ranked in the middle or higher.

Hays and Greer interpret their results as follows: Once you possess enough power to exert basic control over your circumstances, added power doesn't provide many more rewards. But the desire for status is never really satiated because it can never really be *possessed* by the individual once and for all. Since it is esteem given by others, it can always, at least theoretically, be taken away. Interpersonal status is subject to the potentially changeable evaluations of others. Others' views of your competence and value to the group can change (what have you done for us lately?) and so might others' sense that you are working in the group's interest. And as a consequence, interpersonal status is experienced psychologically as insecure rather than a settled matter. How worthy are you, compared to that other person, in the eyes of others? Couldn't you always be more worthy than you are now? In social relational contexts, the answers are for others to decide, and you cannot fully control how they make the decision.

Based on such reasoning, Nicholas Hays and Corrine Bendersky argue that at a psychological level, people experience status evaluations as inherently *mutable*—you can always jockey for more, and you are always at risk of losing what you have.[54] A distinctive effect of this subjective sense that status is changeable and insecure is that gaining status in interpersonal contexts makes people orient toward others as they closely monitor what others think in an attempt to maintain the status that they have and maybe increase it. Steven Blader and his colleagues, for instance, have shown that people who are high status in an interpersonal context, compared to low-status participants, engage in higher levels of implicit perspective-taking in which they attempt to understand how the other sees things in the situation.[55] This is in contrast to occupying a position of high rather than low power, which makes people more egocentric in focus so that they pay less attention to the other's views.[56]

The perspective-taking of high-status people, however, is relatively self-interested (what do you think of me?). Other research shows that lower-status people are actually more accurate role-takers of others, as measured by predicting their behavior.[57] Also, the other-oriented, perspective-taking effect of high status is specific to the local, social relational contexts in which the exchange of status for perceived value to the group actually takes place. To the extent that a local status position (say, as a respected colleague) is transformed into an organizational or societal position of power and resources (say, a boss), the subjective effects also change to the ego-focused ones of power rather than the other-focused ones of high interpersonal status.[58]

If people subjectively experience status in social relations as mutable, what are the implications for the stability of status structures? This is a good question and one we will turn to shortly. As we will see, the implications for the stability of status structures are not as simple as it may seem. For the moment, however, our point is that status takes the form of a reward that is highly desirable, but whose attainment cannot be fully predicted or controlled. And desirable but unpredictable rewards are the kind that, according to classic studies of learning, induce the most persistent behavioral strivings for their attainment.[59]

Incentivizing Acceptance of Low Status

Now that we have a sense of what a persistent motivator status is for individuals, the question arises of how the norms of status relations manage the competitive forces this unleashes. If status is a normative system for managing situations of *cooperative* goal interdependence, how is cooperation and basic stability sustained in the face of such tensions? Considering these issues will give us deeper insights into how status hierarchies really work.

The first issue we need to take up in this regard is a nagging one that has run throughout our examination of how important status is for people. For status hierarchies to function, some people must be induced to accept low status in the group. Low-status members must not only defer to others' influence and prominence and accept less esteem in the group, but also continue to contribute to the group effort by supporting the efforts of the high-status members. The loss of involvement by low-status members is a centrifugal force that threatens the ability of status hierarchies to manage cooperative goal interdependence. Do the norms of interpersonal status hierarchies incentivize the continuing involvement of low-status members? If so, how do these norms do so, given the greater desirability of high status?

We have already seen some of the factors that encourage people to defer to others whom the group believes are more valuable to the group effort than they are. For one thing, they face negative sanctions, like being disliked and criticized, if they resist.[60] And on the positive side, if they do defer to someone who is better able to help the group succeed at its goal, this will benefit them as well, since low-status members receive a share, if a lesser one, of the proceeds of the group's success.[61] Also, low-status members are usually seen as nicer and warmer than high-status members, which offers them a modest compensation for accepting their lower position in the group.[62] In addition, if a group is prestigious, even its low-status members bask in its glory.[63] (Of course, many groups are neither highly successful nor prestigious.) Finally, of course, groups can offer benefits of belonging and acceptance even to their low-status members.[64] Yet the fact remains that to attain whatever benefits of group membership and task success are available, low-status members are asked to pay an emotional price in social esteem that higher-status members are not.

Do the implicit normative processes through which status hierarchies are enacted—the workings of the cultural schema of status itself—also provide additional, systematic, if modest, rewards for the acceptance of low status—rewards that help buffer the costs of being less esteemed in the group? Sandra Nakagawa and I have argued that they do.[65] This system of rewards emerges as an indirect effect of the governing consensus in the group about each member's relative value to the group goal effort. Status relations are inherently comparative, and when a social comparison process leads to a consensually shared definition of a situation—in this case, the rank order of members' perceived value in the group—research shows that definition takes on a quality of validity or reality for the participants.[66] To the extent that this consensual reality draws on common knowledge status beliefs to rank some as better than others, the presumption is that "most people" outside the group, if they were members themselves, would also concur with the consensus, which strengthens its apparent sense of being valid and "right."[67] In this way, the sense that the group's evaluative ranking of the members is shared and consistent with broader status beliefs makes it seem to be a correct, legitimate, and objectively reasonable assessment of who is really better at what the group values.[68]

With this in mind, consider a situation in which a member ranked lower in expected competence by the group finds that her opinion on a goal-related matter disagrees with that of a higher-ranked member. She could persist with her distinctive opinion, but instead, the lower-ranked member defers and agrees to go along with the views of the higher-ranked member. From the group perspective, this deference behavior shows good judgment. Her behavior is eminently reasonable, since the higher-ranked member is presumed to be legitimately more competent at the goal effort. In effect, the lower-ranked member's deference endorses the group's "reasonable" consensus about who is more competent and status-worthy in the situation, and this effect, in turn, makes the lower-ranked member look as if she is *reasonable* as well.

This performance of good judgment and reasonable deference, Nakagawa and I argue, is likely to cause other group members to view the low-status member with a basic measure of *respect* and approval. Being respected as reasonable, in turn, is a modest reward that can increase the low-status member's commitment to the group and its goal efforts. Three studies we conducted support this argument.[69]

In the first study, higher-status participants in a task-oriented group were asked how they would view the low-status member if he or she reacted with either deference or resistance in a disagreement with one of the higher-status members. They reported that they would be highly likely to view the low-status member with respect and as reasonable if the member deferred, but were very unlikely to do so if he or she resisted. Significantly, the participants were just as likely to respect the low-status member when he or she deferred to another high-status member as when the deference was to self. This suggests that the granting of respect is a *normative* process and not simply a matter of high-status members rewarding a low-status member who defers to them personally.

A second study put participants in the position of being the low-status member in this situation and asked how they would be viewed by the others if they deferred or resisted in a disagreement with a higher-status member.[70] Again, participants reported that they were highly likely to be respected and viewed as reasonable if they chose deference, but not otherwise. Furthermore, 70 percent said that deference was the strategy they would choose if faced with such a disagreement when interacting in the group. These two studies together, by showing that participants reward normatively expected deference to another similarly to deference to self and that, when low status, they accurately anticipate such rewards, provide further empirical evidence that people are indeed following a shared normative schema as they enact status relations, just as the cultural schema theory argues.

In the third study, low-status group members in one condition were put in the position of deferring to a higher-status member in a disagreement and then told that others respected their behavior as reasonable.[71] These low-status members reported significantly more commitment to the group and willingness to help it do well than low-status members in another condition who did not receive respect for their deference. Respected low-status members also reported that they were much less likely to leave the group even if they could. Thus, being respected as reasonable does indeed increase low-status members' commitment to the group, despite having to accept low status.

The respect that the low-status members earn by deferring as expected is less than the esteem given to high-status members. It is a baseline respect for the deferrer as at least recognizing what is validly "better" for achieving the group's goals, even if he or she is not personally "better." But it still grants the lower-ranked member a certain dignity in the group as an accepted member who understands and shares the group's standards of value. Note that this modest reward for acceptance of low status emerges as a side effect of routine conformity to the normative processes through which the status hierarchy is enacted. In other words, this respected-as-reasonable reward is a systematic result of the twofold cultural schema of status—in particular, the enactment of the basic status norm.

Whether this modest reward is actually sufficient to induce low-status members to accept their position and continue contributing to the group in any given situation is likely to depend on the strength of other, countervailing options and constraints available to them. But this reward for low-status deference and commitment makes the acceptance of low status more appealing than it otherwise would be and systematically bolsters the likelihood that low-status members will stay involved. Moreover, for low-status members whose circumstances constrain them from leaving the group or resisting the hierarchy, being respected as reasonable at least eases an otherwise difficult situation. Such easing is similar to the other compensating factor associated with low status—being thought warmer and more considerate.[72] For low-status members, the modest reward generated by the cultural schema of status means that the price of being seen as "reasonable" in the group is deference. For the group as a whole, however, this systematic reward process, along with the compensation of being "nicer," helps sustain the commitment of those constrained to be low status by the normative processes of the status hierarchy.

The Insecurity of Status and the Stability of Status Structures

If people care so much about status and, as we have seen, experience it as inherently insecure, doesn't that mean that they also will really *compete* with one another for it?[73] Doesn't the motivating power of status threaten to explode the bounds of cooperation in a group of people who must work together to achieve a shared goal?[74] How does this work? How do status hierarchies maintain sufficient stability in order to function in the face of the powerfully centrifugal force of people's motives to attain higher status? This is a second issue we need to examine.

Although for individuals the psychological experience of interpersonal status may be one of contingency and mutability, one of the most common empirical observations of actual status hierarchies is that they tend to be relatively stable. Not only do interpersonal status hierarchies form quickly, but in most cases, once they do, the structure is maintained over repeated reconvenings of the group.[75] That is to say, individuals who are high status after the initial emergence and stabilization of the hierarchy tend to remain high status at later times.[76] It is not that the status hierarchy never changes, but that it tends to have a "stickiness" that resists change rather than a constant, shifting mutability. As we will see in later chapters, there are many contingent factors that can support the stability of interpersonal status hierarchies. Our task here, however, is to clarify the sources of stability that lie within the normative system of status itself.

In an effort to understand the structural stability of interpersonal status hierarchies in the face of people's competitive desires for status and sense of it as mutable, it is useful to go back to the discussion from chapter 2 about the nature of the rough consensus about each group member's relative value to the group that creates the status hierarchy. It is this effective consensus that would have to be unstable if the status hierarchy is unstable. What I have called the basic norm of status, that esteem and deference be granted in exchange for perceived value to the group, can only be enacted and enforced through such a rough consensus about each member's relative value. If, to attain such a consensus, each member's own personal sense of their relative value to the group had to be in accord with each other member's personal assessment of their relative value, then consensus might not be easy to achieve. Sometimes, of course, people willingly agree at a personal level that they are not as competent as another at the group goal and happily defer in the interest of group success and the rewards of being "reasonable." Yet this is not always the case, as at least two studies have shown.[77] Consensus at the ego level of "the status I really deserve" might indeed be destabilized by people's competitive desires for status.

Recall, however, that the evidence suggests that the consensus that enforces the basic status norm is really an agreement about what *others* in the group estimate is the status that I deserve, based on the information those others have about me. When our own first-order expectations about our value to the group conflict with our second-order expectations for how we think others estimate that value, studies show that it is our sense of *others'* expectations that most powerfully drives our claims for status and deference to others.[78] Recall, as well, that there are good reasons for this. When people make claims for higher status than others believe they deserve based on their perceived value to the group, they tend to be disliked, resisted, and even rejected.[79] As we noted earlier, people are accurate estimators of others' evaluations of their perceived value in the group, which they need to be if they are to anticipate the reactions that their status claims are likely to elicit.

The basic status norm is a *norm*—a cultural "rule" of status—precisely because it is enforced by others' sanctioning of status claims that do not conform to it. Thus, consensus among *others* about the relative value to the group of any given member backstops the stability of the status structure in the face of each individual's competitive desires for greater status. At the same time, the threat of sanctions reflected in this consensus among others may well feed the individual's psychological sense that their status is always implicitly at risk and potentially changeable. Also, while sanctions maintain the relative stability of the hierarchy, this does not mean that status conflicts never break out. As we saw in the last chapter, competitive tensions continue to lurk behind the normative status system. In addition, the maintenance of stability through norm enforcement is not always without cost to the group. When there are more private disagreements about who is higher status, despite public consensus, group task performance tends to suffer as the members involved in the disagreements reduce their contributions to the group effort.[80]

This analysis suggests that the stability of interpersonal status hierarchies depends not so much on individual members' assessments of their *own* value and their desires for status, as on the ability of group members to form a general consensus about the relative value of each *other* member. The cultural schema theory of status argues that group members achieve such consensus by each drawing on shared *status beliefs* about the social identities, personal attributes, and behaviors that indicate greater or lesser status-worthiness and specific or general competence at various things. This approach also accords with a broad tradition of sociological research on status characteristics and expectation states theory of status processes.[81] It is because of the vital role of common knowledge status beliefs in allowing interpersonal groups to quickly form a stabilizing consensus about each member's relative value to the group that I have argued that our cultural schema for organizing status relations consists of not only the implicit basic status norm but also a more explicit and variable set of cultural status beliefs.

In the discussion so far, I have emphasized the usefulness of access to shared cultural status beliefs for groups of interdependent individuals who are trying to form assessments of another member's relative value to group. Drawing on shared status beliefs helps them coordinate their evaluations of a given other with the evaluations that other group members are also forming of the same person so that they can all act together effectively. But taking into account the psychological experience of status as having an inherent element of uncertainty and insecurity, it seems likely that people also have a second, more *self-oriented* interest in forming and using clear, slow-to-change status beliefs.

By allowing individuals to anticipate how others in their culture will evaluate their worthiness and competence, given their social identities, attributes, and behaviors, status beliefs are also a tool to assuage psychological uncertainty.[82] Status beliefs at least let you clarify "where you stand" in the eyes of the group or community. Research has shown that when people's sense of control over a social situation is threatened (for instance, by the psychological uncertainty of status), they have an increased preference for structure and hierarchy.[83] Access to a shared set of clear, relatively stable status beliefs that rank social attributes and behaviors provides a form of such structure and hierarchy that meets individual psychological needs as well as collective goals. Thus, personal needs as well as shared, cooperative needs may drive people to form and maintain cultural status beliefs.

By this analysis, then, the capacity of interpersonal status hierarchies to maintain a functional degree of stability depends more on their members sharing clear, stable cultural status beliefs than on the personal, psychological experience of status as changeable and competitively desirable. It is entirely possible, of course, that interpersonal status hierarchies, while relatively stable, really are more changeable over time and the course of contingent events than are the less dynamic status hierarchies among, say, prestigious and less prestigious firms in an industry, or social identity groups based on gender or race. In the next chapter, we will look more closely at status beliefs and their link not only to interpersonal hierarchies but also to status processes among social groups and organizations.

CHAPTER 4

STATUS BELIEFS AND THE ORGANIZATION OF INEQUALITY

OVER THE PAST few chapters, I have made the case that status, at root, is a human cultural invention. It is a blueprint or schema of cultural rules that we use to organize and manage circumstances that we continually find ourselves in because they are basic to the human condition. We are often cooperatively interdependent with others to achieve valued goals and outcomes that we cannot attain alone. Yet that very interdependence creates its own competitive tensions. We reach to the familiar, deeply learned cultural schema of status to manage these tensions and organize ourselves to achieve our goals in the face of them. And as we do so, we spread status concerns and status-based inequalities to one situation after another, weaving it into groups and organizations of all sorts. It is precisely because status is a cultural schema that we can apply it permissively to so many circumstances so that it spreads everywhere.[1]

These are the claims of the cultural schema theory of status that I have put forward. So far, I have done so by focusing on the dynamics of interpersonal status hierarchies—both as the core source of the tensions that create the status schema and the nexus of needs that make us care so much about status. Now it is time to expand our focus to take into account the broader social framework within which interpersonal status hierarchies develop. We need to address the status of our group identities, like race or gender, and the status of the organizations we deal with. The cultural schema theory claims, after all, that the status schema is twofold, consisting of not only a basic status norm for status allocation but also a set of associated *status beliefs* about social differences that are widely understood in the surrounding culture to indicate greater or lesser status-worthiness and competence.

Status beliefs are key to understanding not only how interpersonal status hierarchies work, but also how status involves relations among groups as well as individuals and how it has far-reaching consequences for larger structures of inequality. It is status beliefs that *link* the status of the social groups to which people belong, like their racial group or their occupational group, to the esteem with which they are treated in everyday social interactions, whether in a restaurant or in the workplace. Status beliefs are also the means by which actors *coordinate* their judgments of who is "better," more valuable, and worthy of esteem so that these judgments carry the weight of the group. Through both processes, status beliefs become fundamental to inequality not only at the individual but at the societal level. Besides their impact on the social outcomes and positions that people achieve in society, they also give people distinctive advantages or disadvantages based on the social groups to which they belong rather than just on their personal attributes. It is time now to look more closely at these status beliefs.

At this point, we need a more precise definition to work with. *Status beliefs are widely held cultural beliefs that link a recognized social difference among actors with greater or lesser status-worthiness and competence.*[2] A recognized social difference (for instance, gender, race, occupation, social class) by definition divides actors into contrasting *groups* or categories based on the difference (women versus men, middle-class versus working-class). In this way, status beliefs are always about groups that are characterized by the "types of actors" that define the groups. Examples are rich people versus poor people, whites versus people of color, people who act assertively versus those who act hesitantly, those with special skills versus those without them, and so on.[3] Distinctively, however, status beliefs not only differentiate but *rank-order* the type of actors in one group compared to a contrasting group in terms of who is more status-worthy and generally more competent. Recall that in contemporary Western societies, "value" for the collective, and therefore status, is understood primarily as instrumental competence.[4] Status beliefs, then, are about who—what type of actor—is "better" in the society than another in terms of social esteem and valued competence. This is their link to inequality.

As the preceding discussion suggests, the implied "actors" in status beliefs are typically individuals. This makes sense if we keep in mind that interpersonal status hierarchies are the core source of the status schema. But as people spread the status schema to broader contexts, status beliefs also develop about types of corporate actors, such as investment firms or producers of automobiles or universities. Think of the status implications of being Goldman Sachs versus the credit union, BMW instead of Kia, or Harvard rather than the state college. Even status beliefs about corporate actors, however, imply to some degree "types" of people who act in their roles as representatives of these corporate entities and are understood to be more or less competent and esteemed in their organizational field. An example would be the senior partner representing a prestigious law firm compared to the senior partner from a little-known law firm.

Finally, the social difference around which status beliefs develop can be any easily recognized social characteristic or group distinction. It is worth keeping in mind that the need to form shared status beliefs in order to coordinate everyday status relations itself drives people to look for, exaggerate, and make wider use of the differences that they see among them.[5] Many status beliefs develop around preexisting social distinctions, such as between ethnic groups, genders, neighborhoods, or organizations.[6] But groups can also create their own distinguishing signs to differentiate themselves from others and assert their superiority. Social class groups, for instance, typically develop distinctive tastes or manners as a ready sign that they are better than others.[7] Since status beliefs are consequential for members of social groups, it can be a political project for groups to distinguish themselves in an effort to foster status beliefs that advantage them. But these status beliefs must come to be widely held in the broader community or society for this political project to succeed.

In what follows, I start by examining more deeply the distinctive nature and content of status beliefs. The goal of this discussion will be to understand what gives status beliefs force in social relations and allows them to shape inequality. Central to this discussion will be a focus on the way in which status beliefs, as a form of cultural "common knowledge," allow actors to coordinate their status-related judgments of "value." Next is a brief overview of the evidence about how status beliefs shape broader patterns of inequality among people from different social groups—a topic we will discuss in much greater detail in later chapters. Then I turn to research about how status beliefs about social differences develop in the first place. We will see that status beliefs develop about differences among organizations as well as people. This leads to a brief examination of research on status relations among organizations and what it tells us about the conditions necessary for the status schema to spread beyond the interpersonal hierarchy. I conclude with a discussion of contemporary theoretical models of the processes by which status beliefs create status advantage based on an actor's group identity, a process that lies at the root of the effects of these beliefs on inequality.

The Distinctive Nature of Status Beliefs

Status beliefs, by definition, center on and evaluate social differences. In fact, the mere recognition of social difference is enough to evoke an evaluative response in people, but this response typically is to favor their own "side" of the difference (their own group) as "better." If your group is the Reds and my group is the Blues, then my first thought is *Blues are better.* This has been repeatedly demonstrated in a large body of research associated with social identity theory, a prominent social psychological theory.[8] Such simple own-group favoritism, however, is not enough to create a status belief because it results in competing views about which group is better. For a status belief to form, both those in the social difference group favored as better and those disfavored as lesser must come to *agree,* as a matter of social reality, that those in the favored group are viewed by society as more esteemed and competent than are those from the other group.[9] This is the hallmark of status beliefs—that the evaluative rank order among the groups is acknowledged by all the groups involved. For status beliefs to develop, then, one group must overcome its tendency to see itself as better and accept, or at least concede, that the broader community sees the other group as better than them. As we shall see, this is a process for which theories about the development of status beliefs must account.

As beliefs about how groups are evaluatively ranked by the "community" or "society," status beliefs are distinctively beliefs about what "most people" believe or could be presumed to believe about the groups. Because of their signature nature as widely shared beliefs about what most people think, I and others refer to status beliefs as *third-order beliefs.*[10] That is, people do not understand them as simply their personal beliefs about which group is best (first-order beliefs). They are also not just perceptions of how specific others in a local encounter evaluatively rank the groups (second-order beliefs).[11] Instead, people understand status beliefs as the typical views of the community as a whole, which is a third-order belief about the evaluative perspective of "most" people.

People who hold status beliefs as third-order beliefs often but certainly not always endorse them personally as well (that is, also hold them as first-order beliefs). Personal endorsement of a status belief may be most likely among those whose own group is favored by the belief, but it does occur even when the belief casts their own group as lower status.[12] Studies show, for instance, that men and women share similar gender stereotypes, including status beliefs that favor men.[13] This third-order consensus about what "most" believe, however, does not mean that everyone similarly agrees, at a personal level, that men really are more status-worthy and competent than women. Note that this creates a possibility for a disjuncture between the extent to which a status belief is held as a third-order belief and the extent to which it is endorsed as a first-order belief. That is, at some point, people may still assume that most people respect a group while at a personal level many no longer do. This situation of pluralistic ignorance is likely to be fragile and points to processes by which status beliefs may collapse and change.[14]

Status beliefs' nature as third-order beliefs is what gives them *force* in social relations.[15] If I assume that most people share a status belief, then I expect that they will act in accord with that belief. I assume, as well, that they will judge me according to that belief. As a result, I must take that belief into account in my own decisions and behavior whether or not I personally endorse it. For instance, if I am a state college graduate interviewing with a firm that usually hires Ivy League graduates, I need to anticipate that I may be underestimated and take this into account in figuring out what I can do to counter the interviewer's impression of me. My ability to get the job depends on my ability to estimate their judgments and coordinate my responses accordingly. As this account suggests, then, the third-order nature of status beliefs is what causes people to draw on them to estimate how others will judge an actor's relative status-worthiness and competence. And because the reactions of others will affect the outcomes of the actor's own judgments and behavior in the situation (that is, there is interdependence), the actor uses the status belief to coordinate his or her behavior with the others involved.

Because status beliefs, owing to their third-order nature, lead to an implicit coordination process, they shape the actor's status judgments and behavior in ways that might not occur without them. As they do so, status beliefs create *status advantage*. By status advantage, I mean that actors labeled as high status by status beliefs are treated as more status-worthy and competent than they would be without that label, and those labeled as low status are treated as less worthy and competent than they otherwise would be.[16] To get a sense of status advantage, do the following thought experiment. Think of a person with a BA degree, job-relevant skills, and an assertive but friendly personality. Now imagine this person is a white man who has an upper-middle-class background and therefore comes from high-status social difference groups. Then imagine this person is, instead, an African American woman with a working-class background, who is thus someone who belongs to lower-status groups. How does the initial impression of this person's competence and status-worthiness change with the knowledge of his or her status-valued group identities? This is status (dis)advantage.

Status advantage is fundamental to how status beliefs create inequality, and we will say more about it later in this chapter. For now, however, we need to look more closely at the coordination function of status beliefs because it is important both for how interpersonal hierarchies work and for the implications of status for broader patterns of inequality.

Status Beliefs and Coordination

In past chapters, we have repeatedly seen that people's ability to enact status hierarchies, especially in the real time of interaction, is dependent on their ability to quickly form roughly consensual judgments of each member's perceived value to the group's success. This ability to coordinate judgments of value so that they can act together to enforce the basic status norm is what allows the group to exercise some control over a would-be dominator. It similarly undergirds the stability of the status hierarchy in the face of the centrifugal force of people's individual competitive desires for status. People manage the trick of coordinating judgments, I have argued, by drawing on cultural status beliefs that they share because these beliefs are common knowledge in their society or wider community. The connection between coordination and common knowledge cultural beliefs, like third-order status beliefs, is worth unpacking a bit.

By providing people with a set of cultural codes about the types of actors presumed to be more competent in the wider society, status beliefs clearly offer people in interpersonal groups a shorthand for quickly (if not necessarily accurately) judging the relative value to the group of another member's efforts. But the enactment of status hierarchies requires not just that people make quick judgments of each other's relative value to the group, but that they make shared, roughly *consensual* judgments. In the definition of status beliefs offered earlier, the characteristic that matters most here is their being "widely held" in the relevant community or society in which the group members are acting.[17] In fact, to coordinate consensual judgments, status beliefs need not only to be widely held in that most people in the community know them—that is, to be what is known as shared knowledge. Status beliefs also need to be widely held in the further sense of being commonly recognized as cultural beliefs that most people can reasonably presume are known by most other people (that is, they are widely held as third-order beliefs). This is what is known as "common knowledge."[18]

Many kinds of situations, including many everyday social interactions, pose coordination problems for their participants. That is, for the people involved to achieve their ends, they need to take into account how the other is likely to behave in order to figure out how best to act themselves. Both classic sociologists like Erving Goffman, in his studies of social interaction, and contemporary game theorists have come to the same conclusion about how people typically solve these coordination problems: each draws on the same common knowledge, a kind of shared social script, as the basis for his or her actions.[19] As a result, their joint actions, even though chosen individually, fit together in a coordinated way. At a wedding, for instance, when someone leads you to the dance floor for a ceremonial waltz, you step forward to the music in the anticipation that your partner, also knowing how to waltz, will step back as you turn smoothly around the floor. If the waltz is not common knowledge between the two of you, you will step on each other's feet, and the result is awkward indeed.

Why does it matter if status beliefs are not just shared knowledge but common knowledge? Consider a group of people trying to figure out who seems more competent and who has more to offer the group than whom. In such a context, there is some risk in acting on your judgment of another's value by, say, deferring and going along with the others' view, on the one hand, or resisting and arguing against those views, on the other. How will the others in the group react to your deference or resistance? Will they be supportive? Or will they assume that you are wrong? If you and the others happen to share the same status beliefs (that is, the beliefs are shared knowledge) and use them to make similar judgments of value, the others are likely to support you. But you can't really know this before you take the risk of acting and then seeing the response. By contrast, if the status beliefs are common knowledge—what "everybody knows"—you can presume before you take the risk that the others in the group are likely to share your judgment and support your action. In this way, common knowledge status beliefs allow group members to quickly form roughly consensual judgments that they can confidently act on in a coordinated way to enact the status hierarchy and enforce the basic status norm.

In fact, experiments by psychologists show that people are quite sensitive to common knowledge in deciding whether to engage in risky but potentially beneficial coordination with others.[20] In these studies, participants could make a higher payoff if they chose to work together, but only if they both did so. Participants, it turned out, were more likely to take the risk of coordinating if the payoff rules were public, common knowledge among them than if the rules were just shared or private knowledge. The researchers argue that their studies imply that people represent common knowledge as a distinct cognitive category in their minds that licenses them to coordinate for mutual gain.[21] Since such coordination situations are characteristic of so much of social life, our minds, the researchers suggest, learn to be closely attuned to the kind of information that helps us manage them, much of which is shared as cultural beliefs. What we see here is that cooperative interdependence to achieve a shared goal, which is the context that gives rise to status hierarchies, is just such a coordination situation. And widely held status beliefs are the common knowledge cultural beliefs that people develop and learn to manage them. Because they understand status beliefs as third-order beliefs about what "most people" think, people assume that they can rely on status beliefs to help manage their coordination challenges in goal-oriented situations.

Throughout the discussion so far, I have asserted that status beliefs are widely held as third-order beliefs about what most people think. But what is the empirical evidence that contemporary cultural beliefs that, say, link status-worthiness and competence with gender or race or occupation are in fact common knowledge beliefs among Americans? The evidence comes from studies conducted by the psychologist Susan Fiske and her colleagues of the stereotypes that Americans hold for the commonly recognized social groups in U.S. society.[22] These studies show, first, that status beliefs are clearly embedded in the stereotypes of all the groups by which inequality is patterned in American society, including race, age, gender, class, and occupational and educational groups. That is to say, among the stereotypic beliefs about these groups are beliefs that they differ in status-worthiness and competence. Second, the very similar answers given when diverse samples of Americans are asked to describe the stereotypes of these groups suggest that these beliefs are consensual in that most everybody knows them as cultural knowledge. Finally, these stereotypes and the status beliefs they contain are not simply personally held beliefs but what respondents assume most Americans believe.[23] They are, in other words, not merely shared but common cultural knowledge, and they have the character of third-order beliefs.

The status beliefs that are most consequential for broad patterns of inequality in society are those that are broadly held across the society, like the group stereotypes just discussed. But of course, these are not the only status beliefs that develop and have an impact on interpersonal hierarchies. Communities of all sorts can develop their own particular status beliefs that matter for status relations among their members. Occupational associations, for instance, often have their own distinct status beliefs about the recognized signs of status-worthiness and competence in their community, beliefs that are not always understood or shared by outsiders. For instance, the sociologist Alison Bianchi and colleagues, in a study of open-source programmers, found that they developed status beliefs that were unique to their community about the special signs of status-worthiness and competence that were most important for their judgments of a programmer's value.[24] Interestingly, these open-source programmers also developed shared cultural norms about ignoring some status beliefs from the wider society, like those based on education and age, in judging competence and value in the programming community. On the other hand, it is likely that these same programmers, in their social relations outside of the open-source community, continued to find that the wider status beliefs about age and education mattered for how others treated them and how they were expected to behave in return. Status beliefs and their effects are typically bounded by the communities that share them as common knowledge. But since people belong to multiple communities, they typically respond to a wide variety of status beliefs as they move from context to context.

The Content of Status Beliefs

The evaluative content of status beliefs lies at the center of their effects on actors' evaluations and behavior toward one another. A little more detailed consideration of this content in terms of status-worthiness and competence will help us understand their broader effects on status hierarchies and inequality.

Competence

Status characteristics and expectation states theory—an empirically well-documented sociological theory of how status beliefs shape interpersonal status hierarchies—is particularly helpful for unpacking the competence content of status beliefs. It distinguishes between two types of status beliefs based on their competence implications.[25] The status beliefs with the broadest, most general implications for inequality are those that link a group difference with differences in overall general competence. The theory labels these *diffuse status characteristics* because the link with general competence makes such status beliefs diffusely relevant to judgments of an actor's competence across a wide variety of tasks and contexts. These general competence assumptions suggest that people from the high-status group can be expected to be diffusely "better" at most things, especially the things that count most in society, than are those from lower-status groups. These diffuse competence expectations even imply that those in the higher-status group would be better at mastering tasks not stereotypically linked to them, if they put their minds to it. Men, for instance, are expected to be the great chefs, even if women are stereotypically linked with cooking. As this suggests, however, in addition to carrying powerful expectations for general competence, diffuse status characteristics also typically carry associations with a number of stereotypic specific skills that have historically been associated with that social difference group (for instance, cooking, math ability, or athleticism).[26]

Evidence suggests that gender, race, education, and occupation are all diffuse status characteristics in that they are linked by status beliefs with assumptions about general competence as well as with varieties of specific skills.[27] Because they act as diffuse status characteristics, these group identities have wide-ranging effects on inequalities in everyday social relations. For that reason, status beliefs that link group differences with general competence will be our primary focus in later chapters that address the role of status in perpetuating inequalities based on differences like race, gender, or social class.

There are other sorts of status beliefs, however, that link more specific social differences with a bounded range of competence that is relevant to some types of task-oriented situations but not others. For example, some people, compared to others, have foreign-language skills, or programming skills, or plumbing expertise. Status characteristics theory calls these *specific status characteristics.*[28] In American society, which values instrumental competence, advanced levels of specialized training or expertise are generally seen as carrying a degree of esteem and status. But the contexts in which specific status characteristics measurably shape judgments of an actor's value to the group are generally limited to those in which the associated competence is relevant to the group's goal effort. In a group traveling abroad, the member with foreign-language skills will be esteemed and given influence, but that expertise may count for little when the group returns home and takes up a very different task. When we examine the microdynamics of status hierarchies in the next chapter, we will discuss in more detail how specific and diffuse status characteristics work together to shape judgments of value to the group.

Status-Worthiness

The other ingredient of status beliefs, status-worthiness, represents the relative level of social esteem that society associates with a social difference group and the type of actors who make up that group. Social difference groups are esteemed for the extent to which they are perceived as offering, or having the capacity to offer, value to the larger community or society, however the community defines that value. Although beliefs about a group's relative esteem and status-worthiness are the fundamental, defining ingredient of status beliefs, in some ways they are the most complex and least well understood empirically. To some extent, the status-worthiness element in American status beliefs just represents the esteem and honor that American culture associates more broadly with assumptions about greater or lesser competence. In her studies of common group stereotypes in the United States, Susan Fiske found beliefs about a group's status and its competence to be so closely related (correlations of about $r = .90$) that the two concepts virtually defined one another.[29]

Other evidence suggests, however, that status-worthiness may incorporate, at least tangentially, another dimension in addition to the esteem attached to competence. This other stream of research suggests that there is something of a moral element to the social honor and esteem represented by beliefs about status-worthiness.[30] The moral implications of status-worthiness derive from the tensions between leaders and followers in groups that we alluded to at the end of chapter 2. In granting an actor high status and influence, the other members need to see the actor not only as competent but as someone who can be trusted to use her competence to help the group rather than just for her self-interest.[31] This is the moral trust factor in interpersonal status hierarchies. We have referred to this factor as a perception of the actor as group-motivated rather than as self-motivated. As we will see in the next chapter, how important this factor is for granting status varies greatly with the group context but generally it is less important than competence.[32]

How are these moral concerns that arise from tensions in interpersonal status hierarchies reflected in cultural status beliefs about types of actors (that is, groups or categories of actors)? There is not sufficient research to answer this question with certainty. However, the research that does exist suggests that the answer may not be simple. Fiske's studies of group stereotypes that demonstrated the association of status and competence also showed another provocative association: as a general pattern, higher-status groups (for instance, men, whites, professionals) were perceived as less warm and communal, even if more agentic and competent, than lower-status groups (women, people of color, blue-collar workers).[33] Other psychological research offers further evidence that North Americans have a general cultural schema of high- and low-status actors in which high-status actors are seen as more agentic and competent and not as communal as low-status actors.[34] To some extent, this schema reflects the behavioral context of interpersonal status hierarchies in which high-status actors are proactive and agentic while lower-status actors are cast into the role of reacting to and agreeing with others.[35] But according to research by the organizational scholars Oliver Hahl and Ezra Zuckerman, part of the difference between high- and low-status actors may also be due to the moral suspiciousness of high-status actors in the eyes of the group (are they self- rather than group-interested?).[36] The slight aura of moral suspiciousness that attends high status (at least in American culture), these researchers argue, makes people presume that high-status actors are less warm and "authentic," unless they demonstrate their good intentions behaviorally.[37]

Taken together, this stream of research suggests that widely held status beliefs about social groups in American society do not, in themselves, contain full assurances of the moral, group-oriented nature of those in high-status groups. Rather, the status-worthiness and esteem attributed to groups in these beliefs derives primarily from the presumed general competence of those in high-status groups and the acknowledged position of respect that this superior competence grants them in society. In other words, the recognized, common knowledge nature of the status beliefs that represent one group as more respected and generally more competent than another itself creates a sense that they are "better" and "status-worthy."

Status Beliefs and Inequality among Types of People

People's use of common knowledge status beliefs about social differences to coordinate their judgments of who is "better" in their everyday, goal-oriented encounters has far-reaching implications for social inequality. We will discuss this process in considerable detail in subsequent chapters. Right now, however, to appreciate the significance of status beliefs, it is useful to have a framing outline of their implications for linking interpersonal status hierarchies to broader patterns of inequality.

If people in groups reach to their cultural knowledge of status beliefs to make quick, consensual sense of each other's likely value to their group effort, then this has an obvious implication. People's social identities as members of high- or low-status groups will significantly shape their perceived competence and value and therefore the esteem with which they are treated and the influence they attain in the local group context. This *status generalization* process, as it is called, has been observed in empirical studies for decades.[38] For instance, an influential study of juries in the 1950s found that jurors' gender and the status of their occupations were among the major determinants of their influence and prominence in the proceedings.[39]

Status characteristics and expectation states theory, the sociological theory of interpersonal status, provides a detailed explanation for the status generalization process that we will review in the next chapter.[40] In brief, the theory argues that whenever people come together to work on a shared task or goal, cultural status beliefs about their social characteristics will become implicitly salient for them either if they differ on the characteristic (for example, the setting is mixed-occupation or mixed-gender) or if the characteristic is culturally understood to be relevant to the group's goals (the setting is gender-typed or occupationally typed). When status beliefs are implicitly salient, they bias group members' expectations for their own and the others' competence and suitability for status in the group. Members' biased self-other expectations, which they are rarely conscious of, have self-fulfilling effects in turn on what transpires in the group. Biased expectations subtly shape who feels emboldened to act assertively and who hesitates, how a member is able to perform in the group, how others evaluate that performance independent of its actual quality, what ability the group attributes to the member, and consequently, the influence and esteem the member attains in the situation.[41]

In these ways, status-biased expectations create apparent differences between otherwise similar actors from higher- or lower-status groups in how outspoken and competent they seem and how influential and prominent they become in the situation. In a business meeting, a job interview, or an encounter between a patient and doctor, for instance, actors from status-advantaged groups like whites or men are presumed to be a little more competent and appropriate for leadership than are otherwise similar actors from status-disadvantaged groups like people of color or women. As a result, a woman in a similar position with similar pay as a man may still be slightly disadvantaged for a promotion, compared to him, by the implicit, status-based presumption that she is not quite as broadly competent and worthy of leadership as he is. Note that the advantage that gender status beliefs give the man is not based on his individual attributes but on his *group identity* as a man. This is among the ways in which status beliefs play a central role in reproducing inequality based on group identities like race, gender, or social class.[42]

As this suggests, it is the biasing effect of macrolevel status beliefs about group differences on everyday microlevel status hierarchies that makes such hierarchies more than mere random noise in broader inequality processes. Goal-oriented encounters taking place in educational settings, the workplace, health institutions, and elsewhere mediate people's access to the rewards, like money and power, and the life outcomes, like health, by which we judge inequality in society. Because of status beliefs, interpersonal hierarchies independently enacted over these diverse but consequential goal-oriented contexts take on systematically similar shapes in terms of the categories of people who end up more or less advantaged within them and revealed as "better." To the extent that status beliefs about group differences create a corresponding interpersonal hierarchy, that hierarchy provides its participants with a vivid, apparently valid demonstration of the greater apparent competence and worthiness of those from high-status difference groups. This, in turn, reinforces cultural status beliefs. In this way, status beliefs are key to how actor-level status evaluations of who is "better" interweave inequality based on group differences into modern "meritocratic" organizations of resources and power. We will take these points up in greater detail in chapter 6.

How Do Status Beliefs Develop?

If status beliefs are so important for people's ability to coordinate judgments and manage cooperative encounters and also so significant for inequality between social groups, then one might imagine that we would know a great deal about how they develop. Surprisingly, this is not the case. There are a few theories and some research, but we need to know much more.

Max Weber observed a century ago that, historically speaking, social groups (the occupational group of bankers, for example, or an immigrant group) generally acquire material resources and wealth in a society first and then later, over time, acquire status as well.[43] Weber's observation is appealing and well known. We noted earlier that given how much people value status and the real advantages it brings, a group can implicitly or explicitly take on the political project of fostering status beliefs that favor their group over others. But we also noted that it is not enough for a group to want such beliefs—these beliefs must become accepted and widely held in the broader society.

Weber's observation alone, then, does not really explain how—that is, through what processes—status beliefs could develop about a group difference. It merely points to a particular structural condition in a society that might foster such beliefs. Keep in mind that any theory about how status beliefs develop needs first to explain how a group difference becomes associated with corresponding differences in status-worthiness and competence, and second, how such beliefs become widely held in the society. Recall that in order to be widely held, a status belief must come to be accepted not just by the group it deems high status but also by the groups it deems lower status. This means that, to become a consensual, common knowledge part of society's culture, even those in the lower-status group must come to accept, as a matter of social reality, the status belief that "most people" would rate those in the higher-status group as more respected and generally more competent than those in the lower-status group. How might this happen?

Status Construction Theory

Status construction theory is a theory of one way in which status beliefs might develop and become widely held.[44] It argues that the processes it describes are sufficient to create widely held status beliefs about a social difference but are unlikely to be the only way this happens. The theory focuses on goal-oriented encounters that take place between people from different social groups in the course of their everyday experience as an important source of status beliefs. These can be any such encounters—in trade, business, the workplace, or the community, including those among family and kin. Under certain conditions, the theory argues, these local encounters create experiences that encourage those involved to form shared status beliefs about their social difference. These encounters also spread status beliefs as those who hold the beliefs treat others according to them, encouraging those others to adopt the beliefs as well. This creates a diffusion process that can lead to widely held status beliefs, the theory claims.

What circumstances would lead cooperative, goal-oriented encounters between people from different groups to foster status beliefs about their difference? In these encounters, hierarchies of esteem and influence are likely to develop quickly, as we know they nearly always do. The theory argues that if something about the conditions in which these encounters take place gives people from one group a systematic advantage over those from the other group in appearing competent and becoming influential in these encounters, then the encounters will encourage those involved to form status beliefs favoring the advantaged group. A variety of circumstances, such as greater wealth, relevant knowledge, or control over technology, could give members of one social difference group a systematic advantage in appearing competent in their encounters with members of the other group.

But how does an encounter in which people from one difference group are perceived as more competent and influential than people from another group induce all participants to form status beliefs about their difference? The theory points out that hierarchies of influence and esteem, even when biased by some outside circumstance, typically develop implicitly through small behaviors that those involved in the encounter rarely notice. Events in the encounter simply seem to reveal that some (those in the advantaged group) are more competent and prominent than others (those in the less advantaged group). Because the actual source of the influence hierarchy is obscure in the situation, but the social difference between the participants is salient for them, the theory argues that there is a chance that they will associate their group difference with their relative esteem and apparent competence in the context. In so doing, those involved in the encounter begin to form a status belief about their social difference.

If subsequent encounters repeat the same experience for those involved, in which people in the advantaged group seem more competent and influential, then the likelihood increases that they will form a status belief about the social difference. And of course, given the systematic advantage that those in one group have in these encounters, such experiences are indeed more likely to be repeated than not. After multiple encounters like this, even those in the less advantaged group, because they also experience the situational "superiority" of those in the more advantaged group, are pressured to believe that "most people" would see the typical member of the other group as more status-worthy and competent than typical members of their own group. In this way, repeated encounters create shared status beliefs about social differences. And once people acquire a status belief, they teach it to others by treating them according to it in subsequent encounters, potentially spreading it widely in the population.

Empirical tests of status construction theory have supported several parts of this argument, particularly those about the power of encounters between socially different people to foster status beliefs about the difference. First tests of the theory took on Weber's argument. They examined whether, if one group gained an average advantage in material resources over another group, that would systematically bias their perceived competence and influence in repeated encounters with the other group. This, in turn, would lead to status beliefs favoring the advantaged group.[45]

A series of experiments created an artificial social difference between participants based on a purported test of "personal response style" and paid those with one response style slightly more than those with the other style. After only two decision-making encounters in which these pay differences led to influence differences between team members who (supposedly) differed in response style type, participants formed status beliefs favoring the pay-advantaged response group. That is, participants in both response style groups formed beliefs that "most people" would rate the typical members of the better-paid, more influential group as higher status, more respected, and more competent—but also as not being as considerate as the typical member of the other style group. Such status beliefs did not form when participants merely knew the pay differences between the groups but did not experience the influence hierarchy between them.[46]

It is striking that the beliefs that study participants formed so readily had the full form of status beliefs as we have described them. They were third-order beliefs about what "most people" think, not just beliefs about what the team members thought themselves about people in one response style group compared to the other. The experiences of two consistent encounters, in other words, made participants think that there was a socially valid reality here—those with one style type clearly were more status-worthy and competent than the other and would be rated that way by most people. Finally, these newly formed status beliefs also showed the full, characteristic form of status beliefs: the higher-status group was seen as not as considerate and warm as the lower-status group.[47]

Status construction theory argues that it is the apparently *consensual* acceptance among the participants in local encounters of the emergent influence advantage of those in one difference group over those in another difference group that encourages people to infer third-order status beliefs.[48] When additional encounters repeat the experience, the consensus supporting the hierarchy seems even broader, increasing the apparent social validity of the link between the social difference and status and competence. Eventually, the theory argues, participants make the leap that "most people" would accept that link and that therefore they must, as a matter of social reality, accept it themselves. In this way, they form a status belief about the social difference, even if it disadvantages their own group.

In an experiment confirming this argument, when an association between the social difference and influence and competence in the encounters simply emerged (and thus appeared consensual), status beliefs formed as in previous studies. But when the apparently consensual acceptance of this association was challenged by a participant, those involved did not develop status beliefs about the difference.[49] It seems, then, that people infer a broader consensus about the validity of a status belief from just a few experiences of local consensual acceptance of it.

It may seem surprising that participants in these studies made inferences so quickly not just about their teammates but also about the social difference groups to which they belonged. But other research has shown that this is not unusual. The psychologist David Hamilton and his colleagues showed that people do not just make spontaneous inferences about the dispositional traits of the individuals with whom they interact.[50] When they have even a little evidence that these individuals belong to groups and act similarly as others in the group, they also spontaneously make inferences about the traits of the typical members of the whole group (for instance, that they are respected and competent, but not so considerate). The researchers suggest, as we have here, that because groups are so fundamental to human life, people's very ways of thinking, even at an automatic level, are tuned to groups along with individuals.

Further experiments on how status beliefs form support another important prediction of status construction theory. These studies show that any *biasing factor*, not just material resources like pay, that gives members of one social difference group an influence advantage over members of another group in their joint encounters will foster status beliefs about their social difference.[51] As we mentioned, a variety of factors, like specialized skills, better technology, or superior information, when possessed, on average, more by one difference group than the other, could provide such a systematic advantage in gaining influence. Joseph Berger and Hamit Fisek note, for instance, that when members from one difference group (say, one newly forming occupational group) are advantaged compared to another group by existing diffuse status characteristics (say, the members are disproportionately men while the other group has more women), the value of the members' diffuse status characteristics will spread to the group difference, creating status beliefs favoring the advantaged group.[52]

Once people form status beliefs about a social difference from local encounters, other experiments show, they treat others according to these beliefs in subsequent encounters.[53] And when they do so, by casting those socially different others as higher or lower status in the encounter, they "teach" these beliefs to the others, as additional experiments show.[54] In this way, encounters spread status beliefs in a diffusion process. Computer simulations of this diffusion confirm that status beliefs that are widely held in the population would be a plausible result under many social conditions.[55] In particular, status construction theory predicts that the stronger the association between the social difference and an influence biasing factor (is nearly everyone in one group richer than those in the other group, or just some?) and the higher the rate of encounters between people from the different groups, the more likely this diffusion process is to result in widely held status beliefs about the difference.[56] Using cross-cultural data, Matthew Brashears reports support for this prediction.[57]

A Brief Example: The Construction of Gender as a Status Difference

It is worth pausing a moment to consider the relevance of status construction theory's arguments for the origins of some prominent, long-entrenched status distinctions in contemporary society, such as gender. The actual historical origins of beliefs about men's status superiority in Western or other societies are lost in the past, and I will not try to reconstruct them here. But we can at least note that gender has some distinctive characteristics as a social difference that make it highly likely that the processes described by status construction theory would create status beliefs about it even if other processes might be involved as well.[58]

We can think of gender as a socially constructed difference between people (men and women) linked to the sex categorization of them as male or female based on physical differences. With its link to bodily differences that have implications for reproduction, the social difference of sex/gender is bound to be a highly salient difference, one that people look for and notice in every society. Indeed, people learn to sex-categorize others from infancy on and come to do so automatically and almost instantly.[59] Of course, people may sometimes miscategorize others or encounter people whom they have difficulty categorizing, but they virtually always try to sex-categorize those they encounter. Significantly, sex/gender's relevance to reproduction also means that men and women have a cooperative, functional interdependence with one another to bear and raise children, at least under most circumstances.[60]

These distinctive aspects of sex/gender create two basic conditions that foster status beliefs, according to status construction theory: a difference that is salient to people in virtually all contexts and that leads to frequent, often intimate, cooperative interdependence between people of different sex/gender categories. Under cooperative interdependence, as we know, implicit hierarchies of status and influence are likely to develop. With sex/gender being a salient difference between them, participants are likely to associate their status and influence in these encounters with their difference. But for this to lead to a stable and shared status belief, according to status construction theory, one more condition is required. Something would have to give either men or women a *consistent* advantage in gaining influence and status in their mutual encounters. This is where the role of resources comes in. As the research shows us, a systematic resource advantage will act as a biasing factor that, over multiple encounters, creates status beliefs favoring the advantaged group.

In an extensive review of the cross-cultural evidence, the psychologists Wendy Wood and Alice Eagly found that societies universally develop some type of gendered division of labor in which some tasks become men's work and others become women's work.[61] The evidence suggests that this division of labor stems not from "natural" dispositions but is rooted in men's and women's functional interdependence for reproduction and survival.

The tasks associated with one sex or the other can vary greatly between cultures. But biological factors, such as men's greater average upper body strength and the mobility issues associated with women's childbearing and nursing, do set certain constraints on this division of labor, and these constraints matter more in some environmental and technological circumstances than in others. From their review of the evidence, Wood and Eagly conclude that male dominance, rather than more egalitarian gender divisions of labor, is associated with circumstances (say, reliance on hunting large animals rather than on foraging) in which these biological constraints foster a division of labor that gives men greater control over the production of valued resources than women.[62] The sociologist Joan Huber, from her review of the evidence, makes a similar argument about how the mobility constraints faced by lactating mothers in the past possibly encouraged the development of male dominance via control of resources.[63]

Keep in mind that these are theories, albeit ones consistent with current evidence, and that the actual historical origins of male dominance in Western or other societies are unknown. But from our perspective here, it still is worth noting that if the factors that Wood, Eagly, and Huber point to did result in a gendered division of labor that gave men greater control of resources, this resource control would serve as a biasing factor that tips influence hierarchies to favor men over women in their mutual encounters. This in turn would feed status beliefs about men's systematically greater competence and status-worthiness, through the processes that status construction theory describes. The eventual result would be diffuse status beliefs favoring men that become widely held in the population.[64]

If a division of labor gives men greater control of resources, you might ask, what does it matter if men also become higher status? It matters, as we have seen before, because status beliefs would give men an advantage even over women who are not lactating mothers and who are just as strong as they are. (Not all men are strong, nor are all women weak.) Status beliefs consolidate male dominance by rooting men's superiority in their group identity as men and not in the degree to which they, as individuals, personally possess materially advantaging characteristics like strength. In chapter 6, we will see how status beliefs legitimate inequalities between social difference groups and contribute to their durability over time.

As this discussion makes clear, sex/gender, with its relevance for reproduction, is unique among the social differences that might become significant status distinctions in a society. As a result, the story behind the emergence of gender status beliefs will not be the same as the stories that are likely to emerge about the development of status beliefs about other differences, such as race or class. These status distinctions also have deep and complex histories that I will not try to unpack here. Instead, I will just observe that biasing factors were also present for these distinctions in the past (wealth, guns and technological superiority, slavery), and that these shaped encounters between the social difference groups in ways that would have encouraged the formations of status beliefs about the difference.[65]

Essential Elements for the Formation of Status Beliefs

Research driven by status construction theory provides us with evidence about one means by which status beliefs develop, but the theory itself makes the point that this is unlikely to be the only way they develop. The empirical studies associated with the theory, however, do highlight for us two essential elements in the formation of a status belief that may have broader generality beyond the status construction account. The first element is a local context or experience that makes salient for its participants an association between a recognized group difference and an existing and apparently valid rank order of actors in terms of status-worthiness and competence. In status construction theory, the valid rank order is the apparently consensual influence hierarchy in encounters between socially different actors.

The second essential element for status belief formation is a behavioral validation of the association between difference and status rank by a broader audience or set of participants beyond the initial context who act as though they accept the association, or at least do not challenge it.[66] Social validation of the bond between the difference and the existing status rank seems to allow the status rank to spread to the group difference.[67] Keeping in mind these two elements of situations that foster status beliefs will be useful in considering the scattering of other research on the formation of status beliefs.

Status construction theory's argument about how status beliefs form implies, for instance, that any local context, not just interactional encounters, that creates a socially valid association for participants between a social difference and status and competence will induce them to form status beliefs about the difference.[68] Consistent with this, studies have shown that when a legitimate authority provides apparently valid information linking a group difference (for example, between colleges) to status-ranked life outcomes (say, differences in the economic success of their graduates), participants form status beliefs about the group difference, just as they did in status construction experiments.[69]

Organizational Research on the Formation of Status Beliefs

Most other research on the development of status beliefs comes from research on the emergence or change of status rankings among organizations. The sociologist Michael Sauder and his colleagues, in a broad review of organizational status research, describe evidence for two processes by which beliefs about status rankings develop.[70] First, and most importantly, as we saw for individuals in the last chapter, status among organizations develops and spreads through associations.[71] So if a new organization developing in a field manages to partner with an existing high- (or low-) status organization, people in the field will come to view the new organization as high- (or low-) status too. A new photo messaging app partners with Facebook, for instance, and its status rises instantly. Our argument here would account for this by noting that, in accepting a public partnership with the new organization, the existing organization creates an apparently valid association between itself, including its status, and the new organization, allowing the established organization's status to spread to the new organization. The spread of status through association, of course, creates a politics of association among organizations.

Second, status ranks can develop among organizations through external, third-party evaluators or critics who rate the organizations in terms of their relative "quality"—meaning the apparent competence and value they offer in their field.[72] Examples are restaurant reviewers, wine critics, or quality rankings published by some recognized source, such as the Michelin guides to restaurants or the J. D. Powers ranking of automobiles. Interestingly, these third-party evaluations also seem to create widely accepted status rankings in a broader community through a process of social validation and the spread of status. In the case of restaurant and wine critics, for instance, the rankings seem socially valid because they come from sources—like the New York Times restaurant critic or the Michelin guide—whose own legitimacy and high status as experts is already established in the community.

Occasionally, the evaluating third party does not have preestablished expertise in an area but does have the capacity to combine private evaluations from others and publicize the resulting rankings widely. An example is the *U.S. News & World Report* ranking of colleges and universities. These rankings are often highly consequential even for people in the colleges and universities who themselves are skeptical of the rankings.[73] The trick lies in the very publicity that the magazine produces for the rankings, which makes them common knowledge. Because interested parties—students, faculty, administrators, donors, and so on—assume that "most people" will see and accept these rankings, the actors take the rankings into account in their own decisions as well, thereby behaviorally validating them.[74] Note that the magazine produces these rankings in an entrepreneurial way because it correctly assumes that a large audience actively wants a status belief that they can use to effectively coordinate their choices about colleges and universities with the reactions of others.

Status beyond the Interpersonal Hierarchy

The similarities that we see between the development of status beliefs among organizations and among individuals about "types" of actors make it clear that people use status as a way of organizing social relations well beyond the interpersonal hierarchy. In addition to their dealings with other individuals, people use status to make judgments of and coordinate with others about the schools they go to, the neighborhoods they live in, the organizations they work for, and the objects they buy, just to list a few examples. A central argument of the cultural schema theory put forward in this book is that people's capacity to do this is a direct result of status's nature as a cultural schema. I mentioned early on that status is a structural schema in the sense discussed by the social theorist William Sewell.[75] That is, it is a set of implicit cultural rules by which people enact a particular form of social structure—a status hierarchy. As Sewell points out, once people have a cultural schema for a particular form of social relations, they tend to apply it permissively to manage a wide range of social contexts beyond those of its origins. It is like acquiring a pair of scissors. Once you have them, you think of new things you can cut with them.

We have already seen that status pervades social relations among business firms, educational institutions, and many types of organizations in addition to social identity groups like ethnic or class groups. Studies of status rankings among organizations show that they bias judgments of the organizations' competence and value in a manner comparable to the way status beliefs about group identities bias judgments of the competence of individuals. And in a familiar manner, these status "signals" bring high-status organizations real advantages in the competitive market, structuring inequality among organizations.[76]

As we saw earlier, status processes also shape social relations in communities of online programmers who rarely interact in person. These communities develop their own status beliefs with which to coordinate their judgments of each other's status-worthiness and competence.[77] These status beliefs, in turn, create classic advantages in perceived competence and influence for actors designated as high status. When the name of a programmer who has been deemed high status by these beliefs is attached to a programming suggestion, it is more likely to be accepted in the community.[78] The parallels between status processes among organizations and among individuals, interpersonally or online, show the similar workings of the status schema across the contexts to which people apply it.

The Conditional Range of the Status Schema

If people can spread status widely to a great variety of contexts, what are its limits? What are the boundaries of the circumstances that push people to draw on status as a blueprint for managing the situation and their relationships in it? Clearly, face-to-face interpersonal relations are not necessary to trigger status processes. But two other conditions apparently are. The first is *goal-orientation*. For status to be evoked, the actors, whether individual or corporate, must be trying to accomplish a goal whose outcomes could be more or less successful.[79] Goal-orientation creates the motive to evaluate signs in self and others of greater or lesser competence at the goal effort—something to which the status schema speaks. Goal-orientation is clear when individuals on a team or in a working group are trying to accomplish something they cannot do alone. It is also apparent in the context of online programming communities that are striving to collectively produce better, more powerful applications. It is even diffusely apparent among organizations in a shared field (say, investment banking or higher education) who are competing for customers and other valued resources in that field.

A second, apparently necessary condition for actors to evoke the status schema is *interdependence* with others for the success of the goal effort. That is to say, the success of any one actor's effort to achieve the valued goal is shaped to a non-negligible degree by the responses of others in the context.

Interdependence sets in motion the need to coordinate judgments of competence and value by drawing on shared status beliefs.

The origin context of the status schema, by cultural schema theory, is a situation characterized by cooperative interdependence to achieve shared, collective goals and competitive interdependence to maximize individual outcomes. This particular form of interdependence is especially clear in goal-oriented interpersonal groups, whether they interact in person or online like open source programmers. The interdependence among organizations competing for customers and resources is clear, but, plausibly, the nature of the interdependence shifts further to the competitive. Importantly, however, cooperative affiliations among organizational partners (for instance, suppliers and producers or strategic alliances among technology firms or universities) remain a core part of the process by which organizations pursue valued outcomes in the market.[80] And it is these cooperatively interdependent affiliations among partners, with their nested competitive tensions, that become organized by status.

But what about status rankings among law schools, or among the restaurants in a community? Here we see the full stretch of the status schema. In these status rankings among competing organizations in a market, the goal-orientation remains. So does the interdependence in that each organization needs to anticipate how it and its choices will be evaluated in comparison to other organizations in the market if it is to make choices that best maximize its own outcomes. But notice that the *cooperative* interdependence—what the organizations must all coordinate on—has shifted away from the outcome goal (they are now too competitive to coordinate on market success) to the collective need for a status ranking itself. Even in this largely competitive situation, in which cooperative interdependence aims only to share a way to anticipate the evaluative reactions of relevant others, people seem to reach implicitly for the status schema to manage the situation.[81]

Status Advantage

As we have seen, in all the contexts that become organized by the status schema, the status beliefs evoked in the context create advantages for actors labeled higher status, whether those actors be individuals or organizations. Status advantage means that the high-status actors are perceived as more competent, valuable, and favored for exchange over and above what they would be if they were not ranked high by the status belief. Status advantages are created by two closely related processes.[82]

In the first process, status beliefs create advantages by biasing a decision-maker's own personal (first-order) evaluations of another actor's competence and value in the context, relative to self and others, through a process of *socially endogenous inference*.[83] Status beliefs are perceived by decision-makers to encode the aggregate of a community's evaluation of a type of actor's average competence and status-worthiness. Yet the circumstances in which status beliefs form cause errors and biases to accumulate within them so that what status beliefs encode about competence deviates from "real" average competence. In addition, status beliefs, once formed, by shaping actors' expectations for one another's competence, bias not only perceptions of competence but actual performance, as research has shown for both individuals and organizations.[84] In this way, the errors embedded in status beliefs become self-fulfilling, and these beliefs create unwarranted advantages in decision-makers' personal evaluations of the competence of those ranked as high status by the beliefs and correspondingly disadvantage those ranked as low status.

In a social world already filled with common knowledge status beliefs, status beliefs may shape people's personal judgments of competence and quality through socially endogenous inference even outside the typical boundary conditions of status processes, although the full status schema is not evoked. This happens when people draw on status beliefs as a shorthand way to quickly infer the competence of other actors even when their judgment is purely a personal one that is not interdependent with the reactions of others. People are most likely to take this shortcut when they have personal uncertainties about another's competence or quality and status beliefs help them resolve those uncertainties.[85] For instance, a person uncertain about which brand of chocolate would taste best might rely on the status of the brands to decide which to buy. This example illustrates a kind of halo effect of status beliefs when people use them for personal judgments. But if the person, having tasted all the chocolates, has little uncertainty about which would be best, status beliefs have much less of an impact on his decision.[86]

In most situations in which status beliefs become salient, however, actors are making decisions under some degree of interdependence, in that the outcome of their decision does depend to some extent on how others react to it. In this situation, the full status schema is salient. For instance, when the person is buying chocolate not just for herself but to take to the office party, the "best" choice is not just the brand she personally would prefer, but the brand that also will be well received as a high-quality choice by relevant others. Hiring decisions in the workplace are typically like this. The "best" applicant is not just the one a given evaluator favors, but the one whom other stakeholders will also accept as best.[87]

Situations of this sort (that is, those with a non-negligible degree of outcome interdependence) create status advantage by an additional, second process, called *third-order inference*.[88] To anticipate the choice that others will react to as "best," actors draw on the third-order nature of status beliefs as beliefs about what "most people" think is best. In this way, they coordinate their own evaluations of the choices with the likely reactions of others to make the choice they believe will be most *effectively* successful in the interdependent situation.

Third-order inference creates an additional status advantage for high-status actors even beyond that created by socially endogenous inference by encouraging people to favor high-status actors even when they do not personally evaluate those actors as more competent or better than others from a lower-status group. For instance, a person who thinks that the woman candidate for police chief is slightly better than the male candidate might still favor the man as easier to "sell" to others, as my colleagues and I found in experiments we conducted.[89] Our experiments on third-order inference showed that there are even contexts in which people favor the high-status choice (for example, a job candidate with high-status educational credentials) as the safely conventional "best" choice despite the background information that other stakeholders might be open to unconventional, out-of-the-box choices (say, a high-performing candidate with low-status educational credentials). Decision-makers are most likely to rely on conventionally high-status choices when the background information about the other stakeholders' openness to unconventional choices, though possibly shared knowledge with the decision-maker, is still not public, common knowledge. As a result, there is still some risk for the decision-maker in coordinating her decision on the basis of it.[90]

Status characteristics and expectation states theory, in its well-known account of status processes among individuals, describes status advantage primarily as a process of socially endogenous inference.[91] But it is worth noting that the theory also implicitly recognizes the effects of third-order inference through its research on the effects of second-order expectations (perceptions of others' expectations for self and other) on people's deference and influence behavior in goal-oriented groups.[92] Actually, the third-order inference model offers an explicit explanation for a distinctive empirical finding in this research. Third-order inference accounts for why, when an actor's second-order expectations about self and other are inconsistent with her own first-order expectations, it is the second-order expectations that typically are the most powerful driver of her behavior in the group.[93] The power of third-order inference to create status advantage highlights how the coordinating function of status beliefs in itself helps produce inequality.

In the many situations in which judgments and choices are inter-dependent to some degree, both processes by which status beliefs create advantages for high-status actors typically co-occur.[94] That is, status beliefs not only factor into people's personal (first-order) evaluations of an (individual or corporate) actor's relative competence and quality but also shape how people expect others to evaluate that actor. In many situations, people may not really distinguish between the two as they form an implicit judgment of another's "value" in the situation. Both processes, separately and together, create unwarranted advantages for high-status actors and similar disadvantages for low-status actors. As they do so, status beliefs foster and reproduce inequality among actors (individual and corporate) based on their group identity, and they do so in a way that justifies this inequality on the basis of "merit." It is through status beliefs, then, that inequality based on actors' group identities, rather than just their individual attributes, is interwoven into modern, ostensibly meritocratic institutions.

CHAPTER 5

THE MICRODYNAMICS OF STATUS

UP UNTIL NOW, we have focused somewhat abstractly on status as a form of organization among people. The goal has been to make a case for the schema theory of status by showing how a cultural schema encodes the rules by which people enact status hierarchies and allows them to spread status everywhere. But now it is time to see how this process plays out for individuals as they make their way through their everyday experience. How does the status schema shape social outcomes for individuals, and how do individuals navigate their way through it? As an implicitly normative process, guided by the taken-for-granted basic status norm, status is something that people experience in others' treatment of them. But at the same time, it is something that people actively engage in, both in how they treat others and in how they position themselves in relation to others. This is the micro-dynamic process we want to understand, with a particular focus on how it creates unequal social outcomes among individuals.

The Context Dependence of Status

The specific dynamics of interpersonal status processes—who ends up where in the hierarchy and why—are always *context-dependent*.[1] We will see this play out in many ways throughout the chapter. In fact, contextual factors are so important for the microdynamics of status that it will be useful to begin with a brief consideration of some of the most important framing factors that set the stage for status processes in specific situations. Then we can narrow our contextual focus to the type of status contexts that are most consequential for unequal outcomes in the larger society.

Perhaps the most important contextual factor that frames who ends up where in the status hierarchy is the goal of the group. Is this a group of friends who gather to laugh and socialize? An athletic group? A group of teenagers focused on expressing a valued self-identity? A group of soldiers facing danger? A project team in the workplace? In each of these contexts, following the basic status norm, status is given for perceived value and competence at the goal activities. But what constitutes competence is entirely dependent on the nature of the goal. What makes you high status in one group (an ability to tell amusing stories) will not help you, or could even hurt you, in another group (a serious-minded work group).[2] And despite the generalizing effects of diffuse status characteristics like race, gender, and social class—which systematically advantage people with some group identities compared to others in perceived general competence—no one is so advantaged as to be high status in every social context they encounter, nor is anyone always low status. The wealthy white businessman nevertheless defers to the CEO of his business, to his parents when they visit, and to his child's pediatrician when the child is sick. The Latino yard worker is a respected member of his church and deferred to in local music circles for his skill with a guitar. Thus, virtually everyone has it in their behavioral repertoire to act in both low- and high-status ways, even if some have more experience acting one way rather than the other.

In addition to shaping the types of competencies that are valued by the group, the context also affects the importance for status of that second dimension of perceived value, group-orientation. Recall that group-orientation is perceived commitment to acting in the group's interest, rather than solely in one's self-interest. As we have seen, since high status brings rewards, when individuals pursue it, their motives are inherently ambiguous in the eyes of other group members and potentially suspect unless they act in a generous or prosocial way.[3] But how important judgments of group-orientation are in the granting of status, compared to goal-related competence, depends on the group context. In any cooperative, goal-oriented situation in which the status schema is at play, there will be tensions between acting to help the group and being self-interested. Some situations, however, exacerbate this tension by making actions to help the group costly or risky for the individual, even though all would benefit if they could find a way to cooperate. In these *social dilemma* situations, groups award status and influence to members who jump-start cooperation by making contributions to the group effort despite personal cost, regardless of the contributors' perceived competence.[4]

We see, then, that when it is very hard to get people to contribute to the group goal effort, willingness to take the lead in contributing (that is, group-orientation) becomes a more important component of perceived value and status than the quality of the contribution.[5] On the other side, however, there are also circumstances where cooperation is not difficult but task success is all-important and hard to achieve. In these situations, the group will award status and influence to a highly competent but clearly self-interested member if they have to in the interest of task success.[6] During the big game, for instance, the team is willing to defer to their arrogant, grandstanding teammate if he has the specialized skills to win against the rival team. Overall, however, the evidence suggests that, in most contexts, at least in individualistic Western societies, goal-related competence is the primary component of perceived value and status, while concerns about group-orientation are secondary.[7]

We need to keep in mind these broad ways in which contexts frame the dynamics of status and give everyone varying experiences of status as they move across contexts in their lives. But some social contexts are more consequential than others for the life outcomes by which we typically measure inequality, such as wealth, power, social recognition, and health. Many of these consequential interpersonal contexts are found in organizations or institutions, like schools, the workplace, or the health organizations that distribute these life outcomes.[8] Given our broader focus on the impact of status processes on patterns of inequality in society, these more consequential social contexts are of special interest to us here. And for most of these, the goal focus of the context tends to be on instrumental tasks like decision-making, problem-solving, or a work task or project. In these settings, perceived task competence is the dominant determinant of value and status. These contexts and group tasks are also the primary focus of most theory and research on the microdynamics of interpersonal status, and that focus will be reflected in our discussion here.

The most systematic theory of the microdynamics of status hierarchies in such contexts, and empirically the best documented, is the sociological theory of status characteristics and expectation states.[9] We have referred to this theory briefly in previous chapters, but it will be central to our concerns here. The theory (which is really a family of related theories) limits its scope of application to groups of cooperatively goal-oriented actors.

These conditions cover most of the consequential interpersonal contexts that concern us here. We will also reach, however, beyond expectation states theory to other research that stretches the boundary of those scope conditions. As I have mentioned before, the cultural schema theory of status laid out in previous chapters provides an account of the deeper, more encompassing normative and cultural processes that undergird the specific, more narrowly interpersonal status processes described by expectation states theory. In regard to the microdynamics of interpersonal status that occur within the cooperative, goal-oriented scope conditions of expectation states theory, the two theories are fully consistent with one another.

We start with an expectation states theory account of how status hierarchies emerge out of the impression formation process in the first few moments of interaction. As this account describes the process, actors' initial formation of performance expectations for self compared to others plays a central role in creating, maintaining, and changing the status hierarchy.[10] Given this, we next turn to the sorts of social information that shape these expectations. We focus on how the context shapes the information that becomes salient for actors, the power of its impact on expectations, how multiple types of information combine to affect who ends up where in the hierarchy, and how hierarchies can change over time. With this conceptual framework for understanding status dynamics in hand, we turn to a more detailed consideration of various types of information that shape performance expectations, including status characteristics (which we discussed in the last chapter), social rewards, proactive versus reactive behavioral styles, and direct evaluations of performance in the situation. Then we turn to questions of legitimacy and authority in status hierarchies and issues of backlash against challenges to the hierarchy. Questions of legitimacy lead to a consideration of techniques for overcoming status generalization and navigating through the labyrinth. We conclude with a brief consideration of the way in which status creates a politics of association among individuals, with consequences for inequality.

Status Hierarchy as a Shared Order of Performance Expectations

The Emergence and Stabilization of Status Hierarchies

When people join a group to work on a shared task or goal, they go through an initial period of uncertainty and orientation as they look around the room and try to gain a quick sense of the others present and how they themselves compare to those others.[11] In other words, they try to figure out how the others will behave in order to decide how to behave in the situation themselves. Given their goal focus, expectation states theory argues that this initial impression formation process will lead the actors to develop implicit, often unconscious anticipations of how useful each person's contributions to the goal effort are likely to be compared to their own and those of the others in the group.[12] These anticipations form an implicit rank order of *performance expectations* for self and others in the group. As this definition suggests, self-other performance expectations are the terms that expectation states theory uses to represent the judgments of perceived value to and competence at the shared goal effort around which the basic status norm turns, according to the cultural schema theory of status.

The ranked self-other performance expectations that emerge in the impression formation process, in turn, shape actors' goal-directed behaviors in the group in a self-fulfilling manner, as research shows expectations tend to do.[13] If, for instance, one actor forms a higher expectation for self than for another ("I think I have more to offer in this situation than he does"), then she is likely to speak up confidently with her opinions and to stick with them if the other disagrees. But if the actor's expectation for self is lower than for the other ("he seems like he knows more about this than I do"), then she is more likely to hesitate and wait for the other to speak first. And if the other does offer an opinion, she is more likely to positively evaluate it and, in case of disagreement, change to agree with the other so that the other becomes more influential.

In this way, expectation states theory argues that rank-ordered performance expectations shape actors' goal-directed behaviors to be more or less assertive or deferential, giving rise to a behavioral status hierarchy in terms of who participates more, how their contributions are evaluated, and how influential they are in the group. The behavioral status hierarchy in turn seems to confirm for actors their performance expectations for one another. The result is that the status hierarchy stabilizes and becomes self-maintaining until new information is introduced to change actors' relative performance expectations.[14] Expectation states researchers have gathered a substantial body of evidence that specifically supports this account.[15] It is also consistent with broader reviews of research on the emergence of status hierarchies.[16]

A study by the organizational scholars Gavin Kilduff and Adam Galinsky nicely illustrates for us how the process of the initial behavioral emergence of status works to stabilize the hierarchy in a self-fulfilling way.[17] In a set of experiments, the researchers formed three-person, task-oriented discussion groups in which one randomly selected member had been led to form an initial, self-confident "approach" mind-set, while a second was induced to form a hesitant, "prevention" focus and the third a neutral focus. These were same-sex groups of undergraduates so they were otherwise fairly homogeneous socially.

As predicted, the approach mind-set led the so-oriented member to engage in more proactive, goal-oriented behavior, while the prevention-focused member acted less assertively in the group discussion, and the neutral person was in between. At the end of the discussion, a status hierarchy had emerged in which the approach-minded member was perceived by the other members as higher status (more respected, admired, and influential) than the prevention-minded member. Data analyses confirmed that it was the differences in assertive versus hesitant behavioral style that led to the differences in members' perceived status in the group. Furthermore, once these status differences developed, they stabilized and persisted among group members even when, a day or two later, they returned to the laboratory to work together again on another group task.

There are two points of interest about this study's results for us here. First, expectation states theory would conceptualize Kilduff and Galinsky's self-confident "approach" mind-set as one source of a high-performance expectation for self, compared to others in the group.[18] Seen that way, the study clearly shows how a high self-expectation leads to more assertive and proactive task behavior, which leads to perceived status and influence in the group, which in turn stabilizes the hierarchy, just as expectation states theory argues.

Second, it is striking that stable differences in group members' perceived value to the group, reflected in status and influence, were constructed out of randomly assigned, relatively ephemeral mind-sets that simply shaped the first few moves in the group interaction. This was enough to trigger a self-fulfilling process by which the basic norm of status played out to create a hierarchy. The random assignment of study participants to an approach or prevention mind-set assures us that the resulting status differences were not due to some other preexisting individual differences among the members. But to be sure, the researchers measured and controlled for personality characteristics, like extroversion and dominance, that are known to be related to assertive behavior and showed that the effects of the assigned mind-set were independent of those characteristics. So, among other things, this study reminds us that perceived differences in status and value to the group can arise contingently and need not necessarily imply underlying, preexisting differences in actual task ability among group members. In this case, the researchers did not measure perceptions of competence among the members, but given that high-status members were more admired and granted influence over task decisions, it is highly likely that they were also perceived as more able at the group task. As we will see later on, assertive, proactive behavioral styles can themselves create an impression of competence, compared to reactive, deferential styles.[19]

A Shared Order of Performance Expectations

To analyze the microdynamics of status, it is useful to start with expectation states theory's conception of a status hierarchy as a rank order of performance expectations for group members that in turn drives their goal-oriented behavior (speaking up with task suggestions, evaluating their own and others' suggestions, accepting or rejecting influence) in a mutually reinforcing manner. We know from previous chapters that, for this order of performance expectations to successfully coordinate group behavior and create a status hierarchy, it must be roughly *shared*, or consensual. Expectation states theory argues that group members form initial performance expectations by observing social cues in the situation that are culturally linked to assumptions about greater or lesser status-worthiness and competence.

By generally noticing similar cues that the situation makes salient for them, and by drawing on shared cultural (status) beliefs about the status and competence implications of these cues, groups members independently form roughly shared orders of performance expectations, the theory argues.[20] For instance, in the study discussed, the approach versus prevention mind-sets may have caused the individual participants to start the interaction with a personally high or low self-expectation. Yet it was their consequent assertive or hesitant task behavior that acted as an observable cue that both led *others* to form a correspondingly high or low expectation for them and stabilized their own self-expectation in turn.

By this account, then, who ends up where in a status hierarchy depends on the status cues that become salient for group members in a particular context and on the way in which these shape the shared order of performance expectations. Expectation states research has identified several types of social information that serve as status cues in this way. Powerful among these are diffuse and specific status characteristics (for example, gender, race, or programming expertise), as we defined them in the last chapter. But valued social rewards (say, pay or a corner office), behavioral style (proactive versus reactive), and explicit performance evaluations also act as status cues. We will discuss each of these in more detail shortly.

Salience, Weighting, and Combining of Status Cues

For status cues to shape shared performance expectations, they must become implicitly salient in the situation, because either group members differ on them or the cues are culturally linked to the group context or task.[21] As we have commented before, when people enter a goal-oriented situation and are trying to figure out who has the most to offer in that situation and how they should act themselves, they are attuned to noticing differences among those involved that might imply answers to these concerns. So they will notice prominent status characteristics like gender or race when the people in the room differ on these characteristics, even if they are completely irrelevant to the group's goals. They will also notice differences in the valued rewards that members possess if these become apparent in the situation, as well as differences in behavior and evaluations of task efforts. Finally, they will also notice status cues that are culturally linked to the context or group task, whether or not members differ on these cues. In a culturally gender-typed setting (child care or construction work), for instance, gender will be implicitly salient and shape members' performance expectations even in a same-sex group.

Given that people in cooperative, goal-oriented settings are actively trying to size each other up and figure out what to expect for themselves and others, it is highly likely that multiple status cues will become salient for them in the first few moments of interaction. How does this shape the order of performance expectations that develops? Expectation states theory argues that actors *combine* the positive and negative competence and performance implications of all salient status cues, weighted by their *relevance* to the group goal effort, to form an aggregated performance expectation for one actor compared to another.[22] Thus, a woman with a computer science background in a mixed-sex group working on a web-programming task will be disadvantaged by her gender but advantaged by her skills. And since her skills are more relevant to the goal effort, they will raise performance expectations for her more than her gender will lower them. As a result, she will have higher status and influence in the group than a man without a programming background. But the group's expectations for her and her status and influence in the group will still be less than they would be for a man with a computer science background.[23]

The impact of a given status cue on performance expectations and status is not only shaped by its relevance to the task context but is also subject to an inconsistency effect, whereby a status cue has a bigger impact if the status it implies contradicts what is already known about a person (say, the Harvard-trained surgeon turns out to be African American). There is also an attenuation effect, in which each additional status cue that confirms what is already known (the Harvard surgeon turns out to be white and also financially successful) has a declining marginal impact, according to the theory.[24] A substantial body of evidence shows that people in groups do act as if they were weighting, combining, and aggregating the competence and status implications of status cues in these ways.[25]

With its account of how the social context of interaction—the nature of the group goal and the mix of people involved—makes status cues salient and powerful in some situations and not in others, expectation states theory offers a sophisticated framework for understanding how a given status hierarchy comes to take the shape it does. Especially useful is its nuanced account of the way in which people implicitly weigh multiple sources of status information and combine them into a shared order of performance expectations. I have often commented that interpersonal hierarchies seem to just emerge in the first few minutes of interaction in a process that typically seems obscure or mysterious to the participants. Thinking of this process as the implicit, often unconscious formation of rank-ordered performance expectations for self and others gives us an analytic framework for seeing through this typically opaque process. In the implicit, comparative judgments that people make of themselves and others and that others make of them in turn, and in the self-fulfilling effects of these on behavior, status, and influence, we see how people end up where they do in the hierarchy.

Stability and Change

As we have seen, the self-fulfilling effects of performance expectations on behavior, which in turn reinforce these expectations, give status hierarchies considerable stability. In addition, high-status group members may use their influence and esteem to steer the group in directions that help maintain their own high status, which further maintains the hierarchy. But stability is not the only story in status hierarchies; they also change and evolve.[26] By our account here, they do so through the introduction of new status information that alters the shared order of performance expectations.

People value high status and often jockey for it by strategically introducing new status cues about themselves that will advantage them. Maybe they mention some relevant experience they have, or a reward they have received. Or they attempt to speak up and act more assertively or offer clever task suggestions. For these attempts to succeed, however, *others* in the group must accept the value of the new information and alter their expectations for the actor.[27] And of course, not only do these others have an interest in maintaining their own status position, but they also already have an established performance expectation for the actor and will assess the value of the new information in relation to that. So changing the hierarchy once it emerges is possible but not easy. We will look more closely at this process later in the chapter.

Now that we have an analytic framework for thinking about the microdynamics of status in terms of the formation, maintenance, and change of a roughly shared order of performance expectations, we can look more closely at the impact of different types of status cues. Of primary importance, both for the shape of status hierarchies and larger patterns of inequality, are status characteristics. "Status characteristics" is the term that expectation states theory uses for social differences among people that are delineated in widely held status beliefs as culturally recognized signs of greater or lesser competence and status-worthiness.[28] According to the cultural schema theory, of course, status beliefs are one of the two basic components of the underlying status schema.

Status Characteristics

In the last chapter on status beliefs, we described status characteristics and outlined how they shape interpersonal status hierarchies. Recall that when a status characteristic is salient for actors because they either differ on the characteristic or it is goal-relevant, it triggers a *status generalization* process. That is, the status of the groups and social categories to which people belong in the larger society shape performance expectations for them in the local situation. This, in turn, has self-fulfilling effects on their status and influence in that situation.

Status characteristics create *status advantage* for actors not only by directly biasing perceptions of an actor's relative competence and value but also by serving as the primary means by which other members coordinate their judgments of the actor's value to create the status hierarchy. Recall that status advantage occurs when an actor is more favorably evaluated than she would otherwise be if she lacked the advantaging status characteristic. Examples are more positive evaluations of the same job résumé when it carries the name of a man rather than a woman, or a white person rather than an African American.[29] Because of their importance in creating status advantage, status characteristics are central to the processes by which status shapes larger patterns of inequality in society. And because they coordinate group members' performance expectations for one another through the common knowledge status beliefs they evoke, status characteristics are among the primary determinants of the microdynamics of interpersonal status.

As we saw in the last chapter, all the major social differences by which inequality is patterned in the United States, including gender, race, age, occupation, education, and class, act as status characteristics in interpersonal contexts because they are linked to widely held status beliefs.[30] As axes along which daily social life is organized, some of the most powerful of these, like gender, race, and age, are signaled by actors and read by others on the basis of visual cues.[31] As a result, in contexts in which either the actors differ on these status characteristics or the characteristics are goal-relevant, their status implications become salient for actors almost immediately. The cues by which people detect class background are more complex, but given its social importance, class background also typically becomes salient within a few moments.[32]

As they become salient in the first moments of interaction, these powerful status characteristics frame the performance expectations and general impressions that actors form of one another and themselves in comparison. Subsequent status cues that become salient are nested within these prior understandings of each other as persons of a certain gender, race, age, and social class.[33] And as we learned from the Kilduff and Galinsky study, this initial framing of performance expectations creates self-fulfilling effects that not only shape status and influence in the short term but persist over the long term.[34]

There is a good deal of evidence to support expectation states theory's account of how status characteristics shape status and influence in goal-oriented interpersonal contexts via performance expectations. A meta-analysis of studies examining the impact of a variety of status characteristics, including education, race, and gender, showed that the impact of these characteristics on deference and influence in interaction is not direct but rather mediated through the performance expectations that the characteristics cause group members to form for one another.[35] Experiments also confirm that the mere knowledge of an interactional partner's status characteristics relative to an actor's own is enough to affect the latter's willingness to accept influence from that partner on task decisions.[36] These studies show that the effects of status characteristics on interpersonal judgments, behavior, influence, and esteem are independent of any possible preexisting individual differences in personality or behavior between people from different social groups and cannot be accounted for by such preexisting differences. Rather, they result from the status beliefs associated with these characteristics that link them to cultural assumptions about differences in competence and value.

Socially important status characteristics like gender, race, and class (and also age, education, and occupation) are powerful and broadly significant not only because they typically frame performance expectations from the first moments of interaction, but also because of their nature as diffuse rather than just *specific status characteristics*. Recall that *diffuse status characteristics* are linked to cultural assumptions about *general* competence, particularly at the tasks that count most in society, and not just narrower, specific competencies. When a diffuse status characteristic is salient in a situation, it will shape self-other performance expectations even if it is irrelevant to the group goal or task.[37] A project team, for instance, may be trying to solve a problem, such as analyzing a biochemical process in a research lab, that has no logical link to race or gender. But if those status characteristics are salient in the situation, they will nevertheless shape expectations for how well whites and men will perform on the team compared to people of color and women. Once a powerful diffuse characteristic is salient in a group context, its effects on performance expectations and status may eventually be outweighed by contradicting status cues about a person like specific status characteristics (for example, test scores, training, or experience) that indicate relevant expertise or exceptional performance.[38] But its effects never really go away because the actor disadvantaged by the characteristic has to be otherwise better and more competent than others to be seen as equally worthy of status and influence in the context.

When considering the broad-ranging advantaging or disadvantaging effects of diffuse status characteristics, it is worth keeping in mind their context specificity. A status characteristic like having a bachelor's degree is advantaging among those who did not finish college but disadvantaging in a group of PhDs. Even though some status characteristics are disadvantaging in many more contexts than they are advantaging, like being a woman, a person of color, or a high school dropout, there are still no status characteristics that are universally advantaging or disadvantaging. It always depends on who else is found in the context and the nature of the shared goal.

That said, however, diffuse status characteristics do have a wide range of self-fulfilling effects on status-related outcomes. As we have said, in interpersonal contexts, by shaping performance expectations, they embolden status-advantaged actors to speak up and act more assertively while causing disadvantaged actors to hesitate and react more deferentially.[39] In a study that illustrates this process, the psychologist John Dovidio and his colleagues recorded the assertive verbal behavior (speech initiations, time talking) and nonverbal behavior (gestures, eye gaze patterns) of mixed-sex student dyads as they worked on three sequential discussion tasks, one chosen to be gender-neutral, another to be feminine-typed, and the third masculine-typed.[40] The results showed that the students' assertive behaviors closely reflected the extent to which the salient status characteristic of gender advantaged or disadvantaged them in each of the three goal contexts, confirming the predictions of expectation states theory. When working on a gender-neutral task, men were modestly more assertive than women in their verbal and nonverbal behavior, reflecting the diffuse status advantage of their gender. Men were even more assertive compared to women on the masculine-typed task, where their gender status advantage was directly relevant to the task. But when the dyad turned to the feminine-typed task, where gender status implied that the men would be less competent than the women, the behavioral hierarchy reversed as women became more verbally and nonverbally assertive than the men. It is revealing that nonverbal behavior, which people are often unaware of, responded so subtly to the contextually varying performance expectation advantages and disadvantages that participants in this study felt simply as a result of their status-valued group identities as men or women. Thus, when diffuse status characteristics are salient in a context, the initial performance expectations they create largely drive actors' initial and subsequent proactively assertive versus reactively deferential goal-directed behaviors in the interaction.

Since, by evoking cultural beliefs about diffuse competence differences, status beliefs shape self-other performance expectations from the moment they are salient for actors, diffuse status characteristics affect status-related outcomes not only in interpersonal hierarchies but also in goal-oriented social relational contexts more broadly, according to the cultural schema theory. As we saw in the last chapter, people draw on the status schema to comparatively evaluate self and other and decide how to behave in socially interdependent goal-oriented situations beyond the interpersonal group. In a socially consequential test-taking situation (the SAT, for instance), if a diffuse status characteristic such as gender or race becomes salient for the test-takers, it implicitly shapes their performance expectations for themselves, compared to others, in ways that, in turn, affect their actual test *performance*.[41] In addition to shaping proactive behavior, then, salient status characteristics can also have self-fulfilling effects on the actual *quality* of an actor's goal-related performance.

The confidence boost of a performance expectation advantage is something like a home-team advantage that makes it easier for you to perform at your best at the task. On the other hand, the anxiety of a performance expectation disadvantage—knowing that others and perhaps even you yourself doubt your ability in the moment—shakes confidence and makes it harder to do as well as you otherwise could. This effect, which has been documented by expectation states researchers, is essentially equivalent to the "stereotype threat" effect on performance demonstrated in extensive psychological research.[42] In a study that demonstrates this effect particularly clearly, the psychologist Margaret Shih and her colleagues found that Asian women's performance on a math test, compared to a control condition, went down when their gender status was made salient for them in the situation, but went up when their racial status was made salient instead.[43]

As we have noted before, status characteristics create status advantage in a way that justifies that advantage on "merit." Earlier we saw one way in which this occurs. The effects of status beliefs on performance expectations create an evaluative bias, in which the same idea "sounds better" (or a résumé looks better) coming from a high-status actor, who is presumed to be more competent, than from a low-status actor.[44] Here we see a second way in which status advantage is created. The effects of status beliefs on performance expectations also can make a high-status actor actually perform better in a given situation than an equally skilled low-status actor.

In addition to biasing perceptions of competence and even actual performance, salient diffuse status characteristics create *double standards* for judging ability or merit based on a performance of a given quality.[45] That is to say, when a person who is disadvantaged by a status characteristic does well in a situation, others—and sometimes even she herself—may think, *Prove it again,* before deciding that she has high ability.[46] The sociologist Shelley Correll, for instance, has shown that double standards bias women's self-assessments of their ability at male-typed tasks, like mathematics, and that biased self-assessments shape their willingness to pursue careers, including STEM careers, that involve such tasks.[47] Similarly, a study of investment professionals sharing online recommendations to buy or sell stock found that double standards biased their willingness to attend to stock recommendations from women on the platform.[48] People advantaged by a status characteristic, on the other hand, are not held to such a high standard for proving their ability to themselves and others. For them, a good performance simply confirms that they do indeed have high ability.

Double standards triggered by status characteristics can also take the form of shifting criteria. For instance, Eric Uhlmann and Geoffrey Cohen asked respondents to evaluate applicants for the job of police chief, a masculine-typed job for which we would expect fairly strong gender status biases in competence expectations.[49] Among the applicants, some men had slightly more education and training than women but less experience, while others had more experience but less education. As expected, men were evaluated more favorably for the job than women. But the key finding was that respondents justified their decisions based on whichever criterion (education or experience) favored the men over the women in the applications they considered. In this way, men and women whose résumés reported generally similar total qualifications were construed as unequally qualified through the implicit effects of gender status biases.[50]

Double standards for judging ability can have important effects on an actor's outcomes in many goal-oriented social relational contexts. In a job interview, for instance, or when an employer is reviewing résumés for hiring or conducting performance evaluations for promotions, judgments of underlying ability based on performance can make the difference between getting offered the job or not, and being promoted or not. In this way, status characteristics can once again create status advantage under the guise of "merit."

Social Rewards

Although status characteristics are typically the most powerful status cues that frame performance expectations in goal-oriented social relational contexts, they are not the only such cues. Socially valued rewards like pay, a larger office, or a prestigious award can also shape performance expectations for actors who have received different levels of these rewards.[51] What makes something a reward for status purposes is that its possession is valued by group members. It has long been observed that interpersonal status hierarchies distribute valued social rewards in proportion to group members' rank in the hierarchy.[52] Expectation states theory accounts for this by arguing that performance expectations give rise to corresponding reward expectations. This leads to the theory's most interesting argument about rewards. Because performance expectations and rewards are linked in assumptions about status, reward differences can actually *create* performance expectation differences in a "reverse" process.[53] In other words, if one actor receives a reward of a higher level than another receives—say, a bigger pay raise or a larger office—others in the situation, and even the actor herself, will assume that she must be more competent and deserving of status and influence than the others, an effect confirmed by research.[54] So possession of a higher level of a valued reward than others can raise a person's status and influence in a group.

Although many material rewards, like pay or even a large office, have a use value independent of their status value, some rewards, like a celebratory plaque, have only status value. Yet research shows that even these create higher performance expectations for those who receive them, as indicated by other people's willingness to grant them influence in task-oriented matters. Stuart Hysom and his colleagues told study participants that either they or their teammate had been chosen as a "student honoree" to attend a private reception with a visiting dignitary. When participants and their teammate then worked on a task, the "honorees" were given more influence over group decisions on the task.[55]

Note that the status-valued reward in this study was the "privilege" of associating with high-status people. We have seen in past chapters that status spreads through association, among both people and groups.[56] It is not surprising, then, that being able to claim access to a network of high-status others—that is, to be able to "name-drop"—itself serves as a status cue that people may actively deploy in a bid to improve their esteem, prominence, and influence in a social encounter.

Status spreads not only through social networks but also from actors (either as owners or producers) to objects. The sociologist Shane Thye, for instance, gave participants in an exchange game a supply of chips that all had the same monetary value but different colors: the color of the chips he gave to those participants who had status characteristic advantages was different from the color of the chips given to participants with status characteristic disadvantages.[57] In the subsequent bargaining, participants paid more for the chips with the color associated with the higher-status actors, even though their actual face value was the same. In the same way, shoes worn by a high-status athlete acquire status value and command a higher price than similar-quality shoes associated with ordinary people. People pay more for higher-status objects (an Apple phone, a BMW car) because possessing those objects functions as social reward in expectation states theory terms. That is, it acts as a status cue that induces actors and others to assume that they are more competent and status-worthy than those who do not possess such high-status objects. As Thorstein Veblen observed some time ago, the status value of objects can lead to patterns of "conspicuous consumption" as people jockey for position in the micro-dynamics of status through the objects they display.[58]

Behavioral Style

Throughout this chapter, we have seen that the display of assertive and proactive versus less assertive and more reactive goal-oriented behavior is a central medium through which the dynamics of interpersonal status hierarchies play out. Studies by the psychologist Michael Conway and his colleagues suggest that North American societies share the cultural belief about the behavioral style of high and low status that high-status actors are more assertive, agentic, and competent while low-status actors are more reactive and communal.[59] Expectation states theory refers to these status beliefs about proactive versus reactive behavioral styles as "status typifications."[60] Expectation states research shows that when actors' behavior falls into a behavioral interchange pattern in which one actor speaks up more assertively and the other hesitates or defers, the behavioral differences trigger status beliefs for both of them that cause them to form higher performance expectations for the more assertive actor.[61] And a wide variety of research shows that verbal and nonverbal behaviors that convey confidence, assertiveness, and agency create impressions of competence, at least among North Americans.[62] Recall that performance capacity or "competence" in a goal-oriented group is not just ability but also effort directed toward the task. Proactive, agentic behavior signals such effort. Also, people seem to assume that if you are so confident, it is probably because you actually are competent, even though, of course, this may not be the case.

As we saw earlier in the Kilduff and Galinsky study, when group members are socially homogeneous peers, any personal difference, even mood, that produces behavioral style differences among them serves as a status cue that shapes performance expectations, creating a status hierarchy between them.[63] Personality traits such as extroversion and dominance have been shown to affect interpersonal status and influence by encouraging such behavioral style differences in the initial moments of interaction.[64] Similarly, minor acts of nonconformity (wearing red sneakers, for example) that do not violate the group's basic standards for behavior but attract attention and appear agentic also create an impression of competence that leads to status.[65]

However, many, perhaps most, groups are not socially homogeneous. In them, salient status characteristics or reward-level differences create performance expectation differences among the members from the beginning. And in these groups, as we saw in the study by Dovidio and his colleagues, status characteristics or reward differences drive differences in assertive verbal and nonverbal behavior in a self-fulfilling manner.[66] Recall that, as expectation states research has shown, there is a declining marginal impact to new status cues (here, behavioral style) that simply confirm other salient status cues (status characteristics or rewards), because they do not add much new to the status differentiation among the members.[67]

But what if a member's behavioral style is inconsistent with his or her status advantage or disadvantage? Is this a way that a person with an initial status disadvantage, say a person of color or a woman in a group with white men, can improve the performance expectations held for him or her and rise in status in the group? It turns out that this is complicated.

As we will see shortly when we discuss legitimacy, authority, and back-lash in status hierarchies, when a person with low-status characteristics speaks up assertively rather than acting deferentially, other group members can see this behavior as inappropriate and illegitimate.[68] Since the lower-status person is presumed to be less competent, his assertive behavior seems like a self-interested grab for attention rather than a group-oriented effort to help the group. As a result, the low-status person may face resistance unless he is careful to balance moderate assertiveness with a clear commu-nication of cooperative, group-oriented intent. This is a delicate balance to accomplish—being assertive enough to prove competence but non-challenging and cooperative enough to assuage concerns about illegitimate motives. But if a low-status actor can bring it off, it can raise his status and influence in the group.[69] Note that this is one of the circumstances in which an actor's group-oriented intent and not just his competence becomes a significant factor in other group members' judgments of his value to the group and therefore his status-worthiness and influence.

Explicit Performance Evaluations

The actual quality of a group member's contributions to the group goal is often hard to judge. The goals or tasks that many groups work on are often complex or ambiguous. Objective feedback about success or failure is not common, or it may only be apparent well after the fact. As a result, direct evaluations of one member's performance in comparison with another that might challenge the performance expectations held for both of them are relatively rare. But if they occur, expectation states theory argues that such evaluations will powerfully alter performance expectations and status, potentially undermining a high-status member's position or raising that of a low-status member.[70] For this reason, high-status members may use their influence in the group to steer it away from areas in which they may not perform well and take other active efforts to maintain perceptions of their competence and value to the group. Yet contingent events occur and may accumulate, especially over time, to unmask the actual performance quality of such members in ways that change the status hierarchy.[71]

We have seen that personality traits like being extroverted or dom-inant can lead to initially assertive behavior that in turn is perceived as competent and leads to status. Yet the evidence suggests that neither per-sonality trait is particularly correlated with actual competence.[72] Perhaps it is not surprising, then, that when the organizational scholars Corrine Bendersky and Neha Shah studied teams of MBAs who worked together on assignments, extroverts gained status initially, but over time their status declined.[73] Because the assignments were graded, the teams were working together in the face of relatively clear performance evaluations. Analysis of the team members' perceptions of one another showed that they were gradually disappointed in the performance of the extraverts compared to their original high expectations for them. Other members who were more neurotic in personality were low status initially, but gradually they exceeded the low expectations held for them and rose a bit in status on the teams.

Legitimacy, Authority, and Backlash

We now have a sense of how status cues that become salient in an ongoing situation of action shape and sometimes change a shared order of performance expectations among the members. This shared order, in turn, governs the status and influence they attain. Once the status hierarchy emerges and stabilizes, it acquires varying degrees of legitimacy for its members. *Legitimacy* is the sense that a status hierarchy is not only as it is, but as it *should* be—that is, appropriate and "right" in the eyes of its members.[74] Legitimacy matters because it affects the ability of high-status members to go beyond influence and persuasion to act authoritatively with the expectation that the members will comply.[75]

For this reason, legitimacy is key to the connection between status, leadership, and the exercise of power in the group. For the same reason, legitimacy affects how high-status members treat other members of the group. Reflecting the psychological insecurity of attaining status and the need to assuage doubts about whether they are group- or self-oriented, high-status members typically show more generosity toward other group members (sharing resources, for instance) and engage in more cooperative, ingratiating behaviors than do low-status members.[76] Members facing legitimacy problems that threaten their exercise of status and influence in a group often respond with behaviors that show group-orientation, including generosity.[77] When the status hierarchy acquires greater legitimacy, however, such generosity may disappear as the high-status members feel more secure and gain authority in the group.[78]

Any status hierarchy in which status ranks correspond to the shared order of performance expectations will have a certain baseline legitimacy with its members because it is perceived by its members as conforming to the basic status norm. In that sense, such a status hierarchy is normatively "right" and, as we have seen, will tend to be stable. But beyond this normative baseline, status hierarchies can be further legitimated to greater or lesser degrees based on the nature of the status cues that support the superiority of the high-status member.

Research has shown that members' sense that a hierarchy is legitimate is based not so much on their personal endorsement of it as on their sense that it is socially *valid* to the other members and even outsiders, who will treat it as though it were legitimate.[79] Note the similarity here with the way the shared order of performance expectations depends on consensus at the level of what other members are likely to expect (second-order expectations) rather than on agreement at the level of personal endorsements (first-order expectations). Validity, in turn, depends on other members' behavioral treatment of the hierarchy as legitimate, but also on the sense that the hierarchy accords with widely held cultural beliefs about the types of people expected to hold high- rather than low-status positions.[80]

Here is where the widely held status beliefs that create diffuse status characteristics play a role in the legitimacy that a high-status member enjoys in the group. When a person advantaged by diffuse status characteristics like gender, race, education, or occupation is high status in an interpersonal hierarchy, it looks expected, "right," and therefore more legitimate, in that it accords with broad cultural beliefs about the types of people who are generally high status. When the distinguished-looking white man takes the lead of a government task force, for instance, his legitimacy is strengthened by the fact that he "looks the part" of a leader more than, say, a middle-aged Latina woman would. Greater legitimacy allows such high-status group members to act with more directive authority and receive compliance rather than resistance compared to high-status members without the backing of diffuse status characteristics.[81]

In an experiment that demonstrates this effect, my colleagues and I created same-sex groups in which the high-status member gained influence because of a diffuse status characteristic advantage. In this case, the member who became high status was thirty-five years old and had an MA degree, while the teammate was an undergraduate student in his or her twenties. We also created other groups in which the high-status member's influence was based on scoring higher on a test of task expertise (a specific status characteristic) despite being only a high school graduate, a diffuse status characteristic disadvantage compared to the college student teammate. When these equally influential high-status members went on to make directive commands, the ones with diffuse status characteristic advantages (older and more educated) received significantly higher rates of compliance from their team members.[82] Ironically, then, more "meritocratic" status hierarchies in which the high-status member is influential owing to proven skill despite not being the "right" type of person is often treated as a bit less legitimate by their members, which limits the high-status member's power in his or her group.

An important consequence of the way in which widely held status beliefs about the types of people expected to be high- (or low-) status legitimate interpersonal hierarchies is that they create a "backlash" or resistance reaction to perceived challenges to those hierarchies. Earlier we saw that a person with low diffuse status characteristics who tries to speak up and act more agentically in order to prove competence and rise in status risks triggering resistance unless she can prove her cooperative group-orientation. A number of studies have shown that dominant, self-promotional behavior from a white woman or an African American man in a business or professional job context evokes resistance and dislike from others, reducing their perceived hireability and others' willingness to comply with them compared to a similar white man.[83]

The evidence on these backlash effects specifically shows that the problem for dominant-acting white women is not that they are seen as insufficiently warm, according to gender stereotypes. Rather, they are seen as "too dominant" in a way that challenges the accepted gender status hierarchy.[84] A meta-analysis of studies further shows that it is women's explicit dominance behavior, like directive commands, not their implicit dominance behavior, like an assertive gaze, that triggers negative backlash reactions.[85]

There are important intersectional variations, however, in the backlash response to dominant behavior from people who belong to low-status race and gender groups. Women of color in the United States are culturally viewed as less prototypical of either their gender or their race group than are men of a given race or white women.[86] This gives women of color a certain "intersectional invisibility" that may sometimes allow them to act dominantly in a business or professional context without a backlash reaction simply because their behavior matters less to accepted gender and race status hierarchies.[87] But the same relative invisibility, the sense of being less important for cultural presumptions about status, may nevertheless set constraints on people's willingness to treat women of color as legitimate occupants of high-status positions.[88] As diffuse status characteristics, then, race and gender, among their other effects, create widespread biases against the legitimacy of efforts by people disadvantaged by these characteristics to climb to high status or to effectively wield power and authority once in a high-status leadership position.

Overcoming Status Generalization

Are there any techniques for threading through the many barriers that diffuse status characteristics create for people who are disadvantaged by them in consequential contexts like the workplace? After all, some women, people of color, and people from working-class backgrounds do make it to top organizational and institutional positions. The techniques that have been documented are implied in what we have said already, but it is useful to pull them out and highlight them.

When a disadvantaging diffuse status characteristic like race, gender, or class background is salient in a local setting, it will immediately frame not only others' expectations for the actor's competence and status but also the actor's own self-expectations. So an actor's first step in overcoming status generalization has to be shoring up self-expectations by developing task-relevant skills and expertise that she can be confident about. But as studies have shown, such development is by no means enough.[89] As we have repeatedly seen, the status hierarchy is created and maintained more through others' expectations for one's self than through self-expectations. The trick, then, is changing *others'* performance expectations for the actor—a change those others often resist, not only because they presume that the actor is not competent but also because such a change does not seem legitimate to them and might even affect their own status in the group.

There are two general techniques that have been shown to be effective in assuaging legitimacy concerns and changing performance expectations.[90] The first is to introduce additional legitimate and unambiguous status information that is directly relevant to the group task and that advantages the actor over the others present. Such information works to counter and outweigh the negative competence implications of the disadvantaging diffuse status characteristics. Widely accepted specific status characteristics, such as public test scores or documented training or experience, carry social validity as signs of competence. The socially valid nature of this status information pressures other group members to accept it and combine it with the disadvantaging diffuse characteristics to create an improved performance expectation for the actor.

Note that it is not enough for the actor disadvantaged by diffuse status characteristics to simply claim expertise (even if true)—she needs to provide some valid "proof" of that expertise to overcome others' doubts and suspicions.[91] Sometimes that proof comes in the form of explicit support from an established authority in the setting who vouches for the diffuse status characteristic–disadvantaged actor. Many women who have risen high in the corporate world, for instance, have been backed at some time by powerful men who vouched for their legitimacy.[92]

The second technique, which is not inconsistent with the first, is to combine assertive behavior demonstrating competence with statements and behaviors that clearly communicate a cooperative, group-oriented desire to help the group rather than just selfishly seek status.[93] This technique only works if the actor disadvantaged by diffuse status characteristics really is competent. But if this is the case, her group-oriented behavior, such as generosity toward others and willingness to work for the group, can calm suspicions about her self-interested motivation, allowing the group to attend more closely to her actual performance on the task. And speaking up more assertively gets the actor's actual task ideas on the floor for the group to consider while communicating confidence and competence in doing so. Balancing between being assertive enough to prove competence but not so assertive as to seem aggressive and threatening to others can be a difficult tightrope to walk. But it is likely to work if the actor can bring it off.[94]

Neither of these two general techniques for overcoming status generalization in interpersonal hierarchies is "fair" for the actor who is disadvantaged by diffuse status characteristics. With both, the actor has to work harder, be nicer, and provide more clear-cut evidence of competence just to be treated as equal to rather than less than. But in the many consequential social relational contexts that mediate people's access to life outcomes that are significant for inequality (a job interview, a workplace project team), overcoming status generalization can help people from lower-status groups attain positions of power and influence.

Three Biases That Result from the Framing Effects
of Status Characteristics

As we have seen throughout this chapter, powerful diffuse status characteristics—the ones that correspond to fundamental axes along which inequality in the United States is organized, like race, gender, education, occupation, and class background—frame interpersonal status processes from the beginning. The status beliefs attached to these group identities shape how a person is implicitly evaluated and treated by others in one consequential encounter after another—an evaluation that the person, who also is cognizant of the status beliefs, perceives as well. The effects of these status beliefs, acting in social relational contexts in which they are salient, set in motion three types of biases that systematically advantage those from higher-status groups and disadvantage people from lower-status groups in access to the valued outcomes that consequential encounters mediate. These are status bias, legitimacy bias, and associational preference bias.[95]

Status bias is the term I use for the full range of *evaluative* biases about the relative competence and status-worthiness of different actors that are unleashed by diffuse status characteristics when they become salient in a social relational context. In this chapter, we have seen how these evaluative biases spread throughout the microdynamics of status. Status bias starts with biases in initial performance expectations that trigger self-fulfilling effects on behavior and even task performance. It continues with biases in the way a task performance is evaluated when it comes from an actor advantaged rather than disadvantaged by diffuse status characteristics. It triggers related biases in the willingness to attribute ability to the actor based on a performance of a given, acknowledged quality. And finally, as a consequence of all these biases in perceived value or "merit," status bias leads to an ultimate bias in people's willingness to grant influence and esteem to one actor compared to another in a given context.

Legitimacy biases refer to the biases that people show in their tendency to treat diffuse status characteristics–advantaged actors, like whites, men, or professionals, as more legitimate occupants of high-status positions than disadvantaged actors, like people of color, women, or blue-collar workers. Importantly, such treatment includes the tendency to sanction behavior that challenges the status rankings between groups that are represented in the widely shared status beliefs that constitute diffuse status characteristics. These are the biases that result in resistive, backlash reactions against those who are disadvantaged by diffuse status characteristics, such as African American men or white women, who act in a highly assertive manner in an effort to prove competence and rise in status. They are also the biases that constrain the ability of these disadvantaged actors, once they achieve a high-status position (say, the African American boss), to act in a directive, authoritative manner and receive compliance rather than resistance from subordinates. In this way, legitimacy biases limit the power of actors disadvantaged by diffuse status characteristics in high-status leadership positions, compared to advantaged actors.

We have already alluded to the third form of social relational bias triggered by diffuse status characteristics, *associational preference bias,* but have not yet discussed it specifically. As we have noted before, people's first reaction to group differences is to prefer people like themselves.[96] And in fact, *social homophily,* the tendency to form network ties with similar others, is the dominant strain in people's associations.[97] But as we have also seen, the status of those with whom a person associates affects perceptions of the person's own status and competence because status spreads through association.[98] The fact that associations have status implications introduces a systematic bias into who is preferred by others for association and social exchange.[99] This bias intensifies the in-group preferences of people from high-status social groups who see every reason to prefer people like themselves not only for social reasons but for hiring and promoting in the workplace.[100] But for people who belong to low-status groups, the status implications of associations blunt their in-group preferences.[101] They experience a tension between sticking with their own group and seeking associations with those from higher-status groups.

People's actual patterns of associations, of course, are shaped not only by their preferences but by the constraints of their social environment, which shapes who is available for them to associate with.[102] But at the very least, these associational preference biases undermine solidarity among members of low-status groups while intensifying network ties, and the flow of information and opportunities, among members of high-status groups.[103] Associational preference biases are likely to be stronger in instrumental, goal-oriented social relational contexts, since these are the contexts in which the cultural schema of status most powerfully drives individual behavior. But these instrumentally oriented contexts, which include work, educational, and political contexts, are also the ones that most powerfully mediate individuals' access to valued social outcomes in society.

The advantaging or disadvantaging effects of status, legitimacy, and associational preference biases vary contextually in power and even direction. But the effects of these biases triggered by status beliefs in consequential social relational contexts nevertheless accumulate over situations and lifetimes.[104] As they do so, they create a general pattern of systematic advantage for those from higher-status groups and disadvantage for those from lower-status groups in access to the valued outcomes that consequential social relational contexts mediate. Such outcomes can include a job, a promotion, social recognition, or a position of power. In this way, the microdynamics of status play a powerful role in the creation and maintenance of inequality between social difference groups.

CHAPTER 6

STATUS, DIFFERENCE, AND THE DURABILITY OF INEQUALITY

IN AN ADVANCED industrial society like the contemporary United States, what is the continuing significance of status, as an ancient form of inequality, for the larger structure of inequality? This is a question I have referred to from the beginning, but now it is time to face it squarely. Considering it takes us back to the core questions that have animated the inquiry behind this book: Why is status everywhere? And why does it matter anyway? So far, I have mostly pointed for an answer to people's reliance on a cultural schema of status to manage their fundamental problems of interdependence, problems that are themselves everywhere in social life. But status is everywhere and matters for additional reasons that are especially significant for the nature and stability of larger structures of inequality. These further reasons will be the focus of our concerns in this chapter.

Here we will explore a set of interlinked effects of status processes that are consequential for the fundamental character of the broad patterns of social and material inequality that cleave modern society. First, the enactment of status inequality, as we know from the cultural schema theory, relies on shared status beliefs. These status beliefs rank groups based on social differences such as gender, race, occupation, and class in terms of the types of actors that are presumed to be "better"—more valuable to society—than others. In this way, status processes foster inequality based on socially defined *group differences,* which, as we will see, contribute to the durability of patterns of material inequality. Second, status processes acting through the diffuse status characteristics created by these status beliefs provide an independent means by which inequality based on status-valued group differences autonomously *reproduces* itself. These status processes do so by advantaging those from higher-status groups in access to valued material resources and positions of power. This access, in turn, allows differences like gender, race, and class-as-culture (that is, class as lifestyle and cultural practices, not just wealth) to become systems of inequality in their own right.[1] Finally, this interweaving of status-valued group differences into material structures of inequality, in turn, *legitimates* and *stabilizes* those structures of inequality by tying them to cultural presumptions that they are based on differences among people in competence and worth—in other words, in "merit." Together these effects have a profound impact on the basic structure of inequality even in an advanced industrial society.

In earlier chapters, we noted that status beliefs develop not just about groups defined by types of individuals, such as race and gender, but also about groups understood as organizations that are differentiated and ranked in relation to one another, like law schools or corporations.[2] In both cases, the status ranking is based on cultural beliefs about differences between the groups (individuals or organizations) in presumed competence and worth (or "quality").[3] Status processes among organizations also have a powerful impact on the overall structure of inequality in American society, and they do so through processes that are roughly comparable to the interlinked effects of status processes among groups of individuals. That said, however, my focus here, as it has been throughout, will be on the significance for the overall structure of inequality of status processes among groups of individuals based on social differences. Specifically, I will comment on status and inequality based on gender, race, and class-as-culture.

Before going any further, we need to clarify what I will be referring to as the "overall structure of inequality." Although status or prestige is part of the societal structure of inequality, for analytic clarity, I will discuss this structure more narrowly in terms of the distribution of *material* inequality. This will allow me to distinguish the effects of status processes on the structure of material inequality. Following Weber and the sociological scholar of inequality Charles Tilly, I will define the material structure of inequality simply in terms of two closely related processes.[4] These are control over material resources (wealth and so on) and access to positions of power in the organizations, such as workplaces, government, families, and health and educational institutions, that produce and distribute these resources.

Categorical Difference and Durable Inequality

In his influential book *Durable Inequality*, Charles Tilly points out that structures of inequality built only on individual differences in the organizational control of resources and power are inherently unstable.[5] They give rise to a constant scramble for precedence between dominant and subdominant individuals in which no dominant individual's regime lasts for long. Think of the violent intrigues among pretenders to the throne in a Shakespeare play or in the television series *Game of Thrones*.

For a structure of inequality to persist—that is, for it to become *durable* inequality—control over resources and power has to be consolidated, Tilly argues, with a categorical difference among people like ethnicity, gender, race, or class lifestyle. That is, differences in material inequality have to become associated with corresponding differences among categories, or "types," of people. Of course, differences in types of people are precisely what status beliefs delineate and evaluatively rank.

Why does the consolidation of material inequality with categorical differences stabilize the structure of inequality? Tilly argues that it does so by facilitating people's ability to carry out, and keep carrying out, the primary mechanisms by which material inequality is generated.[6] The first of these mechanisms is exploitation: some people or groups of people appropriating value from the productive work of others. The owner of a sweatshop, for instance, becomes rich by expropriating value from the efforts of her overworked and underpaid employees. The other mechanism is opportunity hoarding: people favor themselves or those like them for opportunities to gain power and resources. Word of a job or promising investment possibility, for instance, if not kept for oneself, is given to others from the same social group. The consolidation of control over resources and power with "us," marked by a boundary of perceived group difference from "them," turns the individual project of exploitation and hoarding into a shared group project. Acting on the basis of a shared group identity, "we" work together to take from "them" and hoard for "us," strengthening and stabilizing the processes by which we maintain dominant control of resources and power even in the face of changing political and economic circumstances.

The basic thrust of Tilly's argument is persuasive. Like several others, however, I believe that his mechanisms of exploitation and opportunity hoarding tell us more about the goals or resultant effects of dominant group actions than about the actual behavioral processes through which these mechanisms are accomplished.[7] To fully understand the processes Tilly describes, we need to incorporate the effects of status processes. Tilly recognizes, by the way, that ideology, which could be seen to include cultural status beliefs, plays a role in stabilizing structures of material inequality. But he sees these status effects as after-the-fact—a gloss that smooths the appearance of inequality rather than as a causal force in itself. I believe this is a mistake.[8]

Status processes, carried out through cultural beliefs about groups that shape events at the relational level, drive inequality based on group difference. As they do so, they play an essential role in the initial and continuing consolidation of material inequality with group difference. They also act as important processes by which exploitation and opportunity hoarding are actually accomplished on an everyday basis in advanced industrial societies. And through the role they play in legitimatizing inequality on the basis of who is "better," status beliefs provide a powerful means by which the consolidation of difference with inequality actually stabilizes structures of inequality and undercuts resistance from below. The next task is to unpack these processes a bit.

Status as the Consolidator of Material Inequality and Group Difference

When one subgroup of a population gains an advantage in the control of resources and power and seeks to stabilize that control, Tilly suggests, they reach out to a boundary of group difference around which to anchor their advantage. Depending on the group's own distinguishing characteristics, its members may recruit a previously recognized difference, like gender or ethnicity, or they may try to create a new, recognizable boundary of difference by adopting distinctive cultural practices or lifestyles.[9] But how does highlighting a group boundary really consolidate advantage? It does so, most fundamentally, either by creating new status beliefs about the highlighted group difference or by exploiting such beliefs if they already exist.

We know from research on status construction theory, which we discussed in chapter 4, that when a recognizable group difference is systematically correlated with a difference in material resources, encounters between people across the boundary of group difference will rapidly create (or reinforce if they already exist) status beliefs about that social difference. Recall that, under these circumstances, research shows that participants quickly link the appearance of mastery in the situation created by the control over resources with the recognizable group difference between them and make inferences about the type of people in each group.[10] In this way, the participants form beliefs that people from the resource-advantaged difference group are not just richer but also more worthy and competent, if less warm, than people from the poorer difference group. Importantly, as this research demonstrates, since participants from both the advantaged and disadvantaged groups experience the apparent "superiority" of the advantaged "type" of person, these status beliefs are shared by those in both groups.

As we also noted in chapter 4, it is plausible that such processes, while not the only factors involved, have played a role in the construction and maintenance of status beliefs about each of the three status distinctions we focus on here—gender, race, and class-as-culture. Although the actual origins of gender as a status characteristic in Western society are simply unknown, current theories posit factors—such as men's superior upper body strength or the mobility constraints of lactating mothers—that at some point in the past led to a division of labor that gave men greater control over the production of needed resources.[11] By our account here, such a systematic control of resources would quickly foster status beliefs that transformed gender into a diffuse status characteristic, creating a status belief that then becomes self-fulfilling. In the complex history of encounters between groups that lie behind the development of American racial status beliefs, we similarly see many factors (superior technology, institutions of control such as slavery and servitude) that would have yielded resource advantages for whites that were transformed in cross-group encounters into status beliefs.[12] And of course, social class is a status distinction that, while enacted through boundary-marking differences in lifestyles and cultural practices, is nevertheless based directly on one group's superior possession of resources compared to another's.

When status beliefs develop across a line of group difference associated with resource advantages and disadvantages, people from both the poorer group and the richer group come to believe that, like it or not, those from the richer group would be seen by "most people" as a superior *type* or category of person. And since they are seen as better, those in the richer group seem to deserve their material advantages on the basis of merit—because of their superiority.[13] In this way, the development of shared status beliefs about a group difference transforms *individual* advantages in the resources and power possessed by individuals in the richer group into a superior right to those advantages based on their *group identity* as a certain type of person. It is status beliefs, in other words, that really do the work of consolidating categorical group difference with inequality. In the process, status beliefs provide the means to stabilize that inequality.

The Reproduction of Difference-Based Inequality

Once we recognize that it is the development of a shared status belief about a group difference that really consolidates it with material inequality, then we can see that the everyday enactment of status processes based on that group difference is an essential element in the processes by which the pattern of material inequality associated with the difference becomes durable. That is, the effects of status processes play a key role in sustaining the pattern of inequality over time and changing social circumstances.

I have said often that it is status, as a social process, that gives patterns of inequality based on social differences like gender or race an autonomous capacity to reproduce themselves. By that I mean that when a group difference such as gender or race becomes a diffuse status characteristic, it gives individuals, holding constant their current levels of resources and power, an added advantage (or disadvantage), based on their group identity alone, in gaining access to future resources and power. The presumption that, for example, a man or white person is just a little more competent and statusworthy than an equally rich and powerful woman or person of color gives that man or white person an edge in getting a bigger raise or being appointed to a new, more powerful position. Seen this way, it is clear that status processes are part of the routine, everyday means by which people from the higher-status difference group appropriate value from those in the lower-status group (exploitation) and hoard opportunities for their own group.[14] And as a consequence, the status value of group differences such as gender, race, and class-as-culture lies behind their persistent durability as core axes of material inequality in the United States.[15] It is worth looking in a little more detail at how status processes carry out the everyday reproduction of difference-based inequality. We will review two general sets of processes through which this occurs. The first will be familiar from what we learned in the last chapter about how diffuse characteristics shape everyday social relations in ways that create inequality. The second looks at the indirect effect of this process on the organizational reproduction of difference-based inequality.

Status Characteristics and Interactional Reproduction

Recall from the last chapter that diffuse status characteristics (that is, status-valued group identities like race, gender, and class that form major axes of inequality) frame interaction in workplaces and other consequential organizational contexts in several ways that systematically direct people from higher-status groups toward more valued resources and positions of power than otherwise similar people from lower-status groups.[16] Specifically, we saw evidence that status characteristics create three types of biases in everyday encounters that favor those from higher-status groups for valued outcomes over and above what they would receive without their status-valued group identity. In the workplace, such valued outcomes can include a recommendation for a job, a positive performance evaluation, a raise, or a promotion.

First, of course, status characteristics acting in consequential contexts unleash *status bias,* which includes a wide range of evaluative biases that start with implicit expectations that frame actors from high-status groups as more competent and able and shape subsequent judgments and behaviors in self-fulfilling ways. Those judged to be more able and competent are given higher rewards and pointed toward more opportunities (a promotion or valued job assignment). To the extent that this evaluative bias is based simply on status associated with group identity, it constitutes both an extraction of value from the lower-status actor, who does not get the same reward for equal work (exploitation), and the hoarding of opportunity for members of the high-status group.

Similarly, status characteristics trigger *legitimacy bias,* which casts actors from lower-status groups as less appropriate and acceptable candidates for positions of authority and evokes resistance to their efforts to challenge the status hierarchy between the groups. Legitimacy biases further blunt the ability of actors from lower-status groups to achieve and act effectively in positions that provide opportunities to improve their material outcomes. Status characteristics also create *associational preference bias,* which favors actors from high-status groups as network contacts with whom to conduct valued social exchange. Taking place in consequential contexts, associational bias advantages actors from high-status groups and disadvantages those from low-status groups in access to information (how much of a raise can I ask for?) and opportunities (an introduction to a key contact) that is useful in attaining added resources and positions of power. Legitimacy and associational preference biases also play powerful roles in the everyday hoarding of opportunities for the higher-status group.

As we have noted before, though the overall status advantage or disadvantage these biases create can be large, in any given encounter it is often small. But the effects of these small biases accumulate over multiple encounters in all the different organizational and institutional settings that are consequential for material inequality. In a clear example of this, Elizabeth Korver-Glenn has shown that the racial status biases acting in real estate transactions systematically produce discrimination in ways that accumulate over the several stages of buying or selling a home.[17] Over time, such everyday status-biased encounters systematically direct actors from higher-status groups toward positions in society with greater resources (a better house at a lower cost) than those that flow to actors from lower-status groups—and do so while giving the appearance that the outcome is based on merit.

The biases triggered by status characteristics in everyday social encounters, because they typically function without much explicit awareness or thought-out intention on the part of the participants, often fly below the radar of what the actors in these consequential contexts think they are doing. In some ways, however, they are more powerful for that. To be sure, people from higher-status groups also take explicit and strategic actions to maintain the material advantages of their group over a lower-status one—effectively engaging in intentional exploitation and opportunity hoarding. High-status actors may explicitly and intentionally exploit status beliefs about social differences, with their self-justifying implications about the actors' own superiority, to stabilize their control of material inequality between themselves and others. But such intentional group-advantaging behavior is supported by a diffuse but sustained and powerful base of everyday implicit biases that continually reproduce material advantage from status-valued group difference.[18]

Interactional Reproduction through Organizational Practices and Procedures

There is a second, also important, way in which status beliefs about social differences reproduce material inequality based on difference. This second means of reproduction is an indirect effect of status beliefs' biasing effects on social relational processes. Thus far, I have primarily discussed status beliefs at the macrocultural level and status hierarchies at the interpersonal, social relational level. This second effect works at the meso level of organizations.

It is well documented that assumptions about the attributes and superiority of dominant groups are often embedded in the structures, practices, and procedures by which workplace, educational, government, and other organizations carry out their work.[19] For instance, as many have pointed out, the very structure of the traditional workweek, with its nine-to-five, Monday-Friday structure, implies an "ideal worker" who does not have primary responsibility for dependent children and therefore is less likely to be a woman than a man.[20] Contemporary organizational practices that reward or even require "overwork" (more than fifty hours a week) in highly paid business and professional jobs similarly create disproportionate obstacles for women, who are more likely to have time-demanding family responsibilities.[21]

Other research shows that in educational institutions common practices for teaching, responding to, and rewarding students reflect class- and race-based assumptions about valued behavioral styles and cultural knowledge. Speaking up to ask questions in class or asking for a teacher's help, for instance, are valued middle-class behavioral styles that may be less familiar to working-class students and students from some nonwhite race or ethnic groups.[22] These embedded class- and race-shaped cultural practices in schools create added obstacles to success for students who are not from the presumed and valued middle-class and white background and are not comfortable with the behavioral styles of that background.[23] Once such gender-, race-, or class-biased organizational practices and procedures develop, they tend to persist through inertia and act as independent factors in the continued production of unequal outcomes in the organization for those of different genders, races, and class backgrounds.[24]

But how do assumptions about the nature and superiority of dominant groups become embedded in organizational structures and practices in the first place? New structures and procedures are typically developed at the social relational level by committees, teams, or small groups of founders who are confronted with problems of organizing their work. Other, more informal norms and practices through which work is actually carried out in an organization emerge implicitly through repeated social interactions among the various actors involved.[25]

I argue that status beliefs about social differences are likely to shape what goes on in these social relational committees, teams, and encounters as procedures and structures are designed or simply emerge. As they do so, status beliefs affect whose voices are heard and whose interests are heeded in the proceedings. Procedures and practices can be shaped in this way not only by who is "at the table" as they develop but also by who is, by implication, not there.

In some cases, in the ways described by status characteristics and expectation states theory, group differences between the participants or implied others they are dealing with in the work make status beliefs about the difference salient for participants in the encounters.[26] The social-legal scholars Robert Nelson and William Bridges, for instance, examined the historical contexts in which several widely used job classification systems were developed that have the effect of paying men's jobs better than women's.[27] The evidence they found clearly documents the biasing effects of gender status processes, effects that shaped whose perspectives and interests carried weight in the social relations and committee proceedings through which these job classification systems were constructed.

Even in highly homogeneous race, gender, or class contexts, however, participants' shared group identity may make status beliefs about their group salient, relative to an implied contrasting group, in ways that add a status taint to the cultural practices they develop. Drawing on their shared identity as a way of relating to one another, participants may implicitly draw on the defining cultural practices of their "type" of people as they organize their work relations. They are particularly likely to do this as they define standards for what will be more highly valued and rewarded in the organization.[28] Thus, students at an elite school are likely to embed class-based values for individuality and autonomy into their preferred cultural practices just as workers in a male-dominated workplace may develop an aggressive "guy culture."[29] But of course, these defining practices, because they help distinguish the group identity, carry with them the implicit status evaluation associated with the group in society's cultural status beliefs.[30] The effect of these relational processes through which many organizational practices develop is to inscribe assumptions about the greater competence and status-worthiness of people from some groups compared to others into the very structure of the way the organization does its work.

Critical Sites for the Status Reproduction of Difference-Based Inequality

As we have just seen, homogeneous group environments play a significant role in the production of difference-based inequality by fostering the production of distinctive cultural practices that mark the superiority of the high-status group and create barriers for those from lower-status groups.

That said, however, the sites that are most critical for the actual differentiation of material outcomes between those from higher- and lower-status groups are sites in which *cross-category* (for example, across gender, race, or class groups) interactions take place. These are the contexts in which status characteristics become distinctly salient and trigger all the status, legitimacy, and associational preference biases that advantage actors from higher-status groups. Thus, these are the encounters in which status-valued group difference is actually translated into material (dis)advantages between otherwise similar actors. Given the importance of these cross-category encounters, we need to consider how the frequency and the institutional contexts of such encounters vary for the status distinctions of gender, race, and class, since this will shape the means through which status processes maintain durable inequality based on them.

In this regard, as in others, gender is uniquely different from race and class because it is rooted in a very high rate of daily, routine, and even intimate cross-category interaction. Most households and kin groups contain members of both sexes and thus have a level of intimate interdependence between gender groups, at least in those contexts, that is not typical for cross-race or cross-class interaction.[31] Furthermore, because gender divides the population into two roughly equal-sized groups, the statistical likelihood of cross-category interactions for both men and women is increased.[32] Finally, gender cross-cuts every other social division in society, including race and class, and thus cross-gender interactions take place within almost all broad social contexts. Despite the sex-segregation of many jobs and occupations, for instance, cross-gender interaction takes place in most workplaces, made up as they are of people with various positions (nurses and doctors, say, or supervisors and clerks). Given the very high rate of everyday encounters between men and women, gender status processes acting through these routine social relations are plausibly the most powerful factors in the continuing, persistent reproduction of material inequality between men and women, despite legal and economic factors that work against it in the contemporary United States.[33] And it is a distinctive aspect of gender that these status processes operate to produce inequality within the household in family decision-making and in the division of household labor as well as in more public institutions such as the workplace, government, health, or educational organizations.

At the other end of the continuum from the frequent and intimate interactions across gender are the much less frequent and largely instrumental interactions that occur across class lines.[34] Cross-class interactions that take place outside of occupationally structured encounters (for instance, a grocery store clerk and a customer) are much less common compared to gender. Patterns of residential segregation by class, race, and income groups substantially limit routine, informal encounters across class and race as well.[35] Everyday social relations are largely lived within class contexts, and as we will see in the following section, this shapes some of the distinctive ways in which class status is enacted through the cultural capital of higher- and lower-status groups.

Race is somewhere between gender and class in the frequency and intimacy of cross-category interactions, but closer to class on the continuum. Although some kinship relations are cross-race, most are not, and patterns of residence are intensely segregated by race in the United States.[36] However, since racial minorities are, in fact, statistical minorities, making their way through the majority-dominated institutions of everyday life forces some degree of routine cross-racial interaction on most people of color. This, of course, is less true for majority whites, although the changing demographic structure of the United States is increasing cross-racial interactions for them as well.

If routine cross-category encounters are less frequent for race and class, does this mean that interactional status processes are not so important for the reproduction of racial and class-based patterns of inequality? Ironically, no. Interactional status processes continue to play a critical role in the production of class and race inequality because encounters with powerful *gateway institutions* are cross-category for actors from lower-status race and class groups.[37]

Gateway institutions are the dominant organizations in society, like schools, workplaces, government, and health organizations, that mediate people's access to valued outcomes like health, money, and positions of power. Their organizational procedures and cultural norms reflect the dominant actors who control them, and these are disproportionately people from higher-status racial groups and middle- or higher-status class groups. Much like women in male-dominated occupations, people of color and poor or working-class people encounter systematic presumptions about their lesser competence, worth, and legitimacy as they try to make their way through these critical gateway encounters.[38] Thus, although cross-category encounters may occur less frequently across race and class lines, they occur in critical organizational contexts that shape people's long-term path to resources and power in society.

Status and the Variable Construction of Difference

As we have seen, status processes mobilize in many ways the cultural construction of boundaries of difference and distinction.[39] It is worth thinking a bit about how these constructions of difference vary for gender, race, and class, since they affect how status biases based on them play out in the contemporary United States. All status beliefs locate difference in a simplified, abstract conception of the attributes of people in one group compared to the other. People, after all, use status beliefs to quickly form anticipations of how one person will perform in the situation compared to another, and to do so they need simplified assumptions about distinguishing, performance-related attributes. But the widely shared understanding of the nature of the attributes that distinguish the groups can vary from assumptions about differences in immutable essences to differences in acquired and changing tastes or knowledge. The latter we might think of as cultural differences between the groups.

In other words, the differences that signal "better" or "lesser" and thus mark status in dominant group stereotypes can be understood as more or less essentialized within the type of person and his or her physical makeup. The distinction I am making here is related but not identical to the traditional distinction in stratification research between ascribed and achieved differences.[40] Rather than a dichotomy, I argue that this is a continuum of relative essentialization and that status beliefs about gender, race, and class all carry some elements at both ends of the range but vary greatly in the proportions of relatively essentialized features.

As we discuss this matter, it is important to keep in mind that what matters for status processes is *not* whether the group difference "actually is" essentialized in people's persons or not, however that is understood. Rather, the issue is whether the difference is *culturally understood* to be essentialized in widely accepted stereotypes. It is these third-order beliefs that most powerfully drive status behaviors and make beliefs about relative essentialization real in their consequences. We should keep in mind that, as ethnomethodological studies have shown, in the everyday encounters in which most status processes play out, gender, race, and class are all interactional accomplishments.[41] That is, people are understood in the situation as members of these various categories through the social cues they display in the interaction.

Gender, understood here as the socially defined, categorical boundary between male and female, is the difference at play *within* the intimate group of family and kin. It is not just a difference between the home group and others. Given the complexity of maintaining a boundary of difference under such conditions of constant mutual influence and shared exposure, perhaps it is not surprising that gender is highly essentialized in dominant cultural beliefs as stably rooted in the body (even if there are also growing challenges to this cultural assumption). In fact, research on social cognition suggests that, in people's thinking, gender is the most essentialized of the various group differences that pattern social inequality in American society.[42]

Belief in the essentialization of gender has always been fed by simplified cultural presumptions that it is straightforwardly linked to physical sex differences associated with sexuality. Yet gender, like all other social category system, is actually read in social interaction through a complex set of imperfectly correlated social cues and variable physical attributes whose meaning varies across situations.[43] Increasing public awareness of transgender and gender-queer identities plausibly is opening up the cultural possibility that the basis of one's essential gender identity can include choice, including bodily choice, rather than simply the body as born into. It may also include categories that are intermediate between male and female.[44] Yet cultural beliefs that gender identity, however conceived, is a powerful, essential voice in the self persist even in the face of changing understandings of the basis for essentialism.[45]

Beliefs that gender is relatively essentialized deeply within the person does not mean that gender difference is not also marked in status beliefs by presumed differences in acquirable skills (cooking versus mechanics) or specialized knowledge (sports expertise).[46] But these beliefs about more acquirable differences between typical men and women coexist with deeply essentialized beliefs about differences in their fundamental natures that undergird assumptions about men's greater agentic, mastering competence and suitability for leadership.[47]

In the U.S. context, race is also relatively essentialized in dominant cultural beliefs as a meaningful and stable difference among people that is rooted in the body.[48] This belief remains dominant despite evidence not only of its historical construction as a status-valued social distinction but also of its implicitly variable interpretation in everyday encounters.[49] Yet the fact that race is not typically a difference within the intimate group but between that group and other groups also encourages an additional highlighting of the cultural practices of the contrasting racial group as another marker of the boundary that indicates the superiority of the high-status group.

As research on the basis of whites' perceived status superiority in contemporary American racial stereotypes shows, this balance of perceived essential and cultural difference plays out differently for different racial group boundaries. The researchers Linda Zou and Sapna Cheryan find that two dimensions of perceived, status-relevant difference between the dominant white group and various nonwhite groups together determine a hierarchy of racial group position.[50] The first dimension is of perceived *(in)competence,* understood as intellectual and economic inferiority that acts, I argue, along with racial categorization itself, as a more essentialized feature of difference presumably rooted in the nature of the person.[51]

Zou and Cheryan's second dimension of difference is cultural *"foreignness,"* which we can think of as a lack of *cultural competence* or "fit" with dominant white culture—a less essentialized, more acquirable difference. According to several sets of data that Zou and Cheryan present, whites are seen and treated as both inherently competent and culturally adept.[52] In contrast, in current racial stereotypes, Asians are seen as inherently competent but culturally very foreign, Latinx people are seen as less competent and somewhat foreign, and African Americans are viewed as lower in inherent competence but only slightly foreign, culturally. This research suggests that the contemporary American racial status hierarchy rests on boundaries marked by beliefs about both essentialized and group cultural forms of competence and worth. It suggests as well that current stereotypes about competence and worth disadvantage all nonwhite groups in relation to whites, but some nonwhite groups, like African Americans, are more disadvantaged than others, such as Asians, especially in beliefs about essentialized forms of competence.

The relative essentialization of gender and race differences in the American context affects how status processes based on them play out. If a group difference is essentialized in the body, once a person is categorized on it in a social relation, it remains a framing understanding of that person throughout the relationship. Once you are categorized as a man or woman, an Asian or an African American or a white person, that never leaves people's understanding of you. Indeed, cognitive research suggests that in our society gender and race are primary categories of person perception on which we categorize, or at least try to categorize, one another almost instantly.[53] This means that gender and race stereotypes and the status beliefs they contain will be cognitively primed and available to shape expectations for and treatment of another person. As we know from status characteristics and expectation states theory, the situational impact of gender and race status beliefs on how a person is treated will vary in strength and direction depending on the specific nature of the situation. But the point here is that the essentialization of gender and race helps propel the status processes based on them and virtually ensures that gender and race status processes will always be going on in interaction. In this way, these status processes powerfully contribute to the durability of material inequality based on gender and race.

If a person's essentialized gender and racial group identities, along with the status they carry, are always with that person in interaction, it also means that a person from a lower-status gender or race group cannot simply learn the distinctive cultural capital of the high-status group and be accepted as "fitting in." The organizational behavior scholar Catherine Turco, for instance, observed this about gender in her study of investors in the elite leveraged buyout industry, an overwhelmingly white male industry.[54] It was very much an aggressive "guy's culture," she found, in which the display of sports knowledge was used to bond with others and smooth business deals. The few investors who were African American men could show their fit within this elite male culture because displaying sports expertise did not contradict their essentialized identities as either men or African Americans.

Women, however, including the very few minority women, encountered a cultural barrier. They usually tried to cultivate an interest in sports, but it was not seen as enough to enable them to really fit in. They were still often excluded from the sports-oriented gatherings through which business ties were negotiated. In this way, gender status persistently shaped outcomes for investors of all races. In a similar process, essentialized beliefs about African Americans that link their lower status to inherently lower capabilities create persistent barriers to African Americans' efforts to prove competence and legitimacy in the workplace. Evidence suggests, for instance, that they are judged more harshly for mistakes, even in leadership positions.[55]

What about racial groups whose lower status relies heavily on cultural fit based on "foreignness," such as Asian Americans? Because their racial identity as Asian is essentialized, simply mastering dominant white cultural practices, as of course second- and higher-generation Asian Americans have done, does not fully erase other people's treatment of them as "foreign," as many accounts have shown.[56] Whatever their cultural expertise, their racial status clings to them and presents status barriers, particularly to their perceived suitability for leadership.[57]

In striking contrast to gender and race, people in the United States believe that class can be achieved and changed and is not primarily a matter of essentialized differences based in the body.[58] This ideological perspective has consequences in that people treat class as less of an inherent essence than they do race or gender, according to psychological research. This is despite the fact that, as Bourdieu's studies of habitus have shown, being raised and living within a particular social class also writes on people's bodies and ways of being.[59] Psychological research shows, for instance, that people reliably read social class (wealth) from people's faces and do so primarily by picking up visual cues of positive emotion and well-being that they use to classify people as higher- rather than lower-class.[60]

Given American beliefs about the achieved, less essentialized nature of class difference, perhaps it is not surprising that the cues that people use to classify one another on class seem to form a sort of "fuzzy set"—a less unified and tightly bounded set of status attributes compared to those that people use to classify each other on race and gender.[61] Class status attributes include occupation, education, accent, dress, cultural tastes, residence, and family background, among others.[62] Across situations, the class attributes that become salient and relevant to status in the context are likely to vary considerably relative to those that evoke race or gender status. As a result, the specific nature and form of status effects based on class may be relatively more variable over contexts and are likely to interact in complex ways with the more essentialized categories of race and gender.[63]

If American beliefs locate the boundary of difference between classes less in immutable essences and more in acquirable attributes like education and tastes, then the maintenance of that boundary depends more heavily on the high-status group possessing *exclusive* cultural capital that lower-class groups do not (yet) have.[64] This is in contrast to the firmer boundaries that essentialization offers for the maintenance of gender and racial status, despite those also having cultural elements. For elite cultural capital to remain elite, of course, it must continually adapt and change as lower-status class groups acquire its earlier forms. In this way, for instance, inside knowledge about what it takes to impress admissions committees of elite colleges or get valued jobs after graduation evolves to maintain the competitive advantage of class-privileged groups.[65]

Material Inequality and the Maintenance of Status Beliefs

As we have seen, status beliefs play an essential role in the consolidation of group difference and inequality that makes the inequality durable. But by the same token, that consolidation provides people with everyday evidence that some types of people are indeed richer, more powerful, and "better" than are others across a line of social difference. Such evidence offers the everyday reinforcement necessary to the durability of the status belief about the group difference.

Status beliefs about the social signs of greater or lesser competence and worth, I have argued, emerge out of people's efforts to anticipate reactions and coordinate relations in goal-oriented, cooperatively interdependent situations. In the workplace and other contexts consequential for inequality, people reach to shared status beliefs to create expectations for relative competence that organize their behavior in such settings and have powerful self-fulfilling effects on the hierarchies of influence and prominence that develop. The status beliefs that constitute diffuse status characteristics such as gender, race, and class carry broadly relevant assumptions about general competence differences that make them especially likely to create self-fulfilling hierarchies in these consequential settings. To the extent that such status beliefs about group differences create a corresponding behavioral hierarchy, that hierarchy, in turn, provides its participants with a vivid, apparently valid demonstration of the greater apparent competence and value of those from high-status groups that reinforces the cultural status beliefs. Thus, status beliefs, especially those about the diffuse status characteristics that act as major axes of inequality, have a powerful capacity for self-validation and self-maintenance, simply through their effects on influence, prominence, and apparent competence in consequential interactional settings.[66]

In the long run, however, status beliefs about group differences are difficult to sustain if they are not seen to also produce *material* evidence of the implied group difference in competence.[67] If status beliefs are held as signals of the superior capacity of a type of people to produce valued outcomes, what is the real evidence of those outcomes? Or as the popular saying has it, "if you are so smart, why aren't you rich?" For status beliefs about a group difference to persist over time and powerfully shape a broad range of consequent interactions, they need to be associated with average differences between the groups in material resources and in the occupation of positions of power in organizations.[68] If the durability of patterns of material inequality depends on status beliefs about group differences, then, the relationship is entirely reciprocal.

A clear implication of the foregoing analyses is that patterns of material inequality based on group differences like gender, race, or class-as-culture cannot be sustainably changed without changing their supporting status beliefs. But these status beliefs, through their self-fulfilling effects at the interactional level, have considerable powers of self-reinforcement. How, then, do status beliefs about social differences change, as they clearly have over historical periods? For instance, Irish Americans and Italian Americans used to be considered low status compared to Anglo-Saxon Americans, but these once-important status differences among white ethnic groups have faded into relative insignificance over the last several decades.

Recall that to be effective, diffuse status beliefs must retain their appearance of being common knowledge in the society—that is, they must seem to be the beliefs of "most people." The presumption that a status belief is widely shared is what causes people to persist in acting on it, whether or not they personally endorse the belief as accurate.[69] And as long as people persist in acting on a status belief, they give the appearance to others through their own behavior that the belief is indeed held as common knowledge.[70] For this reason, then, changes in cultural status beliefs tend to lag behind changes in the material arrangements between social difference groups that support them.[71]

The key to changing status beliefs is to erode their appearance of consensuality. Changing technological, economic, or political conditions may exogenously begin to alter or reduce the material inequality between status-valued difference groups. Say an economic expansion draws lower-status workers into the labor force and improves their pay, or technological change deskills a higher-status group's formerly secure jobs. Also, and sometimes in connection with such changes, people in lower-status groups may begin to engage in overt political actions and form social movements (for example, the women's movement or the civil rights movement) aimed at challenging dominant status beliefs. When such changes occur, people more broadly begin to have more and more interactions with members of those lower-status groups that do not confirm the status beliefs—say with a woman CEO or an African American college professor. Such status beliefs, embedded in group stereotypes as they are, are subject to confirmation biases and do not erode easily.[72] Still, as changing positions of power and resources between the groups cause disconfirming experiences to become more common, personal endorsement of the beliefs may decline in the population. This can create a condition of pluralistic ignorance in which people persist in assuming that most hold the beliefs even when most no longer do.[73] But such a state is inherently fragile and may eventually lead to a collapse of the status belief, at least as a belief with a measurable impact on everyday social relations.[74]

In other, perhaps more common cases, status beliefs may change more modestly and more gradually as they adapt to changing material arrangements between the groups in some spheres of social life but remain strong in others. For instance, gender status beliefs have changed only modestly despite women's massive entrance into the paid workforce because, absent equivalent changes in inequality in family responsibilities, gender status differences have been moderated but not eliminated.[75] In particular, widely held gender beliefs now view women as more similar to men than they used to be in the softer forms of agentic competence associated with status, such as "independence" and "intelligence."[76] These changes probably reflect women's increased labor force involvement. But women still lag men in the stronger forms of agentic competence and status culturally associated with leadership, such as "assertiveness," "competitiveness," and "boldness." And there have been no changes in cultural beliefs that women are much more communally oriented and emotionally warmer than men.[77]

The Legitimation of Inequality Based on Social Difference

Above, all, of course, status beliefs stabilize structures of inequality between social difference groups by legitimating them on the basis of merit. The repeating, everyday goal-oriented encounters in which people from higher-status difference groups like men and whites as well as middle- or upper-class actors emerge as apparently more competent, more leaderlike, and more prominent than those from lower-status difference groups provide daily lessons for all in the superiority of the dominant groups. The obvious implication of such experiences is that the type of people who make up the dominant, higher-status groups have fairly won their resource and power advantages through their own merit and deserve them.

Status beliefs, then, provide a powerful legitimating ideology for structures of inequality based on social difference groups. As the sociologist Mary Jackman pointed out several years ago, without the development of status beliefs as a legitimating ideology, consolidation of material inequality with categorical difference would simply move the scramble for control of resources from the individual to the group level, rather than stabilize the pattern of inequality.[78] As legitimating ideology, status beliefs provide a justifying basis for the actions that those from higher-status groups take to further their own interests. But more importantly, status beliefs blunt the resistance to such actions by people from lower-status groups, greatly enhancing higher-status groups' ability to maintain their advantages in resources and access to positions of power.

As we saw in chapter 4, status beliefs about all the major social differences that pattern inequality in the United States are widely held in the population, including by those in lower-status groups.[79] Indeed, studies show that people in lower socioeconomic status groups, for instance, do not differ from those in higher socioeconomic groups in the status and competence beliefs that they think "most people" hold about their groups.[80] Those in lower-status groups are less likely, of course, to personally endorse such beliefs and are more likely to just hold them as third-order beliefs about what most people think.[81] But in a social world in which most people hold or are presumed to hold a status belief, even those it disadvantages have an unavoidable, if dreary, interest in accepting the belief, at least at some level, in order to effectively coordinate with others and get what they need to survive. And the fact that these status beliefs offer compensating assumptions about the greater warmth and communality of those in lower status groups may further placate resistance to accepting them.[82]

To be sure, people from lower-status groups often try to resist being cast as lesser or receiving lesser outcomes. A Mexican American waiter, for instance, might react frostily when a customer treats him condescendingly based on his ethnic background. Or groups of people may band together in social movements, like Black Lives Matter, to protest their repeated devaluation, with its sometimes fatal consequences, by social institutions like the police.

And yet, in most everyday situations, people, often without thinking about it, find themselves going along to get along. Doing so not only smooths social relations for them but also reduces their sense of uncertainty about events. That, in turn, can have cognitive and emotional benefits despite the costs of being lower-status.[83] Accepting status beliefs, even for those they disadvantage, provides people with a means of justifying and rendering sensible the structure of inequality in which they find themselves, as psychological research on system-justification has demonstrated.[84] In this everyday way, actor-level status evaluations of who is "better" undercut resistance to inequality.

A Sense of Group Position

The widespread recognition and acceptance of status beliefs creates for members of social difference groups what the sociologist Herbert Blumer long ago termed "a sense of group position."[85] We mentioned this briefly in chapter 3, but its consequences for larger patterns of durable inequality bear a little more examination. As research we reviewed in that earlier chapter showed, especially that based on social identity theory, beliefs about the comparative evaluation of the groups to which people belong have a substantial impact on people's own self-esteem, sense of worth, and, we might say, socially acknowledged dignity.[86] This is Blumer's "sense of group position."

Status beliefs about one's gender, race, and educational, occupational, and class background groups, for instance, shape a sense of one's "position" in society. The public nature of the "position" that status beliefs define affects a person's sense of socially recognized worth in society. As such, the comparative worth that status beliefs attach to the significant groups to which individuals belong becomes a powerful dimension through which they experience the larger structure of inequality. This effect of status beliefs occurs above and beyond how such beliefs shape the way an individual is personally treated in social encounters because it causes the individual to experience as personal how he or she believes the *group* to which they belong is treated.

In particular, the sense of group position generated by status beliefs causes people to react with a sense of threat to social changes or policies that appear to undercut their group's status advantage over another group. In one group of social psychological studies, for instance, whites, but not racial minorities, expressed more concerns about unfairness when applying for a job in an organization with pro-diversity policies. In a hiring simulation study, white men in particular showed higher cardiovascular threat in applying to a pro-diversity organization, compared to a neutral one.[87]

Blumer's original point about sense of group position, later developed by Lawrence Bobo, is that the status anxiety evoked for whites by perceived threats to their racial group position is a more powerful driver of their systematic racial prejudice toward nonwhites than personal animus.[88] Similarly, evidence suggests that such perceived group status threats can motivate support for political movements to restore and defend their group's status superiority over the challenging groups.[89] Experiments by the sociologists Rachel Wetts and Robb Willer, for instance, show that, when given evidence suggesting that whites were losing their income and numerical advantage over nonwhites in the United States, whites but not nonwhites increased their opposition to welfare programs thought to benefit minorities.[90] The political scientists Noam Gidron and Peter Hall use cross-national data to argue that threats to subjective social status, precipitated by changing economic and cultural conditions, fuel support for populist right political movements, particularly among white men without a college education.[91] Joan Williams makes a similar argument about socio-economic and cultural changes that have threatened the social dignity of white working-class Americans and fueled conservative political support.[92]

It is worth noting that in most of the examples just cited, the groups reacting to status threats with political action are not the highest-status groups in society. They typically are not, for instance, highly educated, white, and economically well-off business and professional people. Such people have multiple sources of status advantage with which to buffer their sense of group position in the face of changing racial demography or gender status dynamics. In addition, their greater control over dominant institutions ensures that their own cultural values are more clearly represented, rather than threatened, in the cultural messages they see around them. This is not to say that such relatively privileged people never react to gender-, race-, or class-based status threats in interpersonal encounters or do not engage in myriad behaviors to preserve the status quo that supports their status advantages. But being relatively insulated by their several advantages, they may simply have no sense that their group position is especially threatened. Despite some social changes, the system basically still works for them by supporting their superiority.

Instead, it may be people who belong to groups that are status-advantaged on some dimensions, say race or gender, but disadvantaged in others, such as education or socioeconomic class, who are more sensitive to threats to their more modest status advantages. As Hochschild's study of white Louisianans who supported the Tea Party has shown, these are people who have understood themselves to have a respected position in the middle of the U.S. status system as hardworking middle Americans.[93] The dignity of this position is now challenged by the cosmopolitan values and actions of urban elites that they feel privilege people of color over them and no longer respect their hard work. For them, the status threat is powerful enough to motivate political action.

The defense of the status position of one's group is, of course, just another, more collective effect of the same response that produces legitimacy bias against people from lower-status groups who seek to gain influence and authority. As this suggests, the defense of group position is inherently a reaction of a group that perceives itself to be at least somewhat higher in status compared to another against a threat that would undercut their relative superiority. What does this mean about race, gender, or class groups that are lower-status in society (say, a lower-class woman of color)? Do they not experience a sense of group position that is worth defending?

Since status beliefs that evaluatively rank gender, race, and class groups are embedded in widely held, common knowledge stereotypes about those groups, people in lower-status groups know where they stand, however they personally feel about it.[94] They know that people in their social group are considered to be less important and are less valued than those in higher-status groups. Yet recall that status systems also offer lower-status members a compensating sense of value as being warmer, more communal, and more genuine.[95] As we saw in chapter 3, status systems also offer lower-status members a baseline of respect and dignity in exchange for their "reasonable" acceptance of the legitimacy of their status positions.[96] This baseline of dignity offered for deference—to be seen, for instance, as a woman more concerned about others than herself, as a striving member of a racial minority, or as someone who is poor but hardworking—tempts acceptance and undercuts resistance to the status system by those in lower-status groups. In this way, status makes collective action by lower-status group members in defense of their group more difficult and encourages them to look after their personal interests instead—to go along in order to get ahead—in the existing system.[97] Thus, a status-based sense of group position motivates defense of the structure of inequality by middle- and higher-status groups while diluting the motives for change among those in lower-status groups. This is also how status beliefs sustain and legitimate material inequality based on group difference.

The Denial of Status and the Legitimation of Inequality

There is an interesting alchemy to the way status beliefs in the contemporary United States legitimate inequality based on perceived merit. We noted earlier that status beliefs transform the *individual* possession of superior resources and power into a *group* identity as a member of a particular type or category of person who is more competent and worthy. But notice that status beliefs locate the differences that distinguish the groups they rank-order not in the group itself, but in the *personal attributes* (competent, worthy, but less warm versus less competent, less worthy, but warmer) of the people who make up the group. Status beliefs, then, purport to cluster people not so much in groups at all but according to individuals' personal differences in social value. In this way, status beliefs elide how they create advantage based on group identity by locating the source of that advantage in the superior or inferior attributes of the individual group member.

The belief that material rewards should be based on individual achievement through talent and hard work—that what you earn in life should be based not on what group you belong to but on the quality of your character, skills, talents, and willingness to work hard—is a powerful, even foundational ideology in the United States.[98] Indeed, the American Dream is based on the belief that whatever group you come from, you can work hard, become who you want to be, and have a good life. People from materially and status-advantaged groups are more likely to endorse the views that people mostly get what they "deserve" and that therefore the "system is fair," but acceptance of these beliefs is also widespread.[99]

The power of this legitimating ideology, in my view, causes Americans both to be open to accepting status beliefs and to deny or resist acknowledging their advantaging and disadvantaging effects. The ideology of achievement encourages a finely tuned sensitivity to the socially accepted signs of a person's greater or lesser capacity to achieve, since these will be the basis on which the person is judged by self and others. And these signs, of course, are contained in the status beliefs that Americans quickly pick up on in their efforts to manage achievement demands. Even if the status belief is disadvantaging, if it locates your failure to achieve in your own capacities and efforts, it tells you that maybe you have to accept what you receive as fair.[100]

On the other side, to explicitly recognize the effects of status biases is to see that the system is not fair and has not rewarded you based on your individual value and achievement at all. If you are higher status, you see that you did not legitimately earn or deserve your valued outcomes. If you are lower-status, you see that you have been mistreated and discriminated against rather than judged on individual merit. Both reactions, research by the psychologist Brenda Major and her colleagues has shown, evoke unpleasant emotional responses.[101]

In my view, the paradox of status and individual merit causes Americans to be both highly attentive to signs of status and to resist acknowledging this to themselves or others. As a result, status biases based on group differences often play an invisible but powerful role in contemporary American social relations. This is the final irony and paradox of status as a form of inequality in the contemporary United States: although it is fundamental both to the structuring of patterns of material inequality along lines of social difference and to the obdurate nature of those patterns of inequality, we remain stubbornly blind to many of its effects.

CHAPTER 7

CONCLUSION

IN THIS BOOK, I have tried to inquire into what I think of as the deep story behind status as a distinct form of social inequality that is different from the more familiar forms based on wealth and power. Status is easily defined as a social ranking of people, groups, and objects in terms of the social esteem, honor, and respect associated with them. But what is status really? We all feel the power of status inequality in the subtle (and sometimes unsubtle) ways in which we are treated with attention and respect in one context or overlooked and dismissed in the next. Although we sense the accumulating impact of these micro-experiences of status on our lives and our sense of self, the process of status itself remains slightly mysterious and out of sight. And what we can't quite see and understand we can't come to grips with, manage, or change. It is for these reasons that I have argued that we need a deeper explanation of what status really is as a social process. We need to bring into clear view how and why we create status rankings and why it matters that we do.

To find satisfying answers to such questions, we need a conceptual account of status hierarchies and status evaluations that makes sense of their diverse and widespread nature. We need to understand how status goes from an implicit ranking in esteem among people working together in a room to rankings among universities or occupations or firms in a field or among brands of products in a market. Also, what is the nature of status that it seems to have ancient roots in human history and to be universal in human societies? And yet, despite being an old form of inequality, status continues to interpenetrate modern meritocratic institutions in advanced industrial societies. Given that it does continue to be a force in modern societies, what is its significance for broader patterns of social and economic inequality in the contemporary United States?

To address these questions, I have proposed a cultural schema theory of status. By this theory, status hierarchies and rankings are a cultural invention that people have developed to manage a fundamental tension in the human condition. Whether they like it or not, people are repeatedly in situations in which they are cooperatively interdependent with others to achieve what they need and want to survive and prosper. But this shared need to coordinate on a cooperative goal effort creates a nested set of competitive tensions. On whose terms will the cooperative effort be conducted, what costs must each pay, and what benefits will each receive?

Status hierarchies and rankings, as a social form, result from a cultural schema, a blueprint, of learned and shared rules for organizing social relations in order to manage the tensions and coordination problems posed by contexts of cooperative goal interdependence. This is the basic claim of the cultural schema theory of status. Based on a broad body of evidence about how people typically allocate status in cooperatively interdependent settings, I suggest that the cultural schema of status is twofold.[1] The core part of the schema is a deeply learned, basic norm of status allocation: status and deference are granted in proportion to an actor's perceived value to the group's shared goal effort. Associated with this core norm is an equally essential second part of the status schema: a less normative, more descriptive, and historically changing set of cultural status beliefs about the attributes and actions of actors that are widely believed to indicate greater or lesser goal-related competence and status-worthiness in various social contexts. Shared status beliefs act as common knowledge beliefs by which group members coordinate their judgments of each other's value for the group in order to enact and enforce the basic status norm. In this way, as I have often remarked, the basic status norm acts as the social grammar for status relations, while status beliefs provide the vocabulary by which this grammar is enacted to create status hierarchies over varying contexts.

I argue that, at root, status is this twofold cultural schema. By my theoretical account, the origins of this schema lie in interpersonal groups facing the coordination problems and competitive tensions of cooperative goal interdependence. But cultural schemas, once developed, are like a kind of social tool that was developed for a particular purpose but can now be used and applied in new ways across a range of related but not identical contexts.[2] Without a conceptualization of status as rooted in a cultural form, such as a schema of implicit rules, the enormous range of status rankings—from individuals in the room to group identities like gender and race, to organizations like firms, to their product brands—becomes much harder to explain.

Having made the case for this conceptualization of status over the last several chapters, what I want to do here at the end is, first, to highlight several basic takeaways from the argument. That is, I want to review what the cultural schema theory teaches us about status processes beyond what we already know and how it accounts for the many observed aspects of status phenomena around us. For instance, how does it relate to evolutionary accounts of dyadic rank formation and dominance behavior? What does the status schema account reveal about the nature of the consensus among group members that governs a status hierarchy, and how does that hierarchy actually address the problems posed by cooperative goal-orientation? What does this account tell us about the means by which status hierarchies maintain functional stability in the face of people's competitive desires for status? What does the spread of status rankings to groups and even markets suggest about the essential, limiting conditions for the application of the status schema to organize social contexts? And finally, how does status drive patterns of inequality based on social differences and contribute to their durability in society?

After this review of key issues and points, my second goal here is to step back a bit and briefly ask some larger questions. Given what we have learned about status from this analysis, what should we think of it? Is it a good thing or a bad thing for society? And is it inevitable or can its effects be mitigated?

Status as a *Cultural* Schema

To be plausible, a claim that status hierarchies are rooted in a cultural schema must come to grips with long-standing arguments and evidence that people, like other primates, have evolved responses to form rank relations based on dominance behavior and may also have more distinctly human tendencies to form rank relations based on prestige.[3] In dealing with such arguments, it is important to note that a claim that status is rooted in a cultural schema does not require us to deny that people may have evolved reactions to dominance threats and perhaps prestige. Instead, by the analysis put forward here, while status may be laid on a platform of evolved responses, it is nevertheless a cultural construction that is not fully reducible to those responses. Status is like language in this regard and may be almost as basic to the human condition.

As we saw, there is a contingent uncertainty in the formation of hierarchies in groups of three or more that cannot be fully predicted from the outcomes of dyadic rank contests such as those addressed by evolutionary theories of hierarchy formation.[4] This contingent uncertainty and the sensitivity of hierarchy formation to the reaction of third parties who are bystanders to a given dyadic rank contest create an opportunity for the group as a whole to take normative control of the deference/rank process.[5] The motive for group members to take normative control of the deference process, however, comes from the interdependent exchange interests created for members in cooperative goal-oriented situations. Group members, of course, need to organize themselves to pursue the shared and valued goal. But as part of this, members also share a powerful interest in finding a means to control a would-be dominator who would take over the group without contributing to the goal effort. A normative cultural schema of status is invented, I argue, out of people's interdependent need to organize for goal attainment while controlling the uncontributing dominator.

The normative status schema controls a would-be dominator through a system of carrots as well as sticks. By offering esteem, influence, and a greater share of rewards to those perceived by the group as making more valued contributions to the goal efforts, the basic status norm tempts the dominator to redirect his or her assertiveness to the collective effort in a bid for status. On the other side, group members punish efforts to claim status through dominance alone by disliking the dominator and collectively resisting his or her influence attempts.[6]

Indeed, the fact that status is a rank order of esteem, honor, and respect accorded by a group or community in itself implies that status is inherently a cultural-normative process. But a variety of other evidence also supports the view that status is cultural-normative in nature. Norms, of course, can be recognized not only by their enactment but by their enforcement. As we have just seen, studies show that people punish violations of the basic status norm and do so spontaneously.[7] There is also evidence that people reward with approval those who defer as expected according to the basic status norm. In a particularly clear demonstration that this is a normative process, a study shows that people reward expected deference to another very similarly to expected deference to self.[8]

Finally, for evidence in support of the status belief component of the twofold cultural schema, we need only turn to the decades of research on status characteristics theory.[9] This research clearly documents how standing in interpersonal status hierarchies is substantially determined by the status beliefs that people hold about each other's social identities and distinguishing attributes. In addition, stereotype research shows that status beliefs about all the social difference groups according to which inequality is patterned in American society, including gender, race, education, social class, and occupation, are widely held as common knowledge in the U.S. population.[10]

What the Cultural Schema Account of Status Distinctively Explains

The Second-Order Nature of the Governing Status Consensus

Status rankings, whether among individuals in an interpersonal hierarchy, groups in society, or objects of consumption in a market, represent a shared, roughly consensual perspective on each's relative social value, understood as status-worthiness and competence, or quality, in the eyes of a surrounding group or community. This perceived ranking shared by a group or community is what I refer to as the status consensus that governs status relations among the actors involved, be they individuals, groups, or either possessors or producers of the objects. Understanding status as based on a twofold schema by which actors draw on shared status beliefs to coordinate their judgments of value in goal-related contexts clarifies for us that the consensus that governs the status hierarchy is a second-order consensus. That is, it is a consensus about what *others* expect to be the relative value of self and other in the context, based on the shared cultural status beliefs upon which all are drawing.

The nature of the status consensus as an agreement about what others expect is what gives status processes force in social relations.[11] If I believe that others expect a given status relation between me and another, then I must take that into account in my own behavior whether or not I personally endorse that ranking. In this way, status orders can form a coordinating consensus on rankings without requiring that each member fully buy into their own ranking as what he or she "really deserves." Indeed, if in order to function status hierarchies required a first-order consensus among members about what rank each really deserved, they would probably be a much rarer social form than they are.

The insights that the cultural schema account of status gives us into the second-order nature of the status consensus explain an otherwise slightly mysterious set of empirical findings. Studies of situations in which there is conflict between actors' first-order and second-order expectations about their own status relative to another repeatedly show that actors' second-order expectations are the most powerful determinant of their bids for status and of their willingness to defer to another.[12] It might seem counter-intuitive that actors' perceptions of others' expectations for their deference and status would overrule their own expectations, but when we recognize status as a cultural-normative process, these findings make sense. It is actors' perceptions of others' expectations that alert them to whether their claim for status or their act of deference will be rewarded with respect or sanctioned with disapproval.

The second-order status consensus is the means by which group members not only coordinate to enforce the basic status norm but also, in the process, weigh and combine multiple task inputs into a collective line of action directed at the goal effort. Because the status consensus grants actors esteem in proportion to their perceived value for the goal effort, group members are incentivized to contribute to the goal effort and to do so to the best of their ability. Because esteem in the eyes of the group brings influence, it also provides a means for resolving disagreements and forging a shared goal effort. In this way, status hierarchies, enacted through the basic status norm and a second-order consensus based on shared status beliefs, offer an organizational solution to the problems of cooperative goal interdependence.

The Desire for Status and the Stability of Status Hierarchies

To be perceived as worthy and valued in the eyes of the group is something that really matters to people. Given our dependence on social relations with others to attain so much of what we want and need in life, this is not surprising. Indeed, the evidence suggests that the desire for status is a fundamental, independent motive for people that cannot be reduced to other powerful motives such the desire to belong.[13] Status hierarchies can induce people to work hard for the group effort precisely because people so value the reward of esteem conferred by the hierarchy for perceived goal-related competence and effort. But because people do so value status, they will eagerly compete for it.

How do status hierarchies maintain the functional stability necessary to pursue a cooperative goal in the face of people's competitive interests in status? From the earliest empirical studies, it has been shown that interpersonal status hierarchies, while not unchanging, do maintain considerable stability over time.[14] The cultural schema account of status clarifies for us how such stability is achieved. If people are strongly motivated to achieve the shared goal, they may willingly defer to another they personally perceive to be more competent than them at the effort (that is, they may defer on the basis of first-order expectations) in the interest of collective success. But given their desire for status, they may also be tempted to compete with the other, so such voluntary deference cannot always be guaranteed.[15] Here is where the normative pressures created by the status schema make the difference.

The basic status norm, backed by the second-order consensus, tells people that they should defer to another whom the group deems more competent or face negative sanctions. If they do comply by deferring as expected, evidence suggests, they will be modestly rewarded with approval as a reasonable member of the group.[16] Faced with this system of normative rewards and punishments created by the status schema, most do comply as expected in everyday groups. In this way, the second-order consensus of what others expect for one actor's status relative to another backstops the stability of the status hierarchy in the face of people's competitive desire for status.

The Range of Status Rankings and the Limits of the Status Schema

One of the most useful aspects of an account of status as a cultural schema is that it provides analytic insight into how status rankings, as a social form, manage to encompass such a broad range of social phenomena. I have focused in this book on status hierarchies among individuals and status beliefs about the social difference groups to which individuals belong, such as gender, race, or class. But as I briefly noted in chapter 4, there is also an extensive research literature on status rankings among organizations, like law firms, universities, or producers of objects that acquire status value for consumers.[17]

Research on how status processes work among organizations shows a striking similarity to how these processes work in status hierarchies among individuals. In both cases, being ranked higher in the status hierarchy is associated with a perception of being more competent or higher-quality in regard to the goal focus of the organization or the interpersonal group. And in both cases, the status-based assumption of greater competence or quality produces status advantage for the higher-ranked organization or individual, compared to a lesser-ranked one.[18] That is, the higher-ranked individual or organization is judged as "better" (that is, higher-quality) and favored for exchange and association over and above what she or it otherwise would be without that advantaged status rank. Thus, status brings market advantages to organizations in their field just as status advantages individuals in goal-oriented interpersonal contexts in influence and access to resources and positions of power. Finally, status spreads through association among organizations just as it does among individuals.[19]

Why are status processes among organizations so similar in their basic outlines to status processes among individuals? Because, by the theoretical account I have offered here, they are organized according to the same basic cultural schema for structuring relations in conditions of goal-interdependence. As I have said, precisely because of the *cultural* nature of the implicit rules for status, these rules can be repurposed beyond the interpersonal setting to organize other related, although not identical, situations of goal-interdependence. Such an argument, of course, raises questions about the conditions necessary to evoke the status schema and the limits to which the status schema can spread.

It is clear that status relations emerge in situations in which actors, understood as either individuals or groups, are oriented toward the attainment of a valued goal and have some degree of cooperative independence that requires them to coordinate with one another to achieve positive outcomes. Without such goal-interdependence, I would argue, the full structure of status relations is unlikely to develop. But it is clear from the range of phenomena in which status rankings are observed that the cooperative interdependence among the actors involved can be stretched a bit.

In the classic context of an interpersonal group facing a collective task, the cooperative interdependence is for the achievement of positive outcomes on the task; the status ranking that develops is a means to that end, not the end itself. But at the limit of the status schema's spread, among organizations competing for goal outcomes in a field, the cooperative interdependence is for the status ranking itself. That is, the organizations share a cooperative need for a public recognition of what will be taken as better or worse choices in their goal pursuit. Such a public, common knowledge, evaluative ranking serves them all as they try to maximize their outcomes in a competitive market. It does so by providing each organization with a means to anticipate how relevant others will react if they choose one action versus another. Perhaps this is the farthest reach of circumstances in which the implicit rules of the status schema provide actors with a useful means of organizing relations to pursue their goals.

Social Difference, Inequality, and How Status Matters

The cultural schema theory of status, by showing how status is rooted in a twofold schema of rules and status beliefs, distinctively illuminates several key aspects of how status hierarchies and rankings work and how status comes to organize such a broad range of phenomena beyond the interpersonal group. But shining new light on the inner workings of status hierarchies is not, for me, the most important reason to seek a deeper understanding of status as a form of social relations. Rather, for me, what is most significant is gaining a better understanding of how status matters for broader patterns of inequality in society, especially those based on social differences like gender, race, occupation, and social class. And when I say *how* status matters, I mean not only to what extent it matters but also, and importantly, through what processes it affects social inequality. Again, I believe that the cultural schema account helps us penetrate the processes by which status contributes to durable patterns of inequality based on social differences among people.

Because judgments of a person's competence and value in interpersonal settings are shaped by status beliefs about social differences like gender, race, and class, these status-valued group identities create systematic advantages and disadvantages for individuals in their access to social esteem (the respect of their coworkers, family, and community), resources (pay, a nice house), and power in relation to others and events that affect their lives. By shaping expectations for competence that have self-fulfilling effects on subsequent judgments, behavior, and standing in the group, status beliefs about social differences create a whole range of biases that advantage those from higher- compared to lower-status groups. The first set, which I call status biases, include biases in the evaluation of a person's performance, in the person's confidence to speak up and others to listen to them if they do, and in the assessment of the person's underlying ability. A second set of legitimacy biases creates resistance to people from lower-status groups who act too assertively or seek to rise in a way that challenges the status order based on social difference. Finally, status beliefs about social differences bias associations by making those from higher-status groups more sought after and valued as network contacts.

Acting through interpersonal encounters in contexts consequential for inequality, like workplaces, schools, health organizations, and government institutions, these multiple biases accumulate, even if they are often small in a given instance.[20] Over time and over multiple settings, the net effect is to systematically direct people from higher and lower social difference groups toward very different life outcomes. And just as problematically, status beliefs, because they link social differences to differences in worthiness and competence (who is "better"), justify on the basis of merit the different life outcomes that they themselves foster.

Biases evoked by status beliefs about social differences not only create inequality directly through interpersonal encounters but also have a second, equally consequential effect at the organizational level. By shaping what goes on in organizational teams, committees, and start-ups, status processes write assumptions about the greater competence and worth of some types of actors (those from higher-status social difference groups) into the very practices and procedures by which the organizations do their work.[21] As a consequence, standard procedures and taken-for-granted practices in an organizational setting can end up implying an "ideal worker" or "ideal student" (or patient or citizen) who has characteristics more typical of those from higher-status groups, say men or whites or middle-class people.[22] Once established in the organization, such implicitly status-biased practices and procedures act as additional barriers to the success of those from lower-status social difference groups.

Both through their direct effects at the interpersonal level and their indirect effects through the practices and procedures they foster at the organizational level, status beliefs give patterns of inequality based on social differences like gender and race an independent, autonomous capacity to reproduce themselves. That is to say, status beliefs give people systematic advantages or disadvantages based on their group identities alone, independent of their personal attributes or resources. As a result of these status effects, individuals from higher-status social difference groups (a man or a white person) have an added advantage in gaining valued outcomes, even over individuals from lower-status groups (a woman or a person of color) who are otherwise just as rich and powerful as they are. In this way, cultural status beliefs about, say, gender or race, perpetuate patterns of inequality based on those social differences through their biasing effects on status processes in everyday encounters in consequential social contexts. And as they do so, status beliefs about social differences and interpersonal status processes work together to foster durable patterns of inequality based on membership in status-valued social difference groups.

Status as a Double-Edged Sword for People and Societies

If we step back to assess status as a form of inequality, what do we think about it? Is it a good thing or a bad thing for people and societies? No form of inequality seems like a wholly good thing, but are there merely costs associated with the organizational form of a status hierarchy, or are there also payoffs? There are payoffs, naturally, for those who are high status—all forms of inequality provide benefits for those on top. But are there broader payoffs as well as costs for the group or community as a whole? This is an awkward question for egalitarians, including me, but it needs to be considered if we are going to really understand the persistence of status as a form of inequality.

The answer to this question, I believe, may be different for status hierarchies in interpersonal groups facing cooperative interdependence and status rankings among groups in society. In cooperatively interdependent, goal-oriented groups, extensive evidence suggests that status hierarchies do offer a boundedly functional organizational solution to the collective action problems that these settings pose for their participants.[23] That is to say, by incentivizing group members to contribute to the collective goal effort and providing a means for coordinating and combining members' contributions into a collective line of action, status hierarchies do help the group members successfully attain their shared goal. Since even low-status members receive a share—if a lesser share—of the benefits that flow from successful goal attainment, the organizational assistance that status hierarchies provide really can result in a collective payoff for the group and its members.

In addition to utility as an organizational device for successful goal attainment, I have argued that status hierarchies and the cultural schema of rules that govern them offer another payoff for the members of the group. Through the system of rewards and collective sanctions they create, status hierarchies help the group control a potential dominator who would take over the group without contributing to the shared goal effort. In this way, status hierarchies provide some normative means for mobilizing against and protecting the group from a pure tyrant who would create a form of inequality based on intimidation, with few payoffs for the collective good. Indeed, by my account, the need to manage the dominator while also organizing shared goal activities is behind the cultural invention of status as a schema of rules for inequality.

The payoffs of status hierarchies in interpersonal groups come with real costs, of course. To achieve these payoffs, low-status members are asked to pay a price in esteem and treatment as a person of value in the group that higher-status members are not. Also, because status is given for *perceived* competence and effort, there is often inaccuracy and bias in the perceptions of value that underlie status. The status schema itself feeds bias into the process through the status beliefs about social differences that it offers as a shorthand for coordinating judgments of competence and value. Biases in judgments of relative value for the group create injustice in the allocation of status and, at the same time, reduce the efficiency of the hierarchy as a tool for goal attainment. This is why status hierarchies, even at the level of interpersonal groups, are only boundedly functional for the group.

When we shift from hierarchies among individuals in a group to status rankings among groups in a society, there seem to be fewer collective payoffs of status inequality and the negative effects are more apparent and problematic. But keep in mind that, because of the role of status beliefs about social differences in the construction of status hierarchies, status rankings between groups are as inherent to status as a form of inequality as is status among individuals. Thus, the more iniquitous effects of status rankings among groups in society go hand in glove with the bounded utility of status hierarchies in the goal-oriented interpersonal group. Here is where we see the deeply double-edged nature of status as a form on inequality.

As we have seen, status processes foster a focus on social differences among people in a community (or organizations in a field) that can be taken as signs of competence and therefore status-worthiness in different contexts. In this way, status processes reify social differences among people in society and transform them into common knowledge beliefs about what "type" of people (a given social difference group) are "better" (more competent and worthy) than others. The self-fulfilling effects of status beliefs about types of people who are more worthy and competent than others create cascading effects on broader structures of inequality in society.

The effects of status beliefs, acting through interpersonal processes and organizational practices, encourage the consolidation of patterns of resource distribution and control over positions of power along lines of social difference such as gender, race, occupation, and social class. As they have these effects, status beliefs contribute to the durability of patterns of material inequality in society. Status beliefs do this, not least, by justifying these patterns of inequality, not in terms of group difference at all, but in terms of the differential personal merit of the types of people who make up groups. In this way, status beliefs continue to interweave inequality based on social differences like gender, race, and class background even into modern, ostensibly meritocratic institutions.

Is Status Inequality Inevitable?

Status processes are undeniably a conservative force in society. They slow change in patterns of inequality among individuals and groups and legitimate the status quo. What can be done about them? If we are interested in building a more egalitarian society, what can be done to mitigate the effects of status inequality?

In my view, we will never actually eliminate status as a form of inequality. Something as deeply rooted in human culture as status distinctions and status hierarchies is not likely to simply go away. But that does not mean that mitigating some of the most problematic effects of status processes in regard to overall patterns of inequality between social groups in society is impossible. Broad, durable patterns of socioeconomic inequality based on a few, simplified group differences like gender and race are not inevitable. The diffuse applicability of such status characteristics that allows them to shape widespread patterns of inequality can be eroded by undermining the status beliefs behind them.

Reducing the power of the status beliefs behind core dimensions of difference-based inequality like gender and race involves two interrelated processes. Status beliefs can be changed most directly by undermining their perceived consensuality—the widespread sense that they are the beliefs of "most people" and are therefore an appropriate basis for social action. The long-standing cultural belief that gender identity is fixed at birth, for instance, is undergoing increasingly public challenge by transsexuals and gender-queer people in ways that may eventually undermine its perceived consensuality.[24] Increasing public acceptance of gender identity as potentially acquired as well as ascribed, of course, need not immediately reduce the status advantage attached to being perceived on whatever basis as a man rather than a woman.[25] But it does begin to loosen the bonds of gender essentialism. And among the most problematic content in status beliefs about gender and race are cultural beliefs about the essentialized nature of the differences in competence and worth they are assumed to imply.

As this suggests, a change in what is believed to be consensual in a status belief is often also part of the process through which the content of status beliefs is gradually altered. Altering the content of status beliefs by narrowing the competence differences that they imply, in turn, is the second process necessary to reducing their effects on inequality. Gender status beliefs have altered in this way a bit as women's massive entrance into the paid labor force has gradually narrowed, but not yet eliminated, the gender gap in assumed agentic competence. Similarly, beliefs in the general, rather than context-specific, nature of any differences in competence between the groups can also erode so that the situational relevance of gender and race to status processes narrows. As this happens, the social differences of race and gender would become less consistently advantaging or disadvantaging, and their consolidating effects on patterns of material inequality would thus be reduced.

Change is possible, then, if not easy to achieve. Status beliefs about social difference groups have changed in the past and can change in the present. A world without status distinctions may not be achievable. But a world in which only a few status-valued group identities act as powerful determinants of individual life outcomes is not inevitable. In its place, we might have multiple, cross-cutting status distinctions that result in lower overall levels of inequality among individuals in society. But this much, at least, is clear. If we want to change patterns of inequality in society, we will not succeed without taking status processes into account.

NOTES

CHAPTER 1: WHAT IS STATUS AS A FORM OF INEQUALITY?

1. The term "deep story" is borrowed from Hochschild (2016) and refers to an underlying explanatory narrative or theoretical account that makes sense of diverse and sometimes conflicting aspects of a social phenomenon (see also Turco and Zuckerman 2017).
2. Giddens 1984; Sewell 1992.
3. Blader and Yu 2017; Henrich and Gil-White 2001.
4. Cheng et al. 2013; van Vugt and Tybur 2016.
5. Anderson, Hildreth, and Howland 2015; Blader and Yu 2017.
6. Podolny 2005; Thye 2000.
7. Bales 1950, 1970.
8. Bales 1970.
9. Bales (1970) also found that the most talkative, "best ideas" man was often not the best-liked group member. Instead, the best-liked man was typically slightly less talkative and more socially oriented in what he said, leading Bales to propose that groups have separate "task" and "socioemotional" leaders. Although subsequent research has shown that these roles are not always separate, as we will see in later chapters, there is often a tension between the agentic exercise of influence over the goal activities and the perception of warmth and communality (Fiske 2011; Hahl and Zuckerman 2014).
10. Berger and Webster 2018.
11. Bales 1950.
12. Strodtbeck, James, and Hawkins 1957.
13. Berger, Conner, and Fisek 1974; Berger et al. 1977; Berger and Webster 2018.
14. Status characteristics and expectation states theory takes as scope conditions that a group of people are task-oriented and collectively oriented (Berger et al. 1977; Berger and Webster 2018). These scope conditions are consistent with the conditions of cooperative interdependence to achieve a valued goal posited by the cultural schema theory to be the origin and continuing source context of the normative schema of status. However, by cultural schema theory, once created, people spread the use of the

status schema beyond the strict confines of these conditions to related contexts, modifying the status processes that result. These issues will be discussed in later chapters.

15. Torelli et al. 2014.
16. Blader and Yu 2017.
17. Berger, Anderson, and Zelditch 1972; Ridgeway and Nakagawa 2014.
18. Correll et al. 2017; Goode 1978, 13; Sauder 2006.
19. Blader and Yu 2017; Gould 2002.
20. Goffman 1956.
21. Ridgeway and Erickson 2000.
22. For reviews, see Anderson and Kennedy 2012; Anderson and Willer 2014; Berger and Webster 2018; Magee and Galinsky 2008; see also van Vugt and Tybur 2016 on leadership.
23. Anderson et al. 2006; Anderson and Willer 2014; Berger, Conner, and Fisek 1974; Blau 1964; Gould 2002; Homans 1951; Magee and Galinsky 2008; Willer 2009.
24. Halevy, Chou, and Galinsky 2011.
25. Anderson and Willer 2014.
26. Weber 1918/1968.
27. Cook, Cheshire, and Gerbasi 2018; Emerson 1962.
28. Ridgeway 2014.
29. Magee and Galinsky 2008.
30. Ridgeway 2014; Tomaskovic-Devey 2014.
31. Tilly 1998.

CHAPTER 2: FOUNDATIONS FOR A CULTURAL SCHEMA OF STATUS

1. Anderson and Willer 2014.
2. Van Vugt and Tybur 2016.
3. Cheng and Tracy 2014; Henrich and Gil-White 2001; van Vugt and Tybur 2016.
4. Anderson and Willer 2014; Gould 2002; Ridgeway and Nakagawa 2014.
5. Berger, Conner, and Fisek 1974; Berger and Webster 2018.
6. Cheng and Tracy 2014; Lee and Ofshe 1981; Mazur 1973; van Vugt and Tybur 2016.
7. For a review, see van Vugt and Tybur 2016.
8. Henrich and Gil-White 2001.
9. Henrich and Gil-White 2001; van Vugt and Tybur 2016. Here I focus on the currently predominant evolutionary theories specifically of hierarchy formation, which are the theories of dominance and prestige (van Vugt and Tybur 2016). There are a wide variety of other evolutionary and more broadly biosocial approaches to human cognition and social behavior. Some, such as the social evolutionary approaches of Linnda Caporael and Marilynn Brewer, assume, as I do here, that people are *obligately interdependent*, so that coordination in groups becomes an environment to which humans must adaptively respond (Caporael and Brewer 1991; Caporael 1997). The pressures of surviving in groups, this approach argues, encourages the development of shared cognition and the capacity to create shared culture. Relatedly, Robert Boyd and Peter Richerson

(1985) argue for an evolved basis for social learning among people as a foundation for the human capacity to create culture. The cultural schema theory of status I propose here is broadly consistent with these multilevel social evolutionary approaches, in which people are dependent on groups and have a capacity to create shared culture, which is laid on a platform of evolved responses. While generally consistent with such arguments, the cultural schema theory offers a specific account of the nature of status hierarchies that these approaches do not. In doing so, the cultural schema theory also accounts for why the formation of status hierarchies is primarily governed at the level of cultural norms rather than simply determined by evolved deference responses.

10. A background assumption of these theories of dyadic deference relations is that such relations are transitive—that is, if B defers to A and C defers to B, C will defer to A—and that they therefore aggregate straightforwardly to a linear hierarchy in larger groups (van Vugt and Tybur 2016). However, as we will see later on, a contingent uncertainty in this process complicates the emergence of the hierarchy. I argue later that in human groups this contingent uncertainty is consequential for the emergence of norms that govern the status process.

11. Cheng et al. 2013; Lee and Ofshe 1981; Mazur 1985, 2005; van Vugt and Tybur 2016.

12. Cheng and Tracy 2014; Henrich and Gil-White 2001; Ridgeway 1984.

13. Cheng et al. 2013; Cheng and Tracy 2014.

14. Mazur 1973, 1985, 2005.

15. Mazur 1985; Tiedens and Fragale 2003.

16. Mazur 2005.

17. Mazur 1973, 1985, 2005.

18. Ridgeway 1984, 1993.

19. Mazur 2005; Tiedens and Fragale 2003.

20. Cheng and Tracy 2014; Henrich and Gil-White 2001; van Vugt and Tybur 2016.

21. Anderson and Willer 2014; Correll and Ridgeway 2003; Magee and Galinsky 2008.

22. Boehm et al. 1993; Henrich and Gil-White 2001; van Vugt, Hogan, and Kaiser 2008.

23. While Joseph Henrich and Francisco Gil-White (2001) posit prestige as a uniquely human deference response, studies of hierarchies in other primates show that they vary greatly in how agonistic their rank relations are, and that some appear also to have more apparently voluntary, prestige-like deference relations (Seyfarth and Cheney 2013). These same studies show that other primates also sometimes form coalitions to aggress on another—as, of course, people do. It is not my intention in this chapter to distinguish or compare hierarchy formation among people and other primates, but rather to propose a theory that human interpersonal status hierarchies are based on a cultural schema. I am personally persuaded that there is a continuum of sociability and social behavior among humans and other primates.

24. Boyd and Richerson 1985; Henrich and Gil-White 2001.

25. Henrich and Gil-White 2001.

26. Cheng et al. 2013; Cheng and Tracy 2014.

27. Cheng et al. 2013.

28. Cheng and Tracy 2014; van Vugt and Tybur 2016.

29. Van Vugt and Tybur 2016.

30. Anderson and Willer 2014; Ridgeway and Nakagawa 2014. In the initial, fundamental statements of status characteristics and expectation states theory, group members' anticipations of the likely usefulness of one member's task contributions compared to another's, which constitute *performance expectations,* are equivalent to judgments of *performance capacity* as I define them here (Berger et al. 1974, 1977). In some later research, performance expectations are conceptualized as more narrowly based on judgments of "task ability," but the original theory is more expansive. Thus, my argument here is based on status characteristics and expectation states theory as well as on empirical evidence from studies of status in goal-oriented groups. (For a review of this evidence, see Anderson and Willer 2014.)

31. Anderson and Willer 2014; Ridgeway and Correll 2004; Ridgeway 1982; Simpson, Willer, and Ridgeway 2012.

32. Bai 2016; Carrier et al. 2014; Ridgeway 1982; Willer 2009.

33. Anderson and Willer 2014; Correll and Ridgeway 2003.

34. Bai 2016; Cheng et al. 2013.

35. Ridgeway and Correll 2004.

36. Ridgeway 1982; Willer 2009.

37. Kilduff and Galinsky 2013; Ridgeway 1987.

38. Ridgeway and Diekema 1989. The idea that third-party dynamics play an important role in hierarchy formation is not inconsistent with Caporael and Brewer's social evolution approach, which emphasizes cooperation in groups and shared social cognition (Caporael and Brewer 1991; Caporael 1997). Caporael and Brewer, however, offer no specific account of hierarchy formation or the role of third parties in this process.

39. Chase 1974; 1980.

40. Chase et al. 2002; Chase and Seitz 2011; Chase and Lindquist 2016.

41. Chase and Seitz 2011.

42. The situation of cooperative goal interdependence frames these conflicting interests for all of those involved, but of course individuals will vary in how personally motivated they are by each interest and how willing they might be, for instance, to maximize their own outcomes at the expense of the group.

43. Ridgeway 1984; Ridgeway and Diekema 1989.

44. Horne 2004.

45. Ridgeway 1984; Ridgeway and Diekema 1989.

46. Ridgeway and Diekema 1989.

47. Boehm 1999; Boehm et al. 1993.

48. Emerson 1972.

49. Boehm et al. 1993; Ridgeway and Diekema 1989.

50. Ridgeway and Diekema 1989.

51. Anderson and Willer 2014; Correll and Ridgeway 2003; for reviews, see Magee and Galinsky 2008.

52. Anderson and Kilduff 2009.

53. Ridgeway and Diekema 1989.

54. Ridgeway 1987.

55. Ridgeway 1987; Ridgeway, Berger, and Smith 1985.

56. Kennedy, Anderson, and Moore 2013; Kilduff and Galinsky 2013.

57. Horne 2004.
58. Anderson and Kilduff 2009; Ridgeway and Diekema 1989. Recall that here and elsewhere, I use the term "normative" to mean in accord with informal social rules rather than in the sense of denoting a social ideal.
59. Chwe 2001.
60. Festinger 1954.
61. Berger et al. 1998; Ridgeway and Berger 1986; Ridgeway and Correll 2006.
62. Ridgeway and Correll 2006.
63. Ridgeway and Erickson 2000; Ridgeway et al. 2009.
64. Ridgeway and Nakagawa 2017.
65. Ridgeway and Nakagawa 2017.
66. Berger et al. 1977; Ridgeway et al. 1998; Ridgeway and Erickson 2000.
67. Ridgeway et al. 2009.
68. Berger, Rosenholtz, and Zelditch 1980; Cuddy, Fiske, and Glick 2007; Fiske 2011; Fiske et al. 2002.
69. Conway, Pizzamiglio, and Mount 1996; Rucker, Galinsky, and Magee 2018.
70. Bales et al. 1951; Anderson and Kilduff 2009.
71. Berger et al. 1977; Correll and Ridgeway 2003.
72. Moore 1985; Troyer and Younts 1997; Webster and Whitmeyer 1999.
73. Anderson et al. 2006.
74. Troyer and Younts 1997.
75. Anderson, Willer, et al. 2012.
76. Goffman 1967.
77. Kilduff, Anderson, and Willer 2013.
78. Simpson, Willer, and Ridgeway 2012.
79. Anderson and Kilduff 2009; Ridgeway 1993.
80. Halevy et al. 2012.
81. Halevy, Chou, and Galinsky 2011; Maner and Mead 2010.
82. Boehm et al. 1993; Ridgeway and Diekema 1989.
83. Boehm 1999; Ridgeway 1984; van Vugt, Hogan, and Kaiser 2008.
84. Van Vugt et al. 2004.
85. Boehm et al. 1993; van Vugt, Hogan, and Kaiser 2008.
86. Magee and Galinsky 2008.
87. Hahl and Zuckerman 2014.
88. Van Vugt, Hogan, and Kaiser 2008.
89. Hahl and Zuckerman 2014; Hardy and van Vugt 2006; Ridgeway 1982; Willer 2009.
90. Anderson and Cowan 2014; Anderson and Kennedy 2012.

CHAPTER 3: WHY DO WE CARE ABOUT STATUS?

1. Ridgeway and Correll 2004.
2. See, for instance, Anderson, Hildreth, and Howland 2015; Leary, Jongman-Sereno, and Diebels 2014.
3. Anderson, Hildreth, and Howland 2015.
4. Goode 1978.

5. Fiske 2011.
6. Anderson, Hildreth, and Howland 2015.
7. Baumeister and Leary 1995.
8. Anderson, Hildreth, and Howland 2015; Fiske 2011, 28–55.
9. Berger et al. 1986.
10. Steckler and Tracy 2014; Tiedens, Ellsworth, and Mesquita 2000.
11. Ridgeway, Berger, and Smith 1985.
12. Anderson, Hildreth, and Howland 2015.
13. Anderson et al. 2006.
14. Anderson et al. 2006.
15. Miller 2001.
16. Griskevicius et al. 2009.
17. Rudman et al. 2012.
18. Livingston, Rosette, and Washington 2012.
19. Blumer 1958; Bobo 1999.
20. Craig and Richeson 2014; Wetts and Willer 2018.
21. Hochschild 2016.
22. J. D. Vance (2016) makes a related argument about the sense of elite disrespect felt by so-called hillbillies in rural Kentucky, and Jennifer Sherman (2009) describes the implicit disparagement felt by working-class people in rural California who struggle to find paid work and maintain moral dignity.
23. Cramer 2016.
24. Mutz 2018.
25. Cheng and Tracy 2014; van Vugt and Tybur 2016.
26. Fiske 2011.
27. Berger and Webster 2018.
28. Ridgeway and Johnson 1990.
29. Berger et al. 1985; Homans 1951; Willer 2009.
30. For reviews, see Berger and Webster 2018; Correll and Ridgeway 2003.
31. Berger and Webster 2018.
32. Conway, Pizzamiglio, and Mount 1996; Judd et al. 2005. As we noted earlier, competence (status) and warmth seem to be fundamental dimensions of people's judgments of others and groups (Fiske 2011). While competence and warmth can go together under some circumstances, when people are judged comparatively, as they are in a status ranking, they tend to be negatively related (Judd et al. 2005). Thus, high-status members are seen as competent but less warm, while low-status members are seen as less competent but warmer.
33. Anderson, Hildreth, and Howland 2015; Anderson and Willer 2014.
34. Berger et al. 1986; Kilduff and Galinsky 2013.
35. Berger, Anderson, and Zelditch 1972; Ridgeway and Nakagawa 2014.
36. McCall 2013; Owens 2013.
37. Blader and Yu 2017; Schwalbe and Shay 2014.
38. Lovaglia and Houser 1996; Steckler and Tracy 2014; Tiedens, Ellsworth, and Mesquita 2000.

39. Ridgeway and Johnson 1990.
40. Lovaglia and Houser 1996; Steckler and Tracy 2014.
41. Steckler and Tracy 2014; Tiedens, Ellsworth, and Mesquita 2000.
42. Ridgeway and Johnson 1990; Tiedens, Ellsworth, and Mesquita 2000.
43. Anderson, Hildreth, and Howland 2015.
44. Tiedens, Ellsworth, and Mesquita 2000.
45. Anderson, Hildreth, and Howland 2015.
46. Frank 1985.
47. Anderson, Kraus, et al. 2012.
48. Anderson, Kraus, et al. 2012.
49. Anderson, Hildreth, and Howland 2015.
50. Smith, Tyler, and Huo 2003.
51. Weber 1918/1968.
52. Cramer 2016; Hochschild 2016; Mutz 2018.
53. Hays and Greer 2016.
54. Hays and Bendersky 2015.
55. Blader, Shirako, and Chen 2016.
56. Blader, Shirako, and Chen 2016; Fiske 2010.
57. Love and Davis 2014.
58. Blader and Yu 2017; Krauss et al. 2012.
59. Bandura 1977.
60. Anderson et al. 2006.
61. Berger and Webster 2018.
62. Conway, Pizzamiglio, and Mount 1996; Fiske 2011; Judd et al. 2005.
63. Cialdini and de Nicholas 1989.
64. Anderson, Hildreth, and Howland 2015; Leary, Jongman-Sereno, and Diebels 2014.
65. Ridgeway and Nakagawa 2017.
66. Fiske 2011; Hardin and Higgins 1996.
67. Ridgeway and Correll 2006.
68. Johnson, Dowd, and Ridgeway 2006.
69. Ridgeway and Nakagawa 2017.
70. Ridgeway and Nakagawa 2017.
71. Ridgeway and Nakagawa 2017.
72. Fiske 2011. In a societal context in which men have more power and status and yet the sexes are intimately interdependent, the comparative trade-off between status and warmth feeds gender stereotypes of men as agentic and women as communal (see Ridgeway 2011 for a review). In so doing, Peter Glick and Susan Fiske (1999) argue, it also encourages "benevolent sexism" in which women, in exchange for deference to men, are perceived as warm and good (if less competent) and offered protection.
73. Hays and Bendersky 2015.
74. Anderson and Willer 2014; Blader and Yu 2017.
75. Bales et al. 1951; Berger, Conner, and Fisek 1974; Kilduff and Galinsky 2013.
76. Anderson et al. 2001; Bales et al. 1951; Heinicke and Bales 1953.
77. Anderson, Willer, et al. 2012; Kilduff, Willer, and Anderson 2016.

78. Anderson, Willer, et al. 2012; Kalkhoff, Younts, and Troyer 2011; Troyer and Younts 1997.
79. Anderson et al. 2006; Anderson, Ames, and Gosling 2008; Ridgeway and Diekema 1989.
80. Kilduff, Willer, and Anderson 2016.
81. Berger et al. 1977; Berger and Webster 2018; Ridgeway and Nakagawa 2014.
82. Jost and Banaji 1994; Major and Kaiser 2017.
83. Friesen et al. 2014.

CHAPTER 4: STATUS BELIEFS AND
THE ORGANIZATION OF INEQUALITY

1. Sewell 1992.
2. This definition is a modest variation on status characteristics and expectation states theory's definition of a status characteristic (Berger et al. 1977).
3. Correll and Ridgeway 2003; Ridgeway 2014.
4. Berger and Webster 2018; Fiske et al. 2002; Fiske 2011; Torelli et al. 2014.
5. Lamont 2012; Ridgeway 2014.
6. Tilly 1998.
7. Bourdieu 1984.
8. Hogg, Abrams, and Brewer 2017; Tajfel and Turner 1986.
9. Berger, Rosenholtz, and Zelditch 1980; Jost and Banaji 1994; Ridgeway 1991; Tajfel and Turner 1986.
10. Correll et al. 2017; Ridgeway and Correll 2006.
11. Troyer and Younts 1997.
12. Jost and Banaji 1994.
13. Fiske et al. 2002; Fiske 2011.
14. Correll et al. 2017.
15. Ridgeway and Correll 2006.
16. Correll et al. 2017.
17. Berger et al. 1977; Berger and Webster 2018.
18. Chwe 2001; Schelling 1960.
19. Chwe 2001; Goffman 1967.
20. Thomas et al. 2014.
21. Thomas et al. 2014.
22. Cuddy, Fiske, and Glick 2007; Fiske 2011; Fiske et al. 2002.
23. Fiske et al. 2002.
24. Bianchi, Kang, and Stewart 2012.
25. Berger et al. 1977; Berger and Webster 2018.
26. Berger, Rosenholtz, and Zelditch 1980.
27. Correll and Ridgeway 2003; Fiske et al. 2002.
28. Berger et al. 1977; Berger and Webster 2018.
29. Fiske 2011.
30. Bai 2016; Hahl, Zuckerman, and Kim 2017; Hahl and Zuckerman 2014.
31. Bai 2016; Ridgeway 1982; Willer 2009.
32. Anderson and Willer 2014.

33. Cuddy, Fiske, and Glick 2007; Fiske et al. 2002.
34. Conway, Pizzamiglio, and Mount 1996; see also Rucker, Galinsky, and Magee 2018.
35. Berger, Rosenholtz, and Zelditch 1980; Fiske 2011.
36. Hahl and Zuckerman 2014.
37. Hahl, Zuckerman, and Kim 2017. Feng Bai (2016) argues that in East Asian cultures morality and high status are often closely linked.
38. Berger and Webster 2018.
39. Strodtbeck, James, and Hawkins 1957.
40. Berger and Webster 2018; Correll and Ridgeway 2003.
41. For reviews of this research, see Correll and Ridgeway 2003; Ridgeway and Nakagawa 2014.
42. Ridgeway 2014.
43. Weber 1918/1968.
44. Ridgeway 1991, 2018.
45. Ridgeway 1991; Ridgeway et al. 1998.
46. Ridgeway et al. 1998.
47. Fiske 2011; Fiske et al. 2002; Jost and Burgess 2000.
48. Ridgeway and Correll 2006.
49. Ridgeway and Correll 2006.
50. Hamilton et al. 2015.
51. Mark, Smith-Lovin, and Ridgeway 2009; Ridgeway and Erickson 2000; Webster and Hysom 1998.
52. Berger and Fisek 2006.
53. Ridgeway et al. 2009.
54. Ridgeway and Erickson 2000.
55. Ridgeway and Balkwell 1997.
56. Ridgeway 1991.
57. Brashears 2008.
58. See Ridgeway 2011 for a detailed discussion of this issue.
59. Ito and Urland 2003; Zemore, Fiske, and Kim 2000.
60. Wood and Eagly 2002, 2012.
61. Wood and Eagly 2002.
62. Wood and Eagly 2002.
63. Huber 2007.
64. See Ridgeway 2011 for a more thorough discussion of this process.
65. See, for instance, Jackman 1994.
66. Ridgeway and Correll 2006.
67. Berger, Ridgeway, and Zelditch 2002; Thye 2000.
68. Ridgeway 2018.
69. Jost and Burgess 2000.
70. Sauder, Lynn, and Podolny 2012.
71. Podolny and Phillips 1996.
72. Sauder, Lynn, and Podolny. 2012.
73. Espeland and Sauder 2016.

74. Correll et al. 2017.
75. Sewell 1992.
76. Podolny 2005; Sauder, Lynn, and Podolny 2012.
77. Bianchi, Kang, and Stewart 2012; Stewart 2005.
78. Simcoe and Waguespack 2011.
79. Berger et al. 1977.
80. Sauder, Lynn, and Podolny 2012.
81. The cultural schema theory of status argues that status rankings develop in these more competitive situations as people implicitly draw on and stretch the status schema to manage them. But of course, this need not be the only way such status rankings develop. Hahl and Zuckerman (2014) argue that shared status rankings may also arise straightforwardly in competitive situations in which evaluators have parallel, if competitive, goals to rank talent and draw on similar information and metrics to do so, such as in sports.
82. Correll et al. 2017.
83. On first-order evaluations, see Berger, Rosenholtz, and Zelditch 1980; Lynn, Podolny, and Tao 2009. On socially endogenous inference, see Correll et al. 2017; Lynn, Podolny, and Tao 2009; Sauder, Lynn, and Podolny 2012.
84. Berger and Webster 2018; Ridgeway and Nakagawa 2014; Sauder, Lynn, and Podolny 2012.
85. Lynn, Podolny, and Tao 2009.
86. Correll et al. 2017; Lynn, Podolny, and Tao 2009.
87. Rivera 2015.
88. Correll et al. 2017.
89. Correll et al. 2017.
90. Correll et al. 2017.
91. Berger and Webster 2018.
92. Correll and Ridgeway 2003.
93. Anderson, Willer, et al. 2012; Troyer and Younts 1997.
94. Correll et al. 2017.

CHAPTER 5: THE MICRODYNAMICS OF STATUS

1. Anderson et al. 2001; Anderson and Willer 2014; Berger et al. 1977.
2. Anderson, Hildreth, and Howland 2015.
3. Hahl and Zuckerman 2014; Ridgeway 1982.
4. Hardy and van Vugt 2006; Willer 2009.
5. Simpson, Willer, and Ridgeway 2012; Willer 2009.
6. Halevy et al. 2012.
7. Anderson and Willer 2014; Blader and Yu 2017.
8. Ridgeway and Fisk 2012.
9. Berger, Conner, and Fisek 1974; Berger et al. 1977; Berger and Webster 2018; Correll and Ridgeway 2003.
10. Berger, Conner, and Fisek 1974; Berger and Webster 2018.

11. Fiske 2011.
12. Berger, Conner, and Fisek 1974; Berger and Webster 2018; Correll and Ridgeway 2003.
13. Miller and Turnbull 1986.
14. Berger, Conner, and Fisek 1974; Berger and Webster 2018.
15. Berger and Webster 2018; Correll and Ridgeway 2003.
16. Anderson and Kennedy 2012; Anderson and Willer 2014.
17. Kilduff and Galinsky 2013.
18. Kilduff and Galinsky 2013.
19. Fiske 2010; Ridgeway, Berger, and Smith 1985.
20. Berger, Rosenholtz, and Zelditch 1980.
21. Berger et al. 1977; Berger and Webster 2018.
22. Berger et al. 1977; Correll and Ridgeway 2003.
23. Ridgeway 2011.
24. Berger et al. 1992; Pedulla 2018.
25. See Correll and Ridgeway 2003 for a review.
26. Bendersky and Shah 2013.
27. See Cohen and Roper 1972.
28. Berger, Rosenholtz, and Zelditch 1980.
29. Bertrand and Mullainathan 2004; Davidson and Burke 2000; Eagly and Carli 2007, 77; Moss-Racusin et al. 2012.
30. Cuddy, Fiske, and Glick 2007; Fiske et al. 2002.
31. Fiske and Taylor 2008.
32. Ridgeway and Fisk 2012.
33. Fiske, Lin, and Neuberg 1999; Ridgeway 2011.
34. Kilduff and Galinsky 2013.
35. Driskell and Mullen 1990.
36. For reviews, see Correll and Ridgeway 2003 and Ridgeway and Nakagawa 2014.
37. Correll and Ridgeway 2003.
38. Correll and Ridgeway 2003.
39. Berger, Rosenholtz, and Zelditch 1980; Ridgeway, Berger, and Smith 1985.
40. Dovidio et al. 1988.
41. Lovaglia et al. 1998.
42. Lovaglia et al. 1998. On the effects of stereotype threat, see Schmader, Johns, and Forbes 2008; Steele and Aronson 1995.
43. Shih, Pittinsky, and Ambady 1999.
44. Berger and Webster 2018; Correll and Ridgeway 2003.
45. Biernat and Kobrynowicz 1997; Foschi 1996, 2000.
46. Williams and Dempsey 2014.
47. Correll 2001, 2004.
48. Botelho and Abraham 2017.
49. Uhlmann and Cohen 2005.
50. See also Quadlin 2018.
51. Berger et al. 1985.
52. Homans 1951.

53. Berger et al. 1985.
54. Stewart and Moore 1992.
55. Hysom 2009; Hysom, Webster, and Walker 2015.
56. Sauder, Lynn, and Podolny 2012; Thye 2000.
57. Thye 2000.
58. Veblen 1899/1953.
59. Conway, Pizzamiglio, and Mount 1996.
60. Fisek, Berger, and Norman 1991.
61. Webster and Rashotte 2010.
62. Fiske 2010, 946–47; Ridgeway 1987.
63. Kilduff and Galinsky 2013.
64. Anderson and Cowan 2014.
65. Bellezza, Gino, and Keinan 2014; Ridgeway 1981.
66. Dovidio et al. 1988.
67. Berger et al. 1992; see also Pedulla 2018.
68. Cohen and Roper 1972; Ridgeway 1982; Rudman et al. 2012.
69. Eagly and Carli 2007; Ridgeway 1982; Shackleford, Wood, and Worchel 1996.
70. Berger et al. 1998; Goar and Sell 2005.
71. Bunderson 2003.
72. Anderson and Cowan 2014.
73. Bendersky and Shah 2013.
74. Johnson, Dowd, and Ridgeway 2006.
75. Berger et al. 1998; Zelditch 2018.
76. Hays and Blader 2017; Swencionis and Fiske 2018; Willer 2009.
77. Ridgeway 1982.
78. Hays and Blader 2017.
79. Walker 2014; Zelditch and Walker 1984.
80. Berger et al. 1998.
81. Berger et al. 1998.
82. Ridgeway, Johnson, and Diekema 1994.
83. Livingston, Rosette, and Washington 2012; Rudman et al. 2012.
84. Rudman et al. 2012.
85. Williams and Tiedens 2016.
86. Ridgeway and Kricheli-Katz 2013; Sesko and Biernat 2010.
87. Livingston, Rosette, and Washington 2012; Purdie-Vaughns and Eibach 2008; Tinkler et al. 2019.
88. Rosette and Livingston 2012; Tinkler et al. 2019.
89. Cohen and Lotan 1997; Cohen and Roper 1972.
90. Cohen and Lotan 1997; Ridgeway 1982.
91. Cohen and Roper 1972.
92. Burt 1998; Eagly and Carli 2007.
93. Ridgeway 1982; Eagly and Carli 2007.
94. Eagly and Carli 2007; Livingston and Pearce 2009.
95. Ridgeway 2014.

96. Dovidio and Gaertner 2010.

97. McPherson, Smith-Lovin, and Cook 2001.

98. Hysom 2009; Thye 2000.

99. Ridgeway 2014.

100. Rivera 2015.

101. Tajfel and Turner 1986.

102. McPherson, Smith-Lovin, and Cook 2001.

103. Cabrera and Thomas-Hunt 2007; Sauder, Lynn, and Podolny 2012.

104. See, for instance, Korver-Glenn 2018.

CHAPTER 6: STATUS, DIFFERENCE, AND THE DURABILITY OF INEQUALITY

1. Risman 2004.

2. Espeland and Sauder 2007; Sharkey 2014; Sauder, Lynn, and Podolny 2012.

3. Berger et al. 1977; Podolny 2005.

4. Weber 1918/1968; Tilly 1998.

5. Tilly 1998.

6. Tilly 1998.

7. DiTomaso, Post, and Parks-Yancy 2007; Reskin 2003; Tomaskovic-Devey 2014.

8. Ridgeway 2014.

9. Bourdieu 1984; Lamont 2012; Lamont and Fournier 1992; Tilly 1998.

10. Ridgeway et al. 1998; Ridgeway et al. 2009.

11. Huber 2007; Wood and Eagly 2012.

12. Jackman 1994; Morning 2011.

13. Jackman 1994.

14. Tomaskovic-Devey 2014.

15. See, for instance, Ridgeway 2011.

16. Ridgeway and Nakagawa 2014.

17. Korver-Glenn 2018.

18. DiTomaso 2013; Reskin 2012; Ridgeway 2011.

19. Acker 2006; Baron et al. 2002; Ely and Meyerson 2000; Stephens et al. 2012.

20. Acker 1990; Williams 2000.

21. Cha 2010.

22. Calarco 2014.

23. Calarco 2014; Stephens et al. 2012.

24. Baron et al. 2002.

25. Ely and Meyerson 2000.

26. Berger et al. 1977; Correll and Ridgeway 2003.

27. Nelson and Bridges 1999.

28. Ely and Meyerson 2000; Rivera 2015; Turco 2010.

29. Kahn 2011; Turco 2010.

30. Bourdieu 1984.

31. Glick and Fiske 1999.

32. Blau and Schwartz 1984.
33. Correll 2017; Ridgeway 2011.
34. Ridgeway and Fisk 2012.
35. DiPrete et al. 2011; Massey, Rothwell, and Domina 2009.
36. Massey, Rothwell, and Domina 2009.
37. Lareau 2002; Ridgeway and Fisk 2012.
38. Batruch, Autin, and Butera 2017; Lareau 2011; Lutfey and Freese 2005; Wingfield and Alston 2014.
39. Lamont 2012; Lamont and Fournier 1992.
40. See, for instance, Reskin 2003.
41. West and Fenstermaker 1995.
42. Prentice and Miller 2006.
43. West and Zimmerman 1987; Westbrook and Schilt 2014.
44. Risman 2018; Schilt 2011. Of course, for such changing beliefs about the basis and nature of gender categorization to gain broad force in social relations, they would need to spread to become widely held in society as third-order beliefs about the views of most people. In the meantime, they gain traction in subgroups of society and may be planting seeds for broader change in cultural beliefs about gender (Risman 2018).
45. Risman 2018; Westbrook and Schilt 2014.
46. Wagner and Berger 1997.
47. Charles and Grusky 2004; Haslam et al. 2006; Kray et al. 2017; Ridgeway 2011.
48. Morning 2011.
49. Morning 2011; Saperstein and Penner 2012.
50. Zou and Cheryan 2017.
51. Morning 2011; Zou and Cheryan 2017.
52. Zou and Cheryan 2017.
53. Brewer and Lui 1989; Ito and Urland 2003; Johnson, Freeman, and Pauker 2012.
54. Turco 2010.
55. Rosette and Livingston 2012.
56. Wu 2002; Zou and Cheryan 2017.
57. Berdahl and Min 2012; Chen 1999; Tinkler et al. 2019.
58. Kluegel and Smith 1986.
59. For the psychological research, see, for instance, Bourdieu 1977, 1984; Prentice and Miller 2007.
60. Bjornsdottir and Rule 2017.
61. Ridgeway 2014. All cultural systems for categorizing people, including relatively essentialized ones like gender and race, are in fact based on multidimensional sets of cues (Saperstein and Penner 2012; Westbrook and Schilt 2014). But, I argue, the cultural presumption that these cues form tightly bounded, more unified sets is greater for more essentialized social differences.
62. Ridgeway and Fisk 2012.
63. DiMaggio 2012; Rivera and Tilcsik 2016; Ridgeway and Kricheli-Katz 2013.
64. Bourdieu 1984; Veblen 1899/1953.
65. Armstrong and Hamilton 2013; Ridgeway and Fisk 2012; Rivera 2015; Stuber 2006.
66. Correll et al. 2017.
67. Lynn, Podolny, and Tao 2009.

68. Ridgeway 2011; Tilly 1998.
69. Ridgeway 2018; Seachrist and Stangor 2001.
70. Ridgeway and Correll 2006; Willer, Kuwabara, and Macy 2009.
71. Brinkman and Brinkman 1997; Ridgeway 2011, chap. 6.
72. Fiske, Lin, and Neuberg 1999; Fiske 2011.
73. Prentice and Miller 1993, 1996; Willer, Kuwabara, and Macy 2009.
74. Correll et al. 2017.
75. Cotter, Hermson, and Vanneman 2011; England 2010; Garg et al. 2018; Ridgeway 2011.
76. Garg et al. 2018.
77. See Ridgeway 2011 for a review of studies.
78. Jackman 1994.
79. Cuddy, Fiske, and Glick 2007; Fiske et al. 2002.
80. Durante, Tablante, and Fiske 2017.
81. Durante, Tablante, and Fiske 2017.
82. That the compensating beliefs about warmth associated with low status help stabilize inequality is supported by evidence from comparative studies in which countries with greater inequality have greater competence-warmth trade-offs in their widely held status beliefs (Durante, Tablante, and Fiske 2017).
83. Major and Kaiser 2017.
84. Jost and Banaji 1994; Jost, Banaji, and Nosek 2004.
85. Blumer 1958.
86. Anderson, Hildreth, and Howland 2015; Hogg, Abrams, and Brewer 2017; Tajfel and Turner 1986.
87. Dover, Major, and Kaiser 2016.
88. Blumer 1958; Bobo 1999.
89. Cramer 2016; Hochschild 2016; Mutz 2018.
90. Wetts and Willer 2018; see also Craig and Richeson 2014.
91. Gidron and Hall 2017.
92. Williams 2017.
93. Hochschild 2016.
94. Durante et al. 2017; Fiske 2011.
95. Durante et al. 2017; Fiske 2011.
96. Ridgeway and Nakagawa 2017.
97. Jackman 1994.
98. Kluegel and Smith 1986.
99. See Fiske 2011, 8–10; Kluegel and Smith 1986.
100. Major and Kaiser 2017.
101. Major and Kaiser 2017.

CHAPTER 7: CONCLUSION

1. For reviews of this evidence, see Anderson and Willer 2014; Magee and Galinsky 2008; Ridgeway and Nakagawa 2014.
2. Sewell 1992.
3. Cheng and Tracy 2014; van Vugt and Tybur 2016.
4. Chase and Lindquist 2016.

5. Ridgeway and Diekema 1989.
6. Anderson et al. 2006; Anderson, Ames, and Gosling 2008; Ridgeway and Diekema 1989.
7. Anderson et al. 2006; Ridgeway and Diekema 1989.
8. Ridgeway and Nakagawa 2017.
9. Berger et al. 1977; Berger and Webster 2018.
10. Cuddy et al. 2007; Fiske et al. 2002.
11. Ridgeway and Correll 2006.
12. Anderson et al. 2006; Anderson, Willer, et al. 2012; Troyer and Younts 1997.
13. Anderson, Hildreth, and Howland 2015.
14. Bales 1950, 1970.
15. Anderson, Willer, et al. 2012.
16. Ridgeway and Nakagawa 2017.
17. See Sauder, Lynn, and Podolny 2012.
18. Correll et al. 2017; Lynn, Podolny, and Tao 2009.
19. Podolny and Phillips 1996; Thye 2000.
20. Korver-Glenn 2018.
21. See, for instance, Ridgeway 2011, chap. 6.
22. Acker 2006; Ely and Meyerson 2000; Stephens et al. 2012.
23. See, for instance, Anderson and Willer 2014; Halevy, Chou, and Galinsky 2011.
24. Risman 2018.
25. Schilt 2011.

REFERENCES

Acker, Joan. 1990. "Hierarchies, Jobs, Bodies: A Theory of Gendered Organizations." *Gender and Society* 4(2): 139–58.

———. 2006. *Class Questions: Feminist Answers*. Lanham, Md.: Rowman & Littlefield.

Anderson, Cameron, Daniel R. Ames, and Samuel D. Gosling. 2008. "Punishing Hubris: The Perils of Overestimating One's Status in a Group." *Personality and Social Psychology Bulletin* 34(1): 90–101.

Anderson, Cameron, and Jon Cowan. 2014. "Personality and Status Attainment: A Micropolitics Perspective." In *The Psychology of Social Status*, edited by Joey T. Cheng, Jessica L. Tracy, and Cameron Anderson. New York: Springer.

Anderson, Cameron, John A. Hildreth, and Laura Howland. 2015. "Is the Desire for Status a Fundamental Human Motive? A Review of the Empirical Literature." *Psychological Bulletin* 141(3): 574–601.

Anderson, Cameron, Oliver P. John, Dacher Keltner, and Ann M. Kring. 2001. "Who Attains Social Status? Effects of Personality Traits and Physical Attractiveness in Social Groups." *Journal of Personality and Social Psychology* 81(1): 116–32.

Anderson, Cameron, and Jessica A. Kennedy. 2012. "Micropolitics: A New Model of Status Hierarchies in Teams." In *Looking Back, Moving Forward: A Review of Group- and Team-Based Research*, vol. 15 of *Research on Managing Groups and Teams*, edited by Margaret A. Neale and Elizabeth A. Mannix. Bingley, U.K.: Emerald Group Publishing.

Anderson, Cameron, and Gavin J. Kilduff. 2009. "Why Do Dominant Personalities Attain Influence in Face-to-Face Groups? The Competence-Signaling Effects of Trait Dominance." *Journal of Personality and Social Psychology* 96(2): 491–503.

Anderson, Cameron, Michael W. Kraus, Adam D. Galinsky, and Dacher Keltner. 2012. "The Local Ladder Effect: Social Status and Subjective Well-being." *Psychological Science* 23(7): 764–71.

Anderson, Cameron, Sanjay Srivastava, Jennifer S. Beer, Sandra E. Spataro, and Jennifer A. Chatman. 2006. "Knowing Your Place: Self-Perceptions of Status in Face-to-Face Groups." *Journal of Personality and Social Psychology* 91(6): 1094–1110.

Anderson, Cameron, and Robb Willer. 2014. "Do Status Hierarchies Benefit Groups? A Bounded Functionalist Account of Status." In *The Psychology of Social Status*, edited by Joey T. Cheng, Jessica L. Tracy, and Cameron Anderson. New York: Springer.

Anderson, Cameron, Robb Willer, Gavin J. Kilduff, and Courtney Brown. 2012. "The Origins of Deference: When Do People Prefer Lower Status?" *Journal of Personality and Social Psychology* 102(5): 1077–88.

Armstrong, Elizabeth, and Laura Hamilton. 2013. *Paying for the Party: How College Maintains Inequality.* Cambridge, Mass.: Harvard University Press.

Bai, Feng. 2016. "Beyond Dominance and Competence: A Moral Virtue Theory of Status Attainment." *Personality and Social Psychology Review* 21(3): 203–27.

Bales, Robert F. 1950. *Interaction Process Analysis: A Method for the Study of Small Groups.* Cambridge, Mass.: Addison-Wesley.

———. 1970. *Personality and Interpersonal Behavior.* New York; Holt, Rinehart, and Winston.

Bales, Robert F., Fred L. Strodtbeck, Theodore M. Mills, and Mary E. Roseborough. 1951. "Channels of Communication in Small Groups." *American Sociological Review* 16(4): 461–68.

Bandura, Albert. 1977. *Social Learning Theory.* Englewood Cliffs, N.J.: Prentice-Hall.

Baron, James N., Michael T. Hannan, Greta Hsu, and Ozgecan Kocak. 2002. "Gender and the Organization-Building Process in Young High-Tech Firms." In *The New Economic Sociology: Developments in an Emerging Field*, edited by Mauro F. Guillén, Randall Collins, Paula England, and Marshal Meyer. New York: Russell Sage Foundation.

Batruch, Anatolia, Frederique Autin, and Fabrizio Butera. 2017. "Re-establishing the Social-Class Order: Restorative Reaction against High-Achieving, Low-SES Pupils." *Journal of Social Issues* 73(1): 42–60.

Baumeister, Roy F., and Mark R. Leary. 1995. "The Need to Belong: Desire for Interpersonal Attachments as a Fundamental Human Motivation." *Psychological Bulletin* 117(3): 497–529.

Bellezza, Silvia, Francesca Gino, and Anat Keinan. 2014. "The Red Sneakers Effect: Inferring Status and Competence from Signals of Nonconformity." *Journal of Consumer Research* 41(June): 35–54.

Bendersky, Corinne, and Neha Parikh Shah. 2013. "The Downfall of Extraverts and Rise of Neurotics: The Dynamic Process of Status Allocation in Task Groups." *Academy of Management Journal* 56(2): 387–406.

Berdahl, Jennifer L., and Ji-A Min. 2012. "Prescriptive Stereotypes and Workplace Consequences for East Asians in North America." *Cultural Diversity and Ethnic Minority Psychology* 18(2): 141–52.

Berger, Joseph, Bo Anderson, and Morris Zelditch. 1972. "Structural Aspects of Distributive Justice: A Status-Value Formulation." In *Sociological Theories in Progress*, vol. 2, edited by Joseph Berger, Morris Zelditch, and Bo Anderson. Boston: Houghton Mifflin.

Berger, Joseph, Thomas L. Conner, and M. Hamit Fisek. 1974. *Expectation States Theory: A Research Program.* Cambridge, Mass.: Winthrop.

Berger, Joseph, and M. Hamit Fisek. 2006. "Diffuse Status Characteristics and the Spread of Status Value: A Formal Theory." *American Journal of Sociology* 111(4): 1038–79.

Berger, Joseph, M. Hamit Fisek, Robert Z. Norman, and David G. Wagner. 1985. "The Formation of Reward Expectations in Status Situations." In *Status, Rewards, and Influence: How Expectations Organize Behavior*, edited by Joseph Berger and Morris Zelditch Jr. San Francisco: Jossey-Bass.

Berger, Joseph, M. Hamit Fisek, Robert Z. Norman, and Morris Zelditch. 1977. *Status Characteristics and Social Interaction: An Expectation-States Approach.* New York: Elsevier Scientific Publishing.

Berger, Joseph, Robert Z. Norman, James Balkwell, and Roy F. Smith. 1992. "Status Inconsistency in Task Situations: A Test of Four Status Processing Principles." *American Sociological Review* 57(6): 843–55.

Berger, Joseph, Cecilia L. Ridgeway, M. Hamit Fisek, and Robert Z. Norman. 1998. "The Legitimation and Delegitimation of Power and Prestige Orders." *American Sociological Review* 63(3): 379–405.

Berger, Joseph, Cecilia Ridgeway, and Morris Zelditch. 2002. "Construction of Status and Referential Structures." *Sociological Theory* 20(2): 157–79.

Berger, Joseph, Susan J. Rosenholtz, and Morris Zelditch Jr. 1980. "Status Organizing Processes." *Annual Review of Sociology* 6: 479–508.

Berger, Joseph, and Murray Webster Jr. 2018. "Expectations, Status, and Behavior." In *Contemporary Social Psychological Theories*, 2nd ed., edited by Peter J. Burke. Stanford, Calif.: Stanford University Press.

Berger, Joseph, Murray Webster Jr., Cecilia Ridgeway, and Susan Rosenholtz. 1986. "Status Cues, Expectations, and Behaviors." In *Advances in Group Processes: Theory and Research*, vol. 3, edited by Edward Lawler. Greenwich, Conn.: JAI Press.

Bertrand, Marianne, and Sendhill Mullainathan. 2004. "Are Emily and Greg More Employable than Lakisha and Jamal? A Field Experiment on Labor Market Discrimination." *American Economic Review* 94(4): 991–1013.

Bianchi, Alison J., Soong Moon Kang, and Daniel G. Stewart. 2012. "The Organizational Selection of Status Characteristics: Status Evaluations in an Open Source Community." *Organization Science* 23(2): 341–54.

Biernat, Monica, and Diane Kobrynowicz. 1997. "Gender- and Race-Based Standards of Competence: Lower Minimum Standards but Higher Ability Standards for Devalued Groups." *Journal of Personality and Social Psychology* 72(3): 544–57.

Bjornsdottir, R. Thora, and Nicholas O. Rule. 2017. "The Visibility of Social Class from Facial Cues." *Journal of Personality and Social Psychology* 113(4): 530–46.

Blader, Steven L., Aiwa Shirako, and Ya-Ru Chen. 2016. "Looking Out from the Top: Differential Effects of Status and Power on Perspective Taking." *Personality and Social Psychology Bulletin* 42(6): 723–37.

Blader, Steven, and Siyu Yu. 2017. "Are Status and Respect Different or Two Sides of the Same Coin?" *Academy of Management Annals* 11(2): 800–824.

Blau, Peter Michael. 1964. *Exchange and Power in Social Life.* New York: John Wiley & Sons.

Blau, Peter M., and Joseph E. Schwartz. 1984. *Crosscutting Social Circles: Testing a Macrosocial Theory of Intergroup Relations.* New York: Academic Press.

Blumer, Herbert. 1958. "Race Prejudice as a Sense of Group Position." *Pacific Sociological Review* 1(1): 3–7.

Bobo, Lawrence. 1999. "Prejudice as Group Position: Microfoundations of a Sociological Approach to Racism and Race Relations." *Journal of Social Issues* 55(3): 445–72.

Boehm, Christopher. 1999. *Hierarchy in the Forest: The Evolution of Egalitarian Behavior.* Cambridge, Mass.: Harvard University Press.

Boehm, Christopher, Harold B. Barclay, Robert Knox Dentan, Marie-Claude Dupre, Jonathan D. Hill, Susan Kent, Bruce M. Knauft, Keith F. Otterbein, and Steve Rayner. 1993. "Egalitarian Behavior and Reverse Dominance Hierarchy." *Current Anthropology* 34(3): 227–54.

Botelho, Tristan L., and Mabel Abraham. 2017. "Pursuing Quality: How Search Costs and Uncertainty Magnify Gender-Based Double Standards in a Multistage Evaluation Process." *Administrative Science Quarterly* 62(4): 698–730.

Bourdieu, Pierre. 1977. *Outline of a Theory of Practice.* Cambridge: Cambridge University Press.

———. 1984. *Distinction: A Social Critique on the Judgment of Taste.* Cambridge, Mass.: Harvard University Press.

Boyd, Robert, and Peter J. Richerson. 1985. *Culture and the Evolutionary Process.* Chicago: University of Chicago Press.

Brashears, Matthew E. 2008. "Sex, Society, and Association: A Cross-National Examination of Status Construction Theory." *Social Psychology Quarterly* 71(1): 72–85.

Brewer, Marilynn B., and Layton N. Lui. 1989. "The Primacy of Age and Sex in the Structure of Person Categories." *Social Cognition* 7(3): 262–74.

Brinkman, Richard L., and June E. Brinkman. 1997. "Cultural Lag: Conception and Theory." *International Journal of Social Economics* 24(6): 609–27.

Bunderson, J. Stuart. 2003. "Recognizing and Utilizing Expertise in Work Groups: A Status Characteristics Perspective." *Administrative Science Quarterly* 48(4): 557–91.

Burt, Ronald S. 1998. "The Gender of Social Capital." *Rationality and Society* 10(1): 5–46.

Cabrera, Susan F., and Melissa Thomas-Hunt. 2007. "'Street Cred' and the Executive Woman: The Effects of Gender Differences in Social Networks on Career Advancement." In *Social Psychology of Gender*, vol. 24, edited by Shelley Correll. Bingley, U.K.: Emerald Group Publishing.

Calarco, Jessica M. 2014. "Coached for the Classroom: Parents' Cultural Transmission and Children's Reproduction of Educational Inequalities." *American Sociological Review* 79(5): 1015–37.

Caporael, Linnda. 1997. "The Evolution of Truly Social Cognition: The Core Configurations Model." *Personality and Social Psychology Review* 1(4): 276–98.

Caporael, Linnda, and Marilynn Brewer. 1991. "Reviving Evolutionary Psychology: Biology Meets Society." *Journal of Social Issues* 47(3): 187–95.

Carrier, Antonin, Eva Louvet, Bruno Chauvin, and Odile Rohmer. 2014. "The Primacy of Agency over Competence in Status Perception." *Social Psychology* 45(5): 347–56.

Cha, Youngjoo. 2010. "Reinforcing Separate Spheres: The Effect of Spousal Overwork on Men's and Women's Employment in Dual-Earner Households." *American Sociological Review* 75(2): 303–29.

Charles, Maria, and David Grusky. 2004. *Occupational Ghettos: The Worldwide Segregation of Women and Men*. Stanford, Calif.: Stanford University Press.

Chase, Ivan D. 1974. "Models of Hierarchy Formation in Animal Societies." *Behavioral Science* 19(6): 374–82.

———. 1980. "Social Process and Hierarchy Formation in Small Groups: A Comparative Perspective." *American Sociological Review* 45(6): 905–24.

Chase, Ivan D., and W. Brent Lindquist. 2016. "The Fragility of Individual-Based Explanations of Social Hierarchies: A Test Using Animal Pecking Orders." *PloS ONE* 11(7): 1–16.

Chase, Ivan D., and Kristine Seitz. 2011. "Self-Structuring Properties of Dominance Hierarchies: A New Perspective." In *Advances in Genetics*, vol. 75, *Aggression*, edited by Robert Huber, Danika L. Bannasch, and Patricia Brennan. San Diego, Calif.: Elsevier.

Chase, Ivan D., Craig Tovey, Debra Spangler-Martin, and Michael Manfredonia. 2002. "Individual Differences versus Social Dynamics in the Formation of Animal Dominance Hierarchies." *Proceedings of the National Academy of Sciences* 99(8): 5744–49.

Chen, Anthony S. 1999. "Lives at the Center of the Periphery, Lives at the Periphery of the Center: Chinese American Masculinities and Bargaining with Hegemony." *Gender and Society* 13(5): 584–607.

Cheng, Joey T., and Jessica L. Tracy. 2014. "Toward a Unified Science of Hierarchy: Dominance and Prestige Are Two Fundamental Pathways to Human Social Rank." In *The Psychology of Social Status*, edited by Joey T. Cheng, Jessica L. Tracy, and Cameron Anderson. New York: Springer.

Cheng, Joey T., Jessica L. Tracy, Tom Foulsham, Alan Kingstone, and Joseph Henrich. 2013. "Two Ways to the Top: Evidence That Dominance and Prestige Are Distinct yet Viable Avenues to Social Rank and Influence." *Journal of Personality and Social Psychology* 104(1): 103–25.

Chwe, Michael Suk-Young. 2001. *Rational Ritual: Culture, Coordination, and Common Knowledge*. Princeton, N.J.: Princeton University Press.

Cialdini, Robert B., and Maralou E. de Nicholas. 1989. "Self-Presentation by Association." *Journal of Personality and Social Psychology* 57(4): 626–31.

Cohen, Elizabeth G., and Rachel A. Lotan. 1997. *Working for Equity in Heterogeneous Classrooms: Sociological Theory in Practice*. New York: Teachers College Press.

Cohen, Elizabeth G., and Susan S. Roper. 1972. "Modification of Interracial Interaction Disability: An Application of Status Characteristics Theory." *American Sociological Review* 37(6): 643–57.

Conway, Michael, M. Teresa Pizzamiglio, and Lauren Mount. 1996. "Status, Communality, and Agency: Implications for Stereotypes of Gender and Other Groups." *Journal of Personality and Social Psychology* 71(1): 25–38.

Cook, Karen S., Coye Cheshire, and Alexandra Gerbasi. 2018. "Power, Dependence, and Social Exchange Theory." In *Contemporary Social Psychological Theories*, 2nd ed., edited by Peter J. Burke. Stanford, Calif.: Stanford University Press.

Correll, Shelley J. 2001. "Gender and the Career Choice Process: The Role of Biased Self-Assessments." *American Journal of Sociology* 106(6): 1691–1730.

———. 2004. "Constraints into Preferences: Gender, Status, and Emerging Career Aspirations." *American Sociological Review* 69(1): 93–113.

———. 2017. "Reproducing Gender Biases in Modern Workplaces: A Small Wins Approach to Organizational Change." *Gender and Society* 31(6): 725–50.

Correll, Shelley J., and Cecilia L. Ridgeway. 2003. "Expectation States Theory." In *The Handbook of Social Psychology*, edited by John DeLamater. New York: Kluwer Academic/Plenum.

Correll, Shelley J., Cecilia L. Ridgeway, Ezar W. Zuckerman, Sharon Jank, Sara Jordan-Bloch, and Sandra Nakagawa. 2017. "It's the Conventional Thought That Counts: How Third-Order Inference Produces Status Advantage." *American Sociological Review* 82(2): 297–327.

Cotter, David, Joan M. Hermsen, and Reeve Vanneman. 2011. "The End of the Gender Revolution? Gender Role Attitudes from 1977 to 2008." *American Journal of Sociology* 117(1): 259–89.

Craig, Maureen A., and Jennifer Richeson. 2014. "'On the Precipice of a Majority-Minority America': Perceived Status Threat from the Racial Demographic Shift Affects White Americans' Political Ideology." *Psychological Science* 25(6): 1189–97.

Cramer, Katherine J. 2016. *The Politics of Resentment: Rural Consciousness in Wisconsin and the Rise of Scott Walker*. Chicago: University of Chicago Press.

Cuddy, Amy J., Susan T. Fiske, and Peter Glick. 2007. "The BIAS Map: Behaviors from Intergroup Affect and Stereotypes." *Journal of Personality and Social Psychology* 92(4): 631–48.

Davidson, Marilyn, and Ronald J. Burke. 2000. "Sex Discrimination in Simulated Employment Contexts." *Journal of Vocational Behavior* 56(2): 225–48.

DiMaggio, Paul. 2012. "Sociological Perspectives on the Face-to-Face Enactment of Class Distinction." In *Facing Social Class: How Societal Rank Influences Interaction*, edited by Susan T. Fiske and Hazel Rose Markus. New York: Russell Sage Foundation.

DiPrete, Thomas A., Andrew Gelman, Julien Teitler, Tian Zheng, and Tyler McCormick. 2011. "Segregation in Social Networks Based on Acquaintanceship and Trust." *American Journal of Sociology* 116(4): 1234–83.

DiTomaso, Nancy. 2013. *The American Nondilemma: Racial Inequality without Racism*. New York: Russell Sage Foundation.

DiTomaso, Nancy, Corinne Post, and Rochelle Parks-Yancy. 2007. "Workforce Diversity and Inequality: Power, Status, and Numbers." *Annual Review of Sociology* 33: 473–501.

Dover, Tessa L., Brenda Major, and Cheryl R. Kaiser. 2016. "Members of High Status Groups Are Threatened by Pro-Diversity Organizational Messages." *Journal of Experimental Social Psychology* 62: 58–67.

Dovidio, John F., Clifford E. Brown, Karen Heltman, Steve L. Ellyson, and Caroline F. Keating. 1988. "Power Displays between Women and Men in Discussions of Gender Linked Tasks: A Multichannel Study." *Journal of Personality and Social Psychology* 55(4): 580–87.

Dovidio, John F., and Samuel L. Gaertner. 2010. "Intergroup Bias." In *The Handbook of Social Psychology*, vol. 2, edited by Susan T. Fiske, Daniel T. Gilbert, and Gardner Lindzey. Hoboken, N.J.: John Wiley & Sons.

Driskell, James E., and Brian Mullen. 1990. "Status, Expectations, and Behavior: A Meta-analytic Review and Test of the Theory." *Personality and Social Psychology Bulletin* 16(3): 541–53.

Durante, Federica, Courtney Bearns Tablante, and Susan T. Fiske. 2017. "Poor but Warm, Rich but Cold (and Competent): Social Classes in the Stereotype Content Model." *Journal of Social Issues* 73(1): 138–57.

Eagly, Alice H., and Linda L. Carli. 2007. *Through the Labyrinth: The Truth about How Women Become Leaders.* Cambridge, Mass.: Harvard Business School Press.

Ely, Robin J., and Debra E. Meyerson. 2000. "Theories of Gender in Organizations: A New Approach to Organizational Analysis and Change." *Research in Organizational Behavior* 22: 103–51.

Emerson, Richard M. 1962. "Power-Dependence Relations." *American Sociological Review* 27(1): 31–41.

———. 1972. "Exchange Theory, Part I: A Psychological Basis for Social Exchange." In *Sociological Theories in Progress*, vol. 2, edited by Joseph Berger, Morris Zelditch, and Bo Anderson. Boston: Houghton Mifflin.

England, Paula. 2010. "The Gender Revolution: Uneven and Stalled." *Gender and Society* 24(2): 149–66.

Espeland, Wendy Nelson, and Michael Sauder. 2007. "Rankings and Reactivity: How Public Measures Recreate Social Worlds." *American Journal of Sociology* 113(1): 1–40.

———. 2016. *Engines of Anxiety: Academic Rankings, Reputation, and Accountability.* New York: Russell Sage Foundation.

Festinger, Leon. 1954. "A Theory of Social Comparison Processes." *Human Relations* 7(2): 117–40.

Fisek, M. Hamit, Joseph Berger, and Robert Z. Norman. 1991. "Participation in Heterogeneous and Homogeneous Groups: A Theoretical Integration." *American Journal of Sociology* 97(1): 114–42.

Fiske, Susan T. 2010. "Interpersonal Stratification: Status, Power, and Subordination." In *The Handbook of Social Psychology*, vol. 2, edited by Susan T. Fiske, Daniel T. Gilbert, and Gardner Lindzey. Hoboken, N.J.: John Wiley & Sons.

———. 2011. *Envy Up, Scorn Down: How Status Divides Us.* New York: Russell Sage Foundation.

Fiske, Susan T., Amy J. C. Cuddy, Peter Glick, and Jun Xu. 2002. "A Model of (Often Mixed) Stereotype Content: Competence and Warmth Respectively Follow from Perceived Status and Competition." *Journal of Personality and Social Psychology* 82(6): 878–902.

Fiske, Susan T., Monica Lin, and Steven Neuberg. 1999. "The Continuum Model: Ten Years Later." In *Dual Process Theories in Social Psychology*, edited by Shelly Chaiken and Yaacov Trope. New York: Guilford.

Fiske, Susan T., and Shelley Taylor. 2008. *Social Cognition: From Brain to Culture.* New York: McGraw-Hill.

Foschi, Martha. 1996. "Double Standards in the Evaluation of Men and Women." *Social Psychology Quarterly* 59(3): 237–54.

———. 2000. "Double Standards for Competence: Theory and Research." *Annual Review of Sociology* 26: 21–42.

Frank, Robert H. 1985. *Choosing the Right Pond: Human Behavior and the Quest for Status.* New York: Oxford University Press.

Friesen, Justin P., Aaron C. Kay, Richard P. Eibach, and Adam D. Galinsky. 2014. "Seeking Structure in Social Organization: Compensatory Control and the Psychological Advantages of Hierarchy." *Journal of Personality and Social Psychology* 106(4): 590–609.

Garg, Nikhil, Londa Schiebinger, Dan Jurafsky, and James Zou. 2018. "Word Embeddings Quantify 100 Years of Gender and Ethnic Stereotypes." *Proceedings of the National Academy of Sciences* 115(16): E3635–44.

Giddens, Anthony. 1984. *The Constitution of Society: Outline of the Theory of Structuration.* Berkeley: University of California Press.

Gidron, Noam, and Peter A. Hall. 2017. "The Politics of Social Status: Economic and Cultural Roots of the Populist Right." *British Journal of Sociology* 68(S1): S57–84.

Glick, Peter, and Susan T. Fiske. 1999. "Gender, Power Dynamics, and Social Interaction." In *Revisioning Gender*, edited by Myra Marx Ferree, Judith Lorber, and Beth B. Hess. Thousand Oaks, Calif.: Sage Publications.

Goar, Carla, and Jane Sell. 2005. "Using Task Definition to Modify Racial Inequality within Task Groups." *Sociological Quarterly* 46(3): 525–43.

Goffman, Erving. 1956. "The Nature of Deference and Demeanor." *American Anthropologist* 58(3): 473–502.

———. 1967. *Interaction Ritual: Essays on Face-to-Face Behavior.* Garden City, N.Y.: Doubleday.

Goode, William J. 1978. *The Celebration of Heroes: Prestige as a Control System.* Berkeley: University of California Press.

Gould, Roger V. 2002. "The Origins of Status Hierarchies: A Formal Theory and Empirical Test." *American Journal of Sociology* 107(5): 1143–78.

Griskevicius, Vladus, Joshua M. Tybur, Steven W. Gangestad, Elaine F. Perea, Jennesa R. Shapiro, and Douglas T. Kenrick. 2009. "Aggress to Impress: Hostility as an Evolved Context-Dependent Strategy." *Journal of Personality and Social Psychology* 96(5): 980–94.

Hahl, Oliver, and Ezra W. Zuckerman. 2014. "The Denigration of Heroes? How the Status Attainment Process Shapes Attributions of Considerateness and Authenticity." *American Journal of Sociology* 120(2): 504–54.

Hahl, Oliver, Ezra W. Zuckerman, and Minjae Kim. 2017. "Why Elites Love Authentic Lowbrow Culture: Overcoming High-Status Denigration with Outsider Art." *American Sociological Review* 82(4): 828–56.

Halevy, Nir, Eileen Y. Chou, Taya R. Cohen, and Robert W. Livingston. 2012. "Status Conferral in Intergroup Social Dilemmas: Behavioral Antecedents and Consequences of Prestige and Dominance." *Journal of Personality and Social Psychology* 102(2): 351–66.

Halevy, Nir, Eileen Y. Chou, and Adam D. Galinsky. 2011. "A Functional Model of Hierarchy: Why, How, and When Vertical Differentiation Enhances Group Performance." *Organizational Psychology Review* 1(1): 32–52.

Hamilton, David L., Jacqueline M. Chen, Deborah M. Ko, Lauren Winczewski, Ishani Banerji, and Joel A. Thurston. 2015. "Sowing the Seeds of Stereotypes: Spontaneous Inferences about Groups." *Journal of Personality and Social Psychology* 109(4): 569–88.

Hardin, Curtis D., and Tory E. Higgins. 1996. "Shared Reality: How Social Verification Makes the Subjective Objective." In *Handbook of Motivation and Cognition*, vol. 3, *The Interpersonal Context*, edited by Richard M. Sorrentino and Tory E. Higgins. New York: Guilford.

Hardy, Charlie L., and Mark van Vugt. 2006. "Nice Guys Finish First: The Competitive Altruism Hypothesis." *Personality and Social Psychology Bulletin* 32(10): 1402–13.

Haslam, Nick, Brock Bastian, Paul Bain, and Yoshihisa Kashima. 2006. "Psychological Essentialism, Implicit Theory, and Intergroup Relations." *Group Processes and Intergroup Relations* 9(1): 63–76.

Hays, Nicholas A., and Corinne Bendersky. 2015. "Not All Inequality Is Created Equal: Effects of Status versus Power Hierarchies on Competition for Upward Mobility." *Journal of Personality and Social Psychology* 108(6): 867–82.

Hays, Nicholas A., and Steven L. Blader. 2017. "To Give or Not to Give? Interactive Effects of Status and Legitimacy on Generosity." *Journal of Personality and Social Psychology* 112(1): 17–38.

Hays, Nicholas A., and Lindred L. Greer. 2016. "Satiability of Power and Status." Paper presented at the annual meeting of the Society for Personality and Social Psychology. San Diego, Calif. (January).

Heinicke, Christoph, and Robert F. Bales. 1953. "Developmental Trends in the Structure of Small Groups." *Sociometry* 16(1): 7–38.

Henrich, Joseph, and Francisco J. Gil-White. 2001. "The Evolution of Prestige: Freely Conferred Deference as a Mechanism for Enhancing the Benefits of Cultural Transmission." *Evolution and Human Behavior* 22(3): 165–96.

Hochschild, Arlie R. 2016. *Strangers in Their Own Land: Anger and Mourning on the American Right.* New York: New Press.

Hogg, Michael, Dominic Abrams, and Marilynn Brewer. 2017. "Social Identity: The Role of the Self in Group Processes and Intergroup Relations." *Group Processes and Intergroup Relations* 20(5): 570–81.

Homans, George Caspar. 1951. *The Human Group.* New York: Routledge.

Horne, Christine. 2004. "Collective Benefits, Exchange Interests, and Norm Enforcement." *Social Forces* 82(3): 1037–62.

Huber, Joan. 2007. *On the Origins of Gender Inequality.* Boulder, Colo.: Paradigm Publishers.

Hysom, Stuart J. 2009. "Status Valued Goal Objects and Performance Expectations." *Social Forces* 87(3): 1623–48.

Hysom, Stuart J., Murray Webster Jr., and Lisa Slattery Walker. 2015. "Expectations, Status Value, and Group Structure." *Sociological Perspectives* 58(4): 554–69.

Ito, Tiffany A., and Geoffrey R. Urland. 2003. "Race and Gender on the Brain: Electrocortical Measures of Attention to the Race and Gender of Multiply Categorizable Individuals." *Journal of Personality and Social Psychology* 85(4): 616–26.

Jackman, Mary R. 1994. *The Velvet Glove: Paternalism and Conflict in Gender, Class, and Race Relations.* Berkeley: University of California Press.

Johnson, Cathryn, Timothy Dowd, and Cecilia Ridgeway. 2006. "Legitimacy as a Social Process." *Annual Review of Sociology* 32: 53–78.

Johnson, Kerri L., Jonathan B. Freeman, and Kristin Pauker. 2012. "Race Is Gendered: How Covarying Phenotypes and Stereotypes Bias Sex Categorization." *Journal of Personality and Social Psychology* 102(1): 116–31.

Jost, John T., and Mahzarin R. Banaji. 1994. "The Role of Stereotyping in System-Justification and the Production of False Consciousness." *British Journal of Social Psychology* 33(1): 1–27.

Jost, John T., Mahzarin R. Banaji, and Brian A. Nosek. 2004. "A Decade of System Justification Theory: Accumulated Evidence of Conscious and Unconscious Bolstering of the Status Quo." *Political Psychology* 25(6): 881–919.

Jost, John T., and Diana Burgess. 2000. "Attitudinal Ambivalence and the Conflict between Group and System Justification in Low Status Groups." *Personality and Social Psychology Bulletin* 26(3): 293–305.

Judd, Charles M., Laurie James-Hawkins, Vincent Yzerbyt, and Yoshihisa Kashima. 2005. "Fundamental Dimensions of Social Judgment: Understanding the Relations between Judgments of Competence and Warmth." *Journal of Personality and Social Psychology* 89(6): 899–913.

Kahn, Shamus Rahman. 2011. *Privilege: The Making of an Adolescent Elite at St. Paul's School.* Princeton, N.J.: Princeton University Press.

Kalkhoff, Will, C. Wesley Younts, and Lisa Troyer. 2011. "Do Others' Views of Us Transfer to New Groups and Tasks? An Expectation States Approach." *Social Psychology Quarterly* 74(3): 267–90.

Kennedy, Jessica A., Cameron Anderson, and Don A. Moore. 2013. "When Overconfidence Is Revealed to Others: Testing the Status-Enhancement Theory of Overconfidence." *Organizational Behavior and Human Decision Processes* 122(2): 266–79.

Kilduff, Gavin, Cameron Anderson, and Rob Willer. 2013. "Consensus and Contribution: Shared Status Hierarchies Promote Group Success." Working Paper 145-13. Berkeley, Calif.: Institute for Research on Labor and Employment.

Kilduff, Gavin, and Adam Galinsky. 2013. "From the Ephemeral to the Enduring: How Approach-Oriented Mindsets Lead to Greater Status." *Journal of Personality and Social Psychology* 105(5): 816–31.

Kilduff, Gavin, Robb Willer, and Cameron Anderson. 2016. "Hierarchy and Its Discontents: Status Disagreement Leads to Withdrawal of Contribution and Lower Group Performance." *Organization Science* 27(2): 373–90.

Kluegel, James R., and Elliott R. Smith. 1986. *Beliefs about Inequality: Americans' Views of What Is and What Ought to Be.* Edison, N.J.: Aldine Transaction.

Korver-Glenn, Elizabeth. 2018. "Compounding Inequalities: How Racial Stereotypes and Discrimination Accumulate across the Stages of Housing Exchange." *American Sociological Review* 83(4): 627–56.

Krauss, Michael, Paul K. Piff, Rodolfo Mendoza-Denton, Michelle L. Reinschmidt, and Dacher Keltner. 2012. "Social Class, Solipsism, Contextualism: How the Rich Are Different from the Poor." *Psychological Review* 119(3): 546–72.

Kray, Laura J., Laura Howland, Alexandra G. Russell, and Lauren M. Jackman. 2017. "The Effects of Implicit Gender Role Theories on Gender System Justification: Fixed Beliefs Strengthen Masculinity to Preserve the Status Quo." *Journal of Personality and Social Psychology* 112(1): 98–115.

Lamont, Michèle. 2012. "Toward a Comparative Sociology of Valuation and Evaluation." *Annual Review of Sociology* 38: 201–21.

Lamont, Michèle, and Marcel Fournier. 1992. *Cultivating Differences: Symbolic Boundaries and the Making of Inequality.* Chicago: University of Chicago Press.

Lareau, Annette. 2002. "Invisible Inequality: Social Class and Childrearing in Black Families and White Families." *American Sociological Review* 67(5): 747–76.

———. 2011. *Unequal Childhoods: Race, Class, and Family Life*, 2nd ed. Berkeley: University of California Press.

Leary, Mark R., Katrina P. Jongman-Sereno, and Kate J. Diebels. 2014. "The Pursuit of Status: A Self-Presentational Perspective on the Quest for Social Value." In *The Psychology of Social Status*, edited by Joey T. Cheng, Jessica L. Tracy, and Cameron Anderson. New York: Springer.

Lee, Margaret T., and Richard Ofshe. 1981. "The Impact of Behavioral Style and Status Characteristics on Social Influence: A Test of Two Competing Theories." *Social Psychology Quarterly* 44(2): 73–82.

Livingston, Robert W., and Nicholas A. Pearce. 2009. "The Teddy-Bear Effect: Does Having a Baby Face Benefit Black Chief Executive Officers?" *Psychological Science* 20(10): 1229–36.

Livingston, Robert W., Ashleigh S. Rosette, and Ella F. Washington. 2012. "Can an Agentic Black Woman Get Ahead? The Impact of Race and Interpersonal Dominance on Perceptions of Female Leaders." *Psychological Science* 23(4): 354–58.

Lovaglia, Michael J., and Jeffrey A. Houser. 1996. "Emotional Reactions and Status in Groups." *American Sociological Review* 61(5): 864–80.

Lovaglia, Michael J., Jeffrey W. Lucas, Jeffrey A. Houser, Shane R. Thye, and Barry Markovsky. 1998. "Status Processes and Mental Ability Test Scores." *American Journal of Sociology* 104(1): 195–228.

Love, Tony P., and Jenny L. Davis. 2014. "The Effect of Status on Role-Taking Accuracy." *American Sociological Review* 79(5): 848–65.

Lutfey, Karen, and Jeremy Freese. 2005. "Toward Some Fundamentals of Fundamental Causality: Socioeconomic Status and Health in the Routine Clinic Visit for Diabetes." *American Journal of Sociology* 110(5): 1326–72.

Lynn, Freda B., Joel M. Podolny, and Lin Tao. 2009. "A Sociological (De)Construction of the Relationship between Status and Quality." *American Journal of Sociology* 115(3): 755–804.

Magee, Joe C., and Adam Galinsky. 2008. "Social Hierarchy: The Self-Reinforcing Nature of Power and Status." *Academy of Management Annals* 2(1): 351–98.

Major, Brenda, and Cheryl R. Kaiser. 2017. "Ideology and the Maintenance of Group Inequality." *Group Processes and Intergroup Relations* 20(5): 582–92.

Maner, Jon K., and Nicole L. Mead. 2010. "The Essential Tension between Leadership and Power: When Leaders Sacrifice Group Goals for the Sake of Self-Interest." *Journal of Personality and Social Psychology* 99(3): 482–97.

Mark, Noah, Lynn Smith-Lovin, and Cecilia L. Ridgeway. 2009. "Why Do Nominal Characteristics Acquire Status Value? A Minimal Explanation for Status Construction." *American Journal of Sociology* 115(3): 832–62.

Massey, Douglas S., Jonathan Rothwell, and Thurston Domina. 2009. "Changing Bases of Segregation in the United States." *Annals of the American Academy of Political and Social Science* 626(1): 74–90.

Mazur, Allan. 1973. "A Cross-Species Comparison of Status in Small Established Groups." *American Sociological Review* 38(5): 513–30.

———. 1985. "A Biosocial Model of Status in Face-to-Face Primate Groups." *Social Forces* 64(2): 377–402.

———. 2005. *Biosociology of Dominance and Deference*. Lanham, Md.: Rowman & Littlefield.

McCall, George J. 2013. "Interactional Perspectives in Social Psychology." In *The Handbook of Social Psychology*, 2nd ed., edited by John Delamater and Amanda Ward. New York: Springer.

McPherson, Miller, Lynn Smith-Lovin, and James M. Cook. 2001. "Birds of a Feather: Homophily in Social Networks." *Annual Review of Sociology* 27: 415–44.

Miller, Dale T. 2001. "Disrespect and the Experience of Injustice." *Annual Review of Psychology* 52(1): 527–53.

Miller, Dale T., and William Turnbull. 1986. "Expectancies and Interpersonal Processes." *Annual Review of Psychology* 37: 233–56.

Moore, Monica M. 1985. "Nonverbal Courtship Patterns in Women: Context and Consequences." *Ethology and Sociobiology* 6(4): 237–47.

Morning, Ann. 2011. *The Nature of Race: How Scientists Think and Teach about Human Difference*. Berkeley: University of California Press.

Moss-Racusin, Corrine A., John F. Dovidio, Victoria L. Brescoll, Mark J. Graham, and Jo Handelsman. 2012. "Science Faculty's Subtle Gender Biases Favor Male Students." *Proceedings of the National Academy of Sciences of the United States of America* 109(41): 16474–79.

Mutz, Diana C. 2018. "Status Threat, Not Economic Hardship, Explains the 2016 Presidential Vote." *Proceedings of the National Academy of Sciences of the United States of America* 115(19): E4330–39.

Nelson, Robert L., and William P. Bridges. 1999. *Legalizing Gender Inequality: Courts, Markets, and Unequal Pay for Women in America*. New York: Cambridge University Press.

Owens, Timothy. 2013. "Self and Self-Concept." In *The Handbook of Social Psychology*, 2nd ed., edited by John Delamater and Amanda Ward. New York: Springer.

Pedulla, David S. 2018. "How Race and Unemployment Shape Labor Market Opportunities: Additive, Amplified, or Muted Effects?" *Social Forces* 96(4): 1477–1506.

Podolny, Joel M. 2005. *Status Signals: A Sociological Study of Market Competition*. Princeton, N.J.: Princeton University Press.

Podolny, Joel M., and Damon J. Phillips. 1996. "The Dynamics of Organizational Status." *Industrial and Corporate Change* 5(2): 453–71.

Prentice, Deborah A., and Dale T. Miller. 1993. "Pluralistic Ignorance and Alcohol Use on Campus: Some Consequences of Misperceiving the Social Norm." *Journal of Personality and Social Psychology* 64(2): 243–56.

———. 1996. "Pluralistic Ignorance and the Perpetuation of Social Norms by Unwitting Actors." *Advances in Experimental Social Psychology* 28: 161–209.

———. 2006. "Essentializing Differences between Women and Men." *Psychological Science* 17(2): 129–35.

———. 2007. "Psychological Essentialism of Human Categories." *Current Directions in Psychological Science* 16(4): 202–6.

Purdie-Vaughns, Valerie, and Richard P. Eibach. 2008. "Intersectional Invisibility: The Ideological Sources and Social Consequences of Non-Prototypicality." *Sex Roles* 59(5): 377–91.

Quadlin, Natasha. 2018. "The Mark of a Woman's Record: Gender and Academic Performance in Hiring." *American Sociological Review* 83(2): 331–60.

Reskin, Barbara. 2003. "Including Mechanisms in Our Models of Ascriptive Inequality." *American Sociological Review* 68(1): 1–21.

———. 2012. "The Race Discrimination System." *Annual Review of Sociology* 38: 17–35.

Ridgeway, Cecilia L. 1981. "Nonconformity, Competence, and Influence in Groups: A Test of Two Theories." *American Sociological Review* 46(3): 333–47.

———. 1982. "Status in Groups: The Importance of Motivation." *American Sociological Review* 47(1): 76–88.

———. 1984. "Dominance, Performance, and Status in Groups: A Theoretical Analysis." In *Advances in Group Processes: Theory and Research*, vol. 1, edited by Edward Lawler. Greenwich, Conn.: JAI Press.

———. 1987. "Nonverbal Behavior, Dominance, and the Basis of Status in Task Groups." *American Sociological Review* 52(5): 683–94.

———. 1991. "The Social Construction of Status Value: Gender and Other Nominal Characteristics." *Social Forces* 70(2): 367–86.

———. 1993. "Legitimacy, Status, and Dominance Behavior in Groups" In *Conflict between People and Groups: Causes, Processes, and Resolutions*, edited by Stephen Worchel and Jeffry A. Simpson. Chicago: Nelson-Hall.

———. 2011. *Framed by Gender: How Gender Inequality Persists in the Modern World.* New York: Oxford University Press.

———. 2014. "Why Status Matters for Inequality." *American Sociological Review* 79(1): 1–16.

———. 2018. "Status Construction Theory." In *Contemporary Social Psychological Theories*, 2nd ed., edited by Peter J. Burke. Stanford, Calif.: Stanford University Press.

Ridgeway, Cecilia L., Kristen Backor, Yan E. Li, Justine E. Tinkler, and Kristan G. Erickson. 2009. "How Easily Does a Social Difference Become a Status Distinction? Gender Matters." *American Sociological Review* 74(1): 44–62.

Ridgeway, Cecilia L., and James W. Balkwell. 1997. "Group Processes and the Diffusion of Status Beliefs." *Social Psychology Quarterly* 60(1): 14–31.

Ridgeway, Cecilia L., and Joseph Berger. 1986. "Expectations, Legitimation, and Dominance Behavior in Task Groups." *American Sociological Review* 51(5): 603–17.

Ridgeway, Cecilia L., Joseph Berger, and LeRoy Smith. 1985. "Nonverbal Cues and Status: An Expectation States Approach." *American Journal of Sociology* 90(5): 955–78.

Ridgeway, Cecilia L., Elizabeth Heger Boyle, Kathy J. Kuipers, and Dawn T. Robinson. 1998. "How Do Status Beliefs Develop? The Role of Resources and Interactional Experience." *American Sociological Review* 63(3): 331–50.

Ridgeway, Cecilia L., and Shelley J. Correll. 2004. "Motherhood as a Status Characteristic." *Journal of Social Issues* 60(4): 683–700.

———. 2006. "Consensus and the Creation of Status Beliefs." *Social Forces* 85(1): 431–53.

Ridgeway, Cecilia L., and David Diekema. 1989. "Dominance and Collective Hierarchy Formation in Male and Female Task Groups." *American Sociological Review* 54(1): 79–93.

Ridgeway, Cecilia L., and Kristan Glasgow Erickson. 2000. "Creating and Spreading Status Beliefs." *American Journal of Sociology* 106(3): 579–615.

Ridgeway, Cecilia L., and Susan R. Fisk. 2012. "Class Rules, Status Dynamics, and Gateway Interactions." In *Facing Social Class: How Societal Rank Influences Interaction*, edited by Susan T. Fiske and Hazel Rose Markus. New York: Russell Sage Foundation.

Ridgeway, Cecilia L., and Cathryn Johnson. 1990. "What Is the Relationship between Socio-emotional Behavior and Status in Task Groups?" *American Journal of Sociology* 95(5): 1189–1212.

Ridgeway, Cecilia L., Cathryn Johnson, and David Diekema. 1994. "External Status, Legitimacy, and Compliance in Male and Female Groups." *Social Forces* 72(4): 1051–77.

Ridgeway, Cecilia L., and Tamar Kricheli-Katz. 2013. "Intersecting Cultural Beliefs in Social Relations: Gender, Race, and Class Binds and Freedoms." *Gender and Society* 27(3): 294–318.

Ridgeway, Cecilia L., and Sandra Nakagawa. 2014. "Status." In *Handbook of the Social Psychology of Inequality*, edited by Jane McLeod, Edward J. Lawler, and Michael Schwalbe. New York: Springer.

Ridgeway, Cecilia L., and Sandra Nakagawa. 2017. "Is Deference the Price of Being Seen as Reasonable? How Status Hierarchies Incentivize Acceptance of Low Status." *Social Psychology Quarterly* 80(2): 132–52.

Risman, Barbara J. 2004. "Gender as a Social Structure: Theory Wrestling with Activism." *Gender and Society* 18(4): 429–50.

———. 2018. *Where the Millennials Will Take Us: A New Generation Wrestles with the Gender Structure*. New York: Oxford University Press.

Rivera, Lauren A. 2015. *Pedigree: How Elite Students Get Elite Jobs*. Princeton, N.J.: Princeton University Press.

Rivera, Lauren, and András Tilcsik. 2016. "Class Advantage, Commitment Penalty: The Gendered Effect of Social Class Signals in an Elite Labor Market." *American Sociological Review* 81(6): 1097–1131.

Rosette, Ashleigh S., and Robert W. Livingston. 2012. "Failure Is Not an Option for Black Women: Effects of Organizational Performance on Leaders with Single Versus Dual-Subordinate Identities." *Journal of Experimental Social Psychology* 48(5): 1162–67.

Rucker, Derek D., Adam D. Galinsky, and Joe C. Magee. 2018. "The Agentic-Communal Model of Advantage and Disadvantage: How Inequality Produces Similarities in the Psychology of Power, Social Class, Gender, and Race." *Advances in Experimental Social Psychology* 58: 71–125.

Rudman, Laurie A., Corinne A. Moss-Racusin, Julie E. Phelan, and Sanne Nauts. 2012. "Status Incongruity and Backlash Effects: Defending the Gender Hierarchy Motivates Prejudice against Female Leaders." *Journal of Experimental Social Psychology* 48(1): 165–79.

Saperstein, Aliya, and Andrew Penner. 2012. "Racial Fluidity and Inequality in the United States." *American Journal of Sociology* 118(3): 676–727.

Sauder, Michael. 2006. "Third Parties and Status Position: How the Characteristics of Status Systems Matter." *Theory and Society* 35(3): 299–321.

Sauder, Michael, Freda Lynn, and Joel M. Podolny. 2012. "Status: Insights from Organizational Sociology." *Annual Review of Sociology* 38: 267–83.

Schelling, Thomas C. 1960. *The Strategy of Conflict.* Cambridge, Mass.: Harvard University Press.

Schilt, Kristen. 2011. *Just One of the Guys? Transgender Men and the Persistence of Gender Inequality.* Chicago: University of Chicago Press.

Schmader, Toni, Michael Johns, and Chad Forbes. 2008. "An Integrated Process Model of Stereotype Threat Effects on Performance." *Psychological Review* 115(2): 336–56.

Schwalbe, Michael, and Heather Shay. 2014. "Dramaturgy and Dominance." In *Handbook of the Social Psychology of Inequality,* edited by Jane McLeod, Edward J. Lawler, and Michael Schwalbe. New York: Springer.

Seachrist, Gretchen B., and Charles Stangor. 2001. "Perceived Consensus Influences Intergroup Behavior and Stereotype Accessibility." *Journal of Personality and Social Psychology* 80(4): 645–54.

Sesko, Amanda K., and Monica Biernat. 2010. "Prototypes of Race and Gender: The Invisibility of Black Women." *Journal of Experimental Social Psychology* 46(2): 356–60.

Sewell, William H. 1992. "A Theory of Structure: Duality, Agency, and Transformation." *American Journal of Sociology* 98(1): 1–29.

Seyfarth, Robert M., and Dorothy L. Cheney. 2013. "Social Relationships, Social Cognition, and the Evolution of Mind in Primates." In *Comprehensive Handbook of Psychology,* vol. 3, *Biological Psychology and Neuroscience,* edited by Randy J. Nelson and Sheri Mizumor. New York: John Wiley & Sons.

Shackleford, Susan, Wendy Wood, and Stephen Worchel. 1996. "Behavioral Styles and the Influence of Women in Mixed Sex Groups." *Social Psychology Quarterly* 59(3): 284–93.

Sharkey, Amanda J. 2014. "Categories and Organizational Status: The Role of Industry Status in Response to Organizational Deviance." *American Journal of Sociology* 119(5): 1380–1433.

Sherman, Jennifer. 2009. *Those Who Work, Those Who Don't: Poverty, Morality, and Family in Rural America.* Minneapolis: University of Minnesota Press.

Shih, Margaret, Todd L. Pittinsky, and Nalini Ambady. 1999. "Stereotype Susceptibility: Identity Salience and Shifts in Quantitative Performance." *Psychological Science* 10(1): 80–83.

Simcoe, Timothy S., and David M. Waguespack. 2011. "Status, Quality, and Attention: What's in a (Missing) Name?" *Management Science* 57(2): 274–90.

Simpson, Brent, Robb Willer, and Cecilia L. Ridgeway. 2012. "Status Hierarchies and the Organization of Collective Action." *Sociological Theory* 30(3): 149–66.

Smith, Heather J., Tom R. Tyler, and Yuen J. Huo. 2003. "Interpersonal Treatment, Social Identity, and Organizational Behavior." In *Social Identity at Work: Developing Theory for Organizational Work,* edited by S. Alexander Haslam, Daan van Knippenberg, Michael J. Platow, and Naomi Ellemers. Philadelphia: Psychology Press.

Steckler, Conor M., and Jessica L. Tracy. 2014. "The Emotional Underpinnings of Social Status." In *The Psychology of Social Status,* edited by Joey T. Cheng, Jessica L. Tracy, and Cameron Anderson. New York: Springer.

Steele, Claude M., and Joshua Aronson. 1995. "Stereotype Threat and Intellectual Task Performance of African Americans." *Journal of Personality and Social Psychology* 69(5): 797–811.

Stephens, Nicole M., Stephanie A. Fryberg, Hazel R. Markus, Camille S. Johnson, and Rebecca Covarrubias. 2012. "Unseen Disadvantage: How American Universities' Focus on Independence Undermines the Academic Performance of First-Generation College Students." *Journal of Personality and Social Psychology* 102(6): 1178–97.

Stewart, Daniel. 2005. "Social Status in an Open-Source Community." *American Sociological Review* 70(5): 823–42.

Stewart, Penni A., and James C. Moore Jr. 1992. "Wage Disparities and Performance Expectations." *Social Psychology Quarterly* 55(1): 78–85.

Strodtbeck, Fred L., Rita M. James, and Charles Hawkins. 1957. "Social Status and Jury Deliberations." *American Sociological Review* 22(6): 713–19.

Stuber, Jenny M. 2006. "Talk of Class: The Discursive Repertoires of White Working- and Upper-Middle-Class College Students." *Journal of Contemporary Ethnography* 35(3): 285–318.

Swencionis, Jillian K., and Susan T. Fiske. 2018. "Cross-Status Interactions: Concerns and Consequences." *Social Cognition* 36(1): 78–105.

Tajfel, Henri, and John C. Turner. 1986. "The Social Identity Theory of Inter-Group Behavior." In *Psychology of Inter-Group Relations*, edited by Stephen Worchel and William G. Austin. Chicago: Nelson-Hall.

Thomas, Kyle A., Peter DeScioli, Omare Sultan Haque, and Steven Pinker. 2014. "The Psychology of Coordination and Common Knowledge." *Journal of Personality and Social Psychology* 107(4): 657–76.

Thye, Shane R. 2000. "A Status Value Theory of Power in Exchange Relations." *American Sociological Review* 65(3): 407–43.

Tiedens, Larissa Z., Phoebe C. Ellsworth, and Batja Mesquita. 2000. "Sentimental Stereotypes: Emotional Expectations for High- and Low-Status Group Members." *Personality and Social Psychology Bulletin* 26(5): 560–75.

Tiedens, Larissa Z., and Alison R. Fragale. 2003. "Power Moves: Complementarity in Dominant and Submissive Nonverbal Behavior." *Journal of Personality and Social Psychology* 84(3): 558–68.

Tilly, Charles. 1998. *Durable Inequality.* Berkeley: University of California Press.

Tinkler, Justine, Jun Zhao, Yan Li, and Cecilia Ridgeway. 2019. "Honorary Whites? Asian Women and the Dominance Penalty." *Socius* 5(April): 1–13.

Tomaskovic-Devey, Donald. 2014. "The Relational Generation of Workplace Inequalities." *Social Currents* 1(1): 51–73.

Torelli, Carlos J., Lisa M. Leslie, Jennifer L. Stoner, and Raquel Puente, 2014. "Cultural Determinants of Status: Implications for Workplace Evaluations and Behaviors." *Organizational Behavior and Human Decision Processes* 123(1): 34–48.

Troyer, Lisa, and C. Wesley Younts. 1997. "Whose Expectations Matter? The Relative Power of First- and Second-Order Expectations in Determining Social Influence." *American Journal of Sociology* 103(3): 692–732.

Turco, Catherine J. 2010. "Cultural Foundations of Tokenism: Evidence from the Leveraged Buyout Industry." *American Sociological Review* 75(6): 894–913.

Turco, Catherine J., and Ezra W. Zuckerman. 2017. "Verstehen for Sociology: Comment on Watts." *American Journal of Sociology* 122(4): 1272–91.

Uhlmann, Eric L., and Geoffrey L. Cohen. 2005. "Constructed Criteria: Redefining Merit to Justify Discrimination." *Psychological Science* 16(6): 474–80.

Van Vugt, Mark, Robert Hogan, and Robert B. Kaiser. 2008. "Leadership, Followership, and Evolution: Some Lessons from the Past." *American Psychologist* 63(3): 182–96.

Van Vugt, Mark, Sarah F. Jepson, Claire M. Hart, and David De Cremer. 2004. "Autocratic Leadership in Social Dilemmas: A Threat to Group Stability." *Journal of Experimental Social Psychology* 40(1): 1–13.

Van Vugt, Mark, and Joshua M. Tybur. 2016. "The Evolutionary Foundations of Hierarchy: Status, Dominance, Prestige, and Leadership." In *The Handbook of Evolutionary Psychology*, 2nd ed., edited by David M. Buss. New York: John Wiley & Sons.

Vance, J. D. 2016. *Hillbilly Elegy: A Memoir of a Family and Culture in Crisis.* New York: HarperCollins.

Veblen, Thorstein. 1899. *The Theory of the Leisure Class.* New York: New American Library, 1953.

Wagner, David G., and Joseph Berger. 1997. "Gender and Interpersonal Task Behaviors: Status Expectation Accounts." *Sociological Perspectives* 40(1): 1–32.

Walker, Henry A. 2014. "Legitimacy and Inequality." In *Handbook of the Social Psychology of Inequality*, edited by Jane D. McLeod, Edward J. Lawler, and Michael Schwalbe. New York: Springer.

Weber, Max. 1918. *Economy and Society*, edited by Guenther Roth and Claus Wittich, translated by Ephraim Frischoff. New York: Bedminster, 1968.

Webster, Murray, Jr., and Stuart J. Hysom. 1998. "Creating Status Characteristics." *American Sociological Review* 63(3): 351–79.

Webster, Murray, Jr., and Lisa S. Rashotte. 2010. "Behavior, Expectations, and Status." *Social Forces* 88(3): 1021–49.

Webster, Murray, Jr., and Joseph M. Whitmeyer. 1999. "A Theory of Second-Order Expectations and Behavior." *Social Psychology Quarterly* 62(1): 17–31.

West, Candace, and Sarah Fenstermaker. 1995. "Doing Difference." *Gender and Society* 9(1): 8–37.

West, Candace, and Don H. Zimmerman. 1987. "Doing Gender." *Gender and Society* 1(1): 125–51.

Westbrook, Laurel, and Kristen Schilt. 2014. "Doing Gender, Determining Gender: Transgender People, Gender Panics, and the Maintenance of the Sex/Gender/Sexuality System." *Gender and Society* 28(1): 32–57.

Wetts, Rachel, and Robb Willer. 2018. "Privilege on the Precipice: Perceived Racial Status Threats Lead White Americans to Oppose Welfare Programs." *Social Forces* 97(2): 793–822.

Willer, Robb. 2009. "Groups Reward Individual Sacrifice: The Status Solution to the Collective Action Problem." *American Sociological Review* 74(1): 23–43.

Willer, Robb, Ko Kuwabara, and Michael W. Macy. 2009. "The False Enforcement of Unpopular Norms." *American Journal of Sociology* 115(2): 451–90.

Williams, Joan C. 2000. *Unbending Gender: Why Family and Work Conflict and What to Do about It.* New York: Oxford University Press.

———. 2017. *White Working Class: Overcoming Class Cluelessness in America.* Cambridge, Mass.: Harvard Business Review Press.

Williams, Joan C., and Rachel Dempsey. 2014. *What Works for Women at Work: Four Patterns Working Women Need to Know.* New York: New York University Press.

Williams, Melissa J., and Larissa Z. Tiedens. 2016. "The Subtle Suspension of Backlash: A Meta-analysis of Penalties for Women's Implicit and Explicit Dominance Behavior." *Psychological Bulletin* 142(2): 165–97.

Wingfield, Adia, and Renee Skeete Alston. 2014. "Maintaining Hierarchies in Predominantly White Organizations: A Theory of Racial Tasks." *American Behavioral Scientist* 58(2): 274–87.

Wood, Wendy, and Alice H. Eagly. 2002. "A Cross-Cultural Analysis of the Behavior of Women and Men: Implications for the Origins of Sex Differences." *Psychological Bulletin* 128(5): 699–727.

———. 2012. "Biosocial Construction of Sex Differences and Similarities in Behavior." *Advances in Experimental Social Psychology* 46: 55–123.

Wu, Frank. 2002. *Yellow: Race in America beyond Black and White.* New York: Basic Books.

Zelditch, Morris, Jr. 2018. "Legitimacy Theory." In *Contemporary Social Psychological Theories*, 2nd ed., edited by Peter J. Burke. Stanford, Calif.: Stanford University Press.

Zelditch, Morris, Jr., and Henry A. Walker. 1984. "Legitimacy and the Stability of Authority." In *Advances in Group Processes: Theory and Research*, vol. 1, edited by Edward J. Lawler. Greenwich, Conn.: JAI Press.

Zemore, Sarah E., Susan T. Fiske, and Hyun-Jeong Kim. 2000. "Gender Stereotypes and the Dynamics of Social Interaction." In *The Developmental Social Psychology of Gender*, edited by Thomas Eckes and Hanns M. Trautner. Mahwah, N.J.: Lawrence Erlbaum Associates.

Zou, Linda, and Sapna Cheryan. 2017. "Two Axes of Subordination: A New Model of Racial Position." *Journal of Personality and Social Psychology* 112(5): 696–717.